# GOODREADINGGUIDE
# WORLD FICTION

EDITED BY
VINCENT CASSAR
& NIK KALINOWSKI

A & C Black · London

First published 2007
A & C Black Publishers Limited
38 Soho Square
London W1D 3HB
www.acblack.com

© 2007 Vincent Cassar and Nik Kalinowski

ISBN: 978–0–7136–7999–1

A CIP catalogue record for this book is available from the
British Library.

This book is produced using paper that is made from wood
grown in managed, sustainable forests. It is natural, renewable
and recyclable. The logging and manufacturing processes conform
to the environmental regulations of the country of origin.

Typeset in 8.5pt on 12pt Meta-Light

Printed and bound in Great Britain by
CPI Bookmarque, Croydon, CR0 4TD

# CONTENTS

HOWTOUSETHISBOOK ............................... vii

INTRODUCTION ................................... x

## THEAMERICAS ................................. 1

**South America** ................................. 1
General 1 • Argentina 7 • Brazil 11 • Peru 14 • Guyana 16 •
Caribbean 20 • Dominican Republic/Haiti 25 • Trinidad 26
• Jamaica 27 • Cuba 28

**Central America** ................................ 30
General 30 • Mexico 33

**United States of America** ....................... 38
General 38 • East Coast 42 • New York 47 • American South 52
• Midwest/Great Lakes States 57 • Texas/American West 65 •
South West 70 • Los Angeles 75 • North West/Alaska/Hawaii 80

**Canada** ....................................... 89

## AUSTRALASIA ................................. 97

**Australia** ..................................... 97
**New Zealand** .................................. 103
**Pacific Island** ................................. 106

## ASIA ........................................ 108

**South-East Asia** ............................... 108
Indonesia 111 • Thailand 112 • Burma/Myanmar 113 • Vietnam 114

# FAR EAST .................................................... 116

Japan 116 • Tokyo 122 • China 127 •
Hong Kong/Korea/Taiwan/Tibet 132

# INDIAN SUB-CONTINENT ....................... 136

India ........................................................ 136
Mumbai 141
Pakistan/Sri Lanka/Bangladesh ............................ 143

# THE MIDDLE EAST ..................................... 148

General Middle East ....................................... 148
East Middle East .......................................... 149
West Middle East .......................................... 154
Israel ..................................................... 158

# AFRICA ................................................ 164

General Africa ............................................ 164
East Africa ............................................... 165
Kenya ..................................................... 168
Southern Africa ........................................... 171
South Africa .............................................. 174
Central Africa ............................................ 181
West Africa ............................................... 183
Nigeria ................................................... 186
North Africa .............................................. 189
Egypt ..................................................... 193

# EUROPE ................................................ 197

Greece .................................................... 197
Turkey .................................................... 202
Russia/Soviet Union ....................................... 204
Moscow/St Petersburg 209
Eastern Europe ............................................ 214
General Eastern Europe 214

**Czech Republic/Slovakia/Czechoslovakia** ...................216
Prague 217
**Former Yugoslavia** ...............................................220
**Poland** ..............................................................221
**Hungary** ............................................................223
**Other Eastern European Countries** ........................225
**Scandinavia** .......................................................228
Finland 228 • Sweden 230 • Norway 232 • Iceland 235 •
Denmark 237
**Germany** ............................................................242
Berlin 247
**The Netherlands** .................................................251
**Belgium** ............................................................254
**Austria** ..............................................................255
**Switzerland** ........................................................258
**Italy** .................................................................261
Venice 268
**France** ..............................................................274
Paris 280
**Spain** ...............................................................286
Barcelona 290
**Portugal** ...........................................................292
**Republic of Ireland** .............................................296
Dublin 302
**United Kingdom** ..................................................306
**Northern Ireland** ................................................306
**Scotland** ...........................................................310
Edinburgh 314 • Glasgow 316
**Wales** ...............................................................318
**England** ............................................................322
General England 322 • Northern England 326 • The Midlands 329
• Eastern England 331 • Southern England 334 • London 336 •
South-West England 340

# READONATHEME

Motion Studies – Pedals, Wings, Rail 18–19 • Kitchen Confidentials –
Food and Drink 36–37 • In the Driver's Seat – Road Novels 63–64 •
Adventures in the Screen Trade – Hollywood/Movies 78–79 • Pride and
Prejudice – Black in America 84–85 • Typical Americans – The
Asian/Latino in America 86–88 • Shipping News – Nautical Novels
95–96 • Paradise Lost – Utopian Nightmares 107 • Rooms With a View –
Hotel Novels 125–126 • Adventures in Wonderlands – Imaginary Places
134–135 • Pilgrims' Progress – Spiritual Journeys 146–147 • In the
Beginning – Biblical Novels 162–163 • Once Upon a Time – Myths,
Legends, Folktales 179-180 • Ancient Evenings – Ancient Egypt 196 •
Hellenica – Ancient Greece 200–201 • To the Ends of the Earth –
Explorers, Discoverers, Adventurers 212–213 • Clockwork Oranges
– Time-Travel 226–227 • Norse Odes – Vikings 239 • Pole to Pole –
Arctic/Antarctic 240–241 • Travels With or Without Aunts – Fictional
Odysseys 259–260 • Friends, Romans, Countrymen – Ancient Rome
272–273 • Portrait of the Artist – Art and Artists 284–285 • Postcards
from the Edge – Holidays in Fiction 294–295 • Life in the UK –
Black/Asian/Muslim in Britain 342–344 • Anglo-Saxon Attitudes
– English History 344–345

## INDEX ............................................................. 347

# HOWTOUSETHISBOOK

The *Bloomsbury Good Reading Guide to World Fiction* is intended to highlight the best modern novels that reflect the culture of a particular location. It is aimed at anyone who has ever wanted to read a novel and immerse themselves in their surroundings, perhaps a place that they are about to visit, or simply somewhere that has always held a fascination for them. It is hoped that this book will help them to discover a selection of novels that best communicate a sense of the reader's place of interest, and thus encourage wider and more adventurous reading habits.

In order to facilitate the reader's travel experience through the world in fiction we have eschewed the cold rationale of the alphabet in favour of a geographical ordering of the material. We imagined the reader spreading out a map and planting a finger in the far corner of the world from which to begin the expedition of a lifetime. Which is why we begin our journey in South America and navigate our way westwards to end up in the Britain Isles.

The book is arranged geographically by continent, with each continent flowing naturally into the next. From South America, we journey up through North America, round Australasia, on to Asia, across Africa, and then finally into Europe. Each continent is subdivided into countries or, in some cases, into regions, as is the case with the United States and Great Britain. For each section, we have chosen up to four **Key Titles**. These are then followed by a selection of **Read-Ons**, recommendations for further reading. At the beginning of some of the continent sections there is a general section featuring books that satisfy one of four criteria: they cover the continent as a whole; they are collections of short stories; they are set in an unnamed or a fictional country within that continent; or they are set in a country for which no individual heading exists. Where a significant number of novels are set in a particular city, we have given that city its own section within the relevant country or region, as has been done, for example for New York in the USA section.

There are also a number of **Read on a Theme** lists dotted throughout the guide. Some are geographical in nature and are placed under the relevant country heading, as with *Ancient Egypt* in the Egypt section. Other lists deal with subject categories, for example *Art, Food, Road Journeys*, and *Spiritual Journeys*, and these are placed randomly throughout the book.

The Read-On sections contain brief summaries of the novels listed, and although most of them could also have featured as Key Titles, we have reserved that label for

① South America
② North America
③ Australasia
④ Asia
⑤ Africa
⑥ Europe
⑦ UK

those books about which we were particularly passionate. The Key Titles receive more expansive treatment, with details of plot and essential themes and comments on style or content. If a noteworthy film or other adaptation of the book has been made, this is also mentioned. The publication dates given are for the earliest original editions, as far as these dates can be ascertained, not for the date of first UK publication or translation.

We have selected novels that we feel are particularly evocative of the country in which they are set, either because they conjure up a vivid sense of place or because they reflect a nation's sensibility. For example, although *Fictions* by Jorge Luis Borges is not particularly descriptive of Argentinean life, the book expertly reflects an Argentine mentality, whereas in *A Fine Balance*, the reader virtually walks the streets of Mumbai with its author Rohinton Mistry. We settled on the year 1900 as a cut-off date because we felt that for the book to resonate with a contemporary reader it would need to have appeared within the last hundred years or so, even if its setting were historical.

At the time of writing, the great majority of the novels featured are currently in print in this country. Any that have slipped out of print are probably still attainable through the modern-day bazaar that is the internet. We have decided not to include those classic international works that remain sadly untranslated (for example, *The Unknown Soldier* by Väinö Linn, possibly the most representative work of twentieth century Finnish literature), together with those novels that have been so long out of print as to be practically extinct (for example, *Poor Christ of Bomba* by Mongo Beti, widely regarded as one of the best African novels). The inevitable restrictions of space imposed hard editorial decisions, but we have endeavoured to arrive at a fair balance of the sexes and to represent the indigenous population over the foreign, but not exclusively so, for the outsider's experiences and perspective can often be highly illuminating. The relative preponderance of European novels, compared for example with those novels of African or Australasian origin, reflects both the literary tradition of those continents and the availability of the works. It is by no means a comment on quality. As regards names of places, we have used the current name in section headings but of course formerly used names will appear for places that are settings for individual novels.

Any guide such as this is necessarily subjective and we readily admit that it is not a definitive list – no such beast could exist – but we apologise in advance if your particular favourite is not listed and we welcome comments and suggestions for future editions. We hope you enjoy the trip.

# ACKNOWLEDGEMENTS

The authors would like to thank the following for their numerous suggestions, generous assistance and boundless patience: Stephen E Andrews, Frea Buckler, Richard Butler, Sara Cooper, Mariana Depetris, Zinaida Linden, Kate McEwan, Lisa Price, Louise Reece, Peter Royle, Laura Salisbury, Jennifer Waters, and the staff at Bath central library, colleagues, friends and family. And everyone at A& C Black.

# INTRODUCTION

It is, of course, impossible to replicate with a novel the experience of physically being in another country, feeling the effects of its climate, soaking up its atmosphere through its various sounds and smells, hearing its language and seeing the critical makeup of its people written on their faces and in their architecture and art. And nothing can replace the quality of otherness that comes from being taken outside your normal life and self and being set down somewhere immediately and undeniably different. Many of us who travel to faraway places, however, often get to see little more than tourist spots packaged and anaesthetised for the traveller, passing through airports seemingly designed to rob us of our soul, and suffering interminable journeys that take away more energy than we will ever have again. Waiters or hotel staff may be the only people we converse with, as we slavishly follow our guidebook's directions to an 'authentic' restaurant or bar only to find several dozen western tourists have already beaten us to it, they too in search of that genuine experience. Few of us indeed will gain entrance to people's homes, share their food or conversation, see them laugh and cry or watch over them while they sleep and dream of finer things.

However, when we read a novel, we are let loose in the undergrowths of another culture. There you can vicariously meet its people, get to know their food, and learn about its history in an intimate and meaningful way. We are also more likely to understand a country's spiritual truth through the stories it tells itself than through any historical narrative that may be told about it.

This guide is an opportunity to open your mind to the world of fiction, a world as vast and grand as the earth itself. Through its pages you may find yourself observing the sunset on the Serengeti, living the life of a low-caste street cleaner in Delhi or riding across the Steppes with all your belongings strapped to your back.

Most of us come to foreign fiction via translations into English and whilst some people argue that there is no substitute for the original text, what is lost in translation may be no greater than what is gained. A good translator brings a multitude of skills to the task: an excellent command of the foreign language; a deep understanding of the culture; an intelligent and artistic rapport with the work; and a personal prose style that can communicate the material sensitively. All translation may be compromise to a certain degree, but as Robert Chandler points out in his excellent essay, *Translating Soul* (in the Harvill edition of *Soul* by Andrey

Platonov), 'a translator compensate(s) for inevitable sacrifices by making the most of whatever new possibilities are available'. Of course poor translations do exist. When a character from an Austrian work of the 1920s announces 'your ass is driving me crazy', one wonders whether the right tone has been struck. Nevertheless, it is perhaps better to have the experience of a novel through an uncertain translation than not to experience it at all. Where more than one translation is available, we have often recommended a specific edition, but only when we feel that much benefit is to be gained by searching out that particular version.

One of the joys of preparing this guide has been the discovery that so many small or independent publishing companies are still publishing excellent fiction, whether they are reprinting classics (as do Pushkin Press, giving us *Journey by Moonlight* by Antal Szerb) or bringing us new authors such as Stef Penney, whose *The Tenderness of Wolves*, has come to us via Quercus. In this regard, the publishers Harvill, Saqi, Peter Owen, Quartet, Marion Boyars, Canongate, Serpent's Tail, Dedalus and the irrepressible John Calder also deserve a special mention for their tireless global wandering in search of the best foreign fiction over the years. In addition, we are also indebted to Heinemann's long established African Writers series.

When we were planning our trip around the literary world we were struck by how difficult the task of listing places has become, given that so many countries and cities have changed their name over the course of the last hundred years or so. Think of Persia, Rhodesia, Burma and Ceylon, and cities such as Constantinople, Peking, Bombay, and the yo-yo labelling of St. Petersburg. The collapse of the Soviet Union has led to Russian satellite states reasserting their identities, and the break-up of Yugoslavia and other East European countries has meant new old countries have returned and brand new ones created. With the redrawing of borders, one town currently in Poland was accorded three different nationalities during the last century. This is not to mention the political sensitivities that exist in the Middle East. Some novels have been known to begin in Palestine and end up in Israel.

There are more than a thousand novels covered in this guide, and of the many themes presented in them one unfortunate theme reverberates incessantly: subjugation. An alarming number of these stories concern people trying to escape the yoke of repression, whether it be political, sexual, religious or racial. The emotional and physical scars left by various dictatorships around the world, along with those caused by the Soviet regime and the Third Reich, by British and European colonialism, by American imperialism and by Apartheid will, these stories tell us, take a long time to heal. So much of a nation's character has been formed by its reaction to those who seek to control it and if there are lessons to be learned by history, then these are the voices of those who can teach us. Tahar Ben Jelloun's unforgettable novel *This Blinding Absence of Light* shows us the ability of the human will to survive, while *Woman at Point Zero* by Nawal El-Saadawi, gives us a powerful reminder that our repressors can come from within your own culture.

Many of these novels reveal the cruelty human beings are capable of, describing the pitiless systems of control that can destroy a person's life and the individual brutality that can strip a person of all dignity. But as these novels plumb the depths of human darkness, so too do they touch the sky. The hope, love and generosity of spirit that shines through these novels is profound. There is an instinctual call to survival in all humans and the implacable doggedness of spirit is plain to see, for the essence of any place is, in part, its history, its culture, its geography and its religion, but ultimately it is its people.

These texts can be seen as important historical documents, giving us an understanding of the culture of a people. Vladimir Nabokov wrote, 'It is childish to study a work of fiction to gain information about a country', and he may be right but ultimately, it is not information we are seeking: it is knowledge, it is experience, it is understanding. For that perhaps we do need to travel – we simply need to read. It may be reading a work of fiction set in another country is as close as we come to visiting that place and, in an era of increasing anxiety over the carbon emissions generated by international travel, reading such works is certainly the greenest way of setting foot in a far-off place.

Researching and writing this guide has been for us both an education and an entertainment. In unearthing the literary goldmines of countries such as Iran, Hungary and Nigeria, we have learnt about their history, their politics and their geography. Reading the words of the most talented writers the world has ever produced, it has served to remind us of the diversity of this planet and the ingenuity of its people. We have travelled from the wastes of the Arctic Circle, in *Independent People*, to the tropical heat of Brazil in *Dona Flor and Her Two Husbands*; we have eaten sambols in Sri Lanka with Romesh Gunesekera in *Reef* and sampled katsudon in Banana Yoshimoto's *Kitchen*; we have danced the tango in Buenos Aires in *The Tango Singer* and waltzed around fin-de-siècle Austria in *The Radetsky March*. And we have cried and laughed and fallen in love in oh so many places.

So, where do you want to go today?

**VINCENT CASSAR & NIK KALINOWSKI**

# THEAMERICAS

## SOUTH AMERICA

### GENERAL SOUTH AMERICA

**KEY**TITLES

*One Hundred Years of Solitude*, Gabriel García Márquez
*The House of the Spirits*, Isabel Allende
*The War of Don Emmanuel's Nether Parts*, Louis de Bernières

### ONE HUNDRED YEARS OF SOLITUDE (1967)
Gabriel García Márquez

Generally considered to be Márquez's masterpiece, this novel chronicles the life of a fictional town, Macondo, through several generations of the Buendía family, over the course of a century.

It begins with Colonel Aureliano Buendía facing a firing squad and recalling his family history, a long and complicated history in which many of the characters have the same or similar names. The colonel himself has seventeen children called Aureliano! The family's struggles symbolise the history of Colombia in particular, and Latin America in general, as the Buendías become merged with the town itself and end up nothing more than a ghostly memory.

Macondans begin life like the first humans. They have no spoken language, so they use simple hand gestures. Spirits are a major part of their life, as are the forces of nature, but with the arrival of outsiders the elemental essence of life is lost.

As the town of Macondo grows, the national government takes an interest in its affairs and seeks to apply the laws of the land. Before long, jack-booted generals arrive seeking to impose order. They are followed by lawyers who implement the new legal systems, and the bishops who accompany them diminish the people's vision and dilute their dreams. When foreigners start to arrive, a banana plantation is opened nearby. In time, a union-led strike takes place and, when the army is called in, an outright massacre is the result. Macondo is eventually embroiled in a bloody civil war.

Márquez infuses the temporal with the surreal world of the imagination, as we see the Buendías having children with tails, floating with butterflies, and living to be impossibly old. In time, the last of the Buendía line disappears, leaving no more than a trace of how things used to be before the world was made solid.

A beautiful, magical book that weaves the figurative and the factual together seamlessly, it is both comic and tragic and is wholly deserving of its classic status. The excellent translation is by Gregory Rabassa.

*Márquez won the Nobel Prize in 1982. His other novels include the slow-burning* Love in the Time of Cholera *(1985), about a sixty-year love affair, and* The General in His Labyrinth *(1989), a portrait of Simón Bolívar.*

# THE HOUSE OF THE SPIRITS (1985)

Isabel Allende

Allende's debut novel follows the fortunes of an unnamed South American country through three generations of the Trueba family. It tells the history of Chile in all but name. The book opens at the beginning of the last century, with Clara Trueba writing in her diary.

As a child, Clara has psychic abilities and can make objects move at will. After the death of her sister, Rosa the Beautiful, Clara does not speak for nine years. When she finally opens her mouth, it is to announce her wedding to her sister's former fiancé, Esteban. He is a rich man with a violent temper who builds a house for the pair of them to live in. They have a tempestuous relationship: she does not entirely commit to him emotionally and he is constantly unfaithful to her. His anti-communist political activity is at odds with her more spiritual approach to life, and his authoritarian nature alienates their three children. Later, he forces his first-born daughter, Blanca, to marry a mysterious Count after she has disgraced the family in becoming pregnant by a local peasant-cum-revolutionary, Pedro Tercero.

Allende combines perfectly the personal and the political by interposing highly imaginative flights of fancy with the violent reality of the times. The political back-drop to the action is the struggle between Left and Right, which eventually led to the execution of the author's uncle, Salvador Allende (known as 'The President' in the book) in the 1973 coup, an event that ushered in the cold terror of Augusto Pinochet.

With the unique Trueba family, and perhaps especially its strong female charac-ters, Allende blends empathy and passion to produce a human drama saturated in Chilean history but laced with Latin magic.

A film was made in 1993 by Bille August. Allende's *Daughter of Fortune* (1999) and *Portrait in Sepia* (2000) both feature some of the same characters and settings as *The House of the Spirits*, although they are not sequels to it. Most of Allende's early novels, including *Of Love and Shadows* (1987), are set in South America.

# THE WAR OF DON EMMANUEL'S NETHER PARTS (1990)

## Louis de Bernières

The first of a Latin American trilogy of novels set in a fictional South American country, it features a rich spoilt landowner, Dona Constanza, who is seeking to divert the local river to fill her swimming pool. The locals are understandably upset and enlist the help of a dissolute Englishman, Don Emmanuel. This minor dispute turns so nasty that the government sends in a squadron of soldiers, led by the vicious and dim-witted Colonel Figueras.

The novel's grip on reality lessens as the book proceeds and magic realism soon takes over. When a Navantes Indian girl is killed by a land mine, she turns into a cat and ultimately helps to bring down the state. However, in the meantime, torture, bloodshed and plagues of various kinds, including giant cats and laughing fits, finally convince the villagers to leave their town and establish a new settlement in the mountains.

Drawing on the author's own experiences of teaching in Colombia, this is a political satire on tinpot dictatorships. It contains the familiar ingredients of such satires: a corrupt and inept army, a torture-loving colonel, brainless authorities and a self-serving church. Episodes of extreme violence sit side by side with slapstick and ribaldry in an exotic location of jungles and swamps. The book is something of a light-hearted romp through the tempestuous terrain of South America. By not setting any book of the trilogy in a particular named country, de Bernières could lay himself open to the charge of glibly serving up stereotypes and the writing might well be described as Marquez-lite. Nevertheless, despite their lack of weightiness, all three books are wildly inventive and essentially rumbustious fun.

The further books in the trilogy are *Señor Vivo and the Coca Lord* (1991), which deals with the world of drug barons, and *The Troublesome Offspring of Cardinal Guzman* (1992), which takes on religious (ie Catholic) fanaticism.

## 📖 Read ons

*Journey Through the Wilderness*, Moris Farhi
An art restorer goes back to an unnamed country in Latin America to track down the war criminal who murdered his father.

*Nostromo*, Joseph Conrad
In the fictional country of Costaguana, an English émigré entrusts the silver from his mine to an 'incorruptible' mercenary, to keep it from the hands of revolutionaries. Possibly Conrad's finest work.

*The Dark Bride*, Laura Restrepo (Colombia)
A poetic and innovative novel which has a journalist re-telling the story of a legendary prostitute in a small Colombian oil town.

*Rosario Tijeras*, Jorge Franco (Colombia)
Two men love a mysterious woman and each speaks of her past as they wait for her to recover from being shot, in this psychological gangland thriller set in Medellín in the 1980s.

*By Night in Chile*, Roberto Bolano (Chile)
A deathbed monologue narrated by a priest who is attempting to come to terms with his right-wing associations. A short novel by a writer sometimes described as the best South American writer of the last twenty years.

*The Mermaid and the Drunks*, Ben Richards (Chile)
A woman returns to Santiago following the suicide of her exiled father and becomes involved with two men in modern-day Chile. An evocative romantic thriller replete with historical facts.

*The Pleasure of Eliza Lynch*, Anne Enright (Paraguay)
This novel re-imagines the extraordinary life of a beautiful Irish woman in the 1850s who turned into the Eva Peron of her day when she became mistress of a Paraguayan dictator.

*Eva Luna*, Isabel Allende (Venezuela)
It charts the picaresque life of the eponymous heroine, the illegitimate child of a servant, who resorts to fantasy when life becomes unbearable. The sequel is *The Stories of Eva Luna*.

### *Keepers of the House*, Lisa St Aubin de Terán (Venezuela)

17-year-old Lydia travels with her new husband to his decaying, ancestral hacienda in the Andes. As he starts to shut himself off from the world, she takes solace in the tragic and legendary tales of his ancestors.

### *The Shipyard*, Juan Carlos Onetti (Uruguay)

Onetti writes with an almost European sense of existential gloom. The stark, realistic prose tells of a man returning after five years in exile to a town on the River Plate, with a plan to make good. It is a sequel to *Body Snatcher*.

### *The City of Your Final Destination*, Peter Cameron (Uruguay)

A finely written modern comedy of manners about a shambling biographer whose life begins to unwind when he arrives unexpectedly at his dead subject's tiny homestead and spends time with his family and friends.

### *The Old Man Who Read Love Stories*, Luis Sepulveda (Ecuador)

A beautifully written novella about a man who sits on the edges of the Amazonian jungle reading books and recalling his life. It contains some exquisite descriptions of the verdant world around him.

### *Indecision*, Benjamin Kunkel (Ecuador)

A man takes an experimental drug to cure him of his procrastination and he immediately flies to the Ecuadorian jungle with the girl of his dreams. A hilarious novel about the responsibility that comes with maturity.

# ARGENTINA

**KEY**TITLES

*Labyrinths*, Jorge Luis Borges
*The Tango Singer*, Tomás Eloy Martínez

## LABYRINTHS (1962)
### Jorge Luis Borges

A stunning collection of short pieces by the master of intellectual intrigue. He has been cited by almost every major South American author as an influence and his literary imagination is peerless. His 'fictions' are classifiable neither as novels nor as short stories, representing as they do a new form of literary expression: essay fiction. He takes historical situations, embellishes them, convolutes them, and makes them fantastical or puzzling. These 'stories' read like walks in a maze with a kaleidoscope for a guide. They stay trapped in the mind for a long time after reading, and each new reading brings forth more wonders.

This collection includes all the pieces that make up *Fictions*, plus extra essays and parables, including the man who rewrote Don Quixote without changing a word, and the world where anything becomes exactly what you want it to be. In Borges' world, libraries can be infinite and mirrors menacing, and when a person dreams, he or she dreams for the whole of humankind. *The Garden of Forking Paths* deconstructs the mystery story, and in *Funes the Memorious* a boy is driven to insanity because he can recall everything. These are intelligent and intellectual pieces but they are not merely to be enjoyed by bibliophiles and philosophers. Written mainly in the 1940s, these pieces challenge our view of reality by requiring us to think differently about the world around us.

Controversy seems to surround the various Borges translations. All his fictional pieces were collated in *Collected Fictions* (1998), with a new translation by Andrew Hurley. Penguin uses these Hurley versions for its individual short story collections. However, some British readers may find them somewhat Americanised and rather too literal. *Labyrinths* remains a better collection overall, even though a variety of translators have been used, from different periods. The quality is erratic but, when it is good, it reveals Borges at his best.

# THE TANGO SINGER (2004)
## Tomás Eloy Martínez

Bruno Cadogan, an American student, goes to Buenos Aires to track down an elusive tango singer, Julio Martel, hoping it will provide him with much-needed inspiration to write his dissertation on Jorge Luis Borges' essays on the tango.

When Bruno arrives, in September 2001, Argentina is in the grip of hyperinflation and the country is tense with unrest. The poor are camped on street corners and there are demonstrations in the street. Bruno finds himself a room in the hotel that is the setting for Borges' celebrated story *The Aleph*, and this becomes another obsession, as Bruno seeks to find the real Aleph, a point in space that contains all other points in the universe. Just as Martel and his mythical voice are seemingly always out of reach, so is the city itself. Both are elusive and illusive.

Julio Martel is a legendary singer who has never made a recording, sings songs of a much earlier era, often with incomprehensible lyrics, and makes impromptu appearances at unlikely venues. The singer may have 'sunlight in his throat' but he is also a haemophiliac who spends most of his days in a wheelchair. Bruno comes to suspect that Martel's choices of venue are not arbitrary, that instead they adhere to some secret system mapping out the history of the city. He sings in places that are associated with acts of violence against the people: the Athletics Club, which was a place of torture under the military dictatorship; the Jewish Community Centre, where a terrorist bomb killed eighty-five people in 1994; and opposite a factory where striking workers were gunned down in 1919.

Martínez wants the reader to believe that Buenos Aires, that very out-of-the-way city, is the Aleph of the universe, the city that contains all other cities. He makes a convincing case, for the pages come alive when the author is describing the constantly shifting light, the ever-changing street names and the various fascinating characters Bruno encounters. Included are many stories of the capital's fractured past, from when the Spanish were ousted in 1810, through the Peron era, and into the current political turmoil. A short section of notes at the back of the book is a useful aid to those unfamiliar with Argentina's history.

*Tomás Eloy Martínez's previous books include* The Perón Novel *(1985) and* Santa Evita *(1995).*

# 📖Read ons

## *Kiss of the Spider Woman*, Manuel Puig
A classic novel, set in the late 1970s, about a middle-aged homosexual and a Marxist revolutionary who share a prison cell. Initially mutually hostile, they gradually learn to trust each other.

## *The Hare*, Cesar Aira
This is a subtle reflection on love, language and colonial dependency as an English naturalist wanders the Argentine pampas in search of a rare animal. The sightings reported by local Indians, however, make him apprehensive.

## *Hopscotch*, Julio Cortazar
Pablo Neruda famously said, 'People who do not read Cortazar are doomed.' This is metafiction that has the reader jumping wildly from place to place, so much so that it comes with a Table of Instructions. Set in Paris and Buenos Aires, it is about a writer who loses his lover and seeks to find her in all things.

## *The Story of the Night*, Colm Tóibín
Set around the time of the Falklands war, Tóibín's beautifully realised novel tells of a young gay man beginning to explore his sexuality in a country starting to emerge from repressive rule.

## *The Buenos Aires Quintet*, Manuel Vázquez Montalbán
A comic romp about a Catalonian detective, ex-communist and gourmand who is sent to Buenos Aires to look for a missing person. However, he soon finds himself investigating the country's turbulent past.

## *The Seven Madmen*, Roberto Arlt
A neglected work of eccentric genius. In 1929, a failed inventor finds himself involved with various bizarre characters in Buenos Aires in a plot to overthrow the government. There is a sequel, *The Flamethrowers*.

## *Open Door and Other Stories*, Luisa Valenzuela
A collection of short stories imbued with Valenzuela's surrealistic black humour. She writes stories about men and violence, and women in love, in free-flowing, ornate language.

ARGENTINA

### The Invention of Morel, Adolfo Bioy Casares
A hugely influential novella set on a mysterious island where a man on the run believes he is alone until other characters begin to appear. However, it appears they can neither see nor hear him.

### The Moldavian Pimp, Edgardo Cozarinsky
Set in Buenos Aires and Paris in the 1920s and the present day, this novel is based on true accounts of young Jewish girls who were enticed from the Ukraine into a life of prostitution.

### The Honorary Consul, Graham Greene
In a remote border town, a band of rebels kidnap the wrong man. The local physician is brought in to help negotiate his release. However, the doctor is having an affair with the kidnapped man's wife.

# BRAZIL

## KEY TITLES

*City of God*, Paulo Lins
*Dona Flor and Her Two Husbands*, Jorge Amado

## CITY OF GOD (1997)

### Paulo Lins

Cidade de Deus is a real housing project on the west side of Rio de Janeiro. Initially intended for displaced flood victims, it has increasingly become a place where the government dumps poor people as a way of closing its eyes to the social problems inherent in the city. The project is notorious for violence, and shoot-outs regularly take place between drug gangs and the police. The beauty of its surroundings, on the outskirts of a jungle and with an idyllic beach nearby, is contrasted with the ugliness and violence of the favela.

Paulo Lins lived in this hell from the age of seven, and he went back to interview his former friends and collect stories from the locals. The book has a dreamlike feel of story falling in upon story, then unfolding again, mirroring the relentless cycle of violence and drugs it portrays. Nine years in the writing, *City of God* covers three decades, from the 1960s to the 1980s, recounting the stories of mainly teenage gangsters in back-to-back vignettes. Lins's reportage style has a cinematic, mise-en-scène quality: it is as if hundreds of oddly nicknamed individuals come into the field of vision of a stationary camera for a few fleeting moments before disappearing again. Whereas the classic multi-award-winning film concentrated on one or two characters, the book has a more scatter-gun approach and takes in the lives of many young boys as they spend their time robbing, chasing girls, playing with guns and selling or taking drugs.

Dealing as it does with this grim subject matter, the book has an inescapable ugliness and brutality, but Lins communicates a deeper social message about the historical and political causes of the poverty that produces such violence.

First published in Brazil in 1997, it was adapted for the screen in 2002. The

English translation of the book was not published until 2006, not surprisingly given the richness of the original in slang, double meaning and cultural specifics. Alison Entrekin appears to have done a fine job, however. She has certainly captured the rhythm and pace of the book, which flows as freely and as dirtily as the river that oozes past the Cidade de Deus itself.

# DONA FLOR AND HER TWO HUSBANDS (1966)
Jorge Amado

Dona Flor's irresponsible first husband, Vadinho Guimaraes, dies unexpectedly while dancing in a street carnival in Salvador, Bahia. He was a licentious gambler who treated his wife badly but satisfied her sexually. She is modest and conventional by nature, so his early death leaves her feeling abandoned and alone. Not yet thirty years old and with a passionate sexuality, she spends her initial widowhood climbing the walls in sexual frustration, her urgent desires played out in her dreams. She begins to see the sensual in everything and although she appears outwardly calm, inside she is a raging fire.

Dona Flor devotes herself to running her cookery school and, despite her friends' constant exhortations to remarry, she cements her position as a respectable widow. She eventually meets a kind pharmacist, Dr Teodoro Madureria, who proposes marriage, and she decides that his more mature approach to life will suit her well, for he is everything Vadinho was not: considerate, honourable, respectable and good with money. Unfortunately, in bed he is rather incompetent and Dona Flor's sexual dissatisfaction becomes a siren echoing through the spirit world to summon the ghost of her deceased husband. Eventually, Vadinho's spirit is awakened and is ready to perform. What ensues is a bawdy, comic romp through the erotic fantasies of Bahian life, with lashings of ghostly apparitions, witchcraft, home cooking and Samba music – in short a paean to hedonism.

Amado is a political writer and it may seem odd that he has produced such a frivolous novel, especially so soon after the imposition of a military dictatorship in Brazil, but much can be read beneath the surface, in particular the choice the country faces between holding onto the past or embracing a more modern future.

*A highly successful film was made by Bruno Barreto in 1976. Amado was born in the state of Bahia, the setting for most of his novels, including* Gabriela, Clove and Cinnamon *(1958) and* Tent of Miracles *(1969).*

## 📖Read ons

*Inferno*, Patricia Melo
A fast-paced tale of drug trafficking on the mean streets of Sao Paulo, as an eleven-year-old boy has to grow up quickly amid the poverty and violence.

*The Brothers*, Milton Hatoum
An elaborate and descriptive tale of twins whose lives take very different paths and who are constantly competing for familial affection. Set in a Lebanese community on the North Brazilian coast.

*Benjamin*, Chico Buarque
From a renowned musician comes a tale of a middle-aged ex-model whose past life flashes before him as he is about to be shot. The disparate lifestyles of Brazil's rich and poor are vividly brought to life.

*The Club of Angels*, Luis Fernando Verissimo
In the club of epicurean has-beens, greed still lives on. Unfortunately, the diners do not as, one by one, they die in this smart, ruminative take on Brazilian society.

*The Silence of the Rain*, Luiz Alfredo Garcia-Roza
The first in a best-selling trilogy of crime novels featuring jaded intellectual, Inspector Espinosa. Set in Rio de Janeiro, it is a heady mix of exotica and police procedure as Espinosa investigates the apparent suicide of a businessman.

*The Lost Manuscript*, Rubem Fonseca
A thriller set around the Rio carnival, as a film director is caught up in the theft of priceless jewels. The book offers a cavalcade of seriously disturbing characters.

*The War of the End of the World*, Mario Vargas Llosa
A mammoth fictionalised account of the rise and desperate fall of Canudos, a village overcome by Christian fervour that was wiped out by the government in 1897.

# PERU

KEYTITLE

*Death in the Andes*, Mario Vargas Llosa

## DEATH IN THE ANDES (1993)
Mario Vargas Llosa

Ostensibly, this is an investigation into the disappearance of three men in an isolated outpost in the Peruvian Andes, undertaken by a civil guard, Corporal Lituma. The disappeared are presumed to have been kidnapped, and probably murdered, by the Shining Path (Sendero Luminoso), a band of communist freedom fighters who are ruthlessly making their way through the country. However, other suspects soon appear. There is a woman who, with her husband, runs the local bar and is a witch who is said to practise human sacrifice to placate the apus, ancient spirits of the mountains. Also in the frame are the fat-sucking pishtacos, ghouls who live in the caves and attack anyone who travels along the roads at night.

Lituma is initially sceptical about talk of the supernatural, but after questioning the witch and interviewing a few hostile locals, he gradually learns how all is connected, past and present, spirit with body and myth with truth. These impoverished mountain people – 'the real descendents of the Incas' – live in constant fear for their lives from all quarters: the Government, the rebels and the land itself. They can take little comfort from their ancient traditions and beliefs, for it is from their own blood that they have built the landscape.

The Corporal lies awake at night in a makeshift hut listening to his adjutant Tomasito tell the story of his love for a prostitute. Tomasito's passion for his lover is the only respite in a catalogue of gruesome deaths and macabre goings-on. It begins with Tomasito's shooting of the gang boss who is beating her and their subsequent flight together. However, later she steals his money and leaves him broken-hearted.

Also interwoven in this fine mosaic are the yarns of the victims. Characters are introduced in great detail only to die a few pages later. Vargas Llosa gives least sympathetic treatment to the rebels, painting them as mere killing machines with no reason or spirit. There is no denying the mastery of his prose, however, and this is a surprisingly invigorating read for a text saturated with death.

*Of Vargas Llosa's other books,* Aunt Julia and the Scriptwriter *(1977) and* The Notebooks of Don Rigoberto *(1997) are both set in Lima.*

## ⪧Read ons

*The Bridge of San Luis Rey*, Thornton Wilder
When the finest bridge in Peru collapses in 1712, a Franciscan missionary sets out to explore the lives of the five people who died, in the hope of finding some meaning in their futile deaths.

*The Dancer Upstairs*, Nicholas Shakespeare
A military policeman becomes obsessed with finding the leader of a terrorist organisation in this taut, intelligent thriller. *See also* **The Vision of Elena Silves**.

*The Puma's Shadow*, A B Daniel
Two star-crossed lovers are half a world away from each other. While Anamaya weaves her delicate psychic threads in Incan Courts, the rebel nobleman, Gabriel, pits his wits against the Spanish Crown. First in the *Inca Series* trilogy.

*War by Candlelight*, Daniel Alarcon
Short stories by a young author of great promise, set in a world of flux where revolution is not simply in the air, but in the home and in the heart.

# GUYANA

KEYTITLE

*Palace of the Peacock*, Wilson Harris

## PALACE OF THE PEACOCK (1960)
Wilson Harris

There are no two ways about it: this is a difficult read. Set in the sixteenth century and moving back in time, this is ostensibly the tale of the crew of a boat making its way by river, through the jungles of Guyana, in search of the mission of Mariella, each with his own greedy motive. Mariella is also the name of a woman whom the crew's captain abuses, and, as a symbol of all women, she makes frequent and unexpected appearances throughout the novel.

Donne is the anguished leader of the crew – he is both the aggressor and a symbol of a state of mind. He dies many times in the novel, only to live again. The crew is a cross-section of every race that has come to Guyana. Among them are the ship's pilot, Vigilance, an Amerindian; the avaricious Cameron, an Afro-Scot; the Shaman Carroll; an Afro-Caribbean youth; and the avuncular Schomburgh, a German-Indian fisherman. Portuguese twins, an Anglo-Saxon and a Chinese man also feature and all are caught up in a spiritually incestuous relationship, at times becoming a single entity, a homogestalt, symbolic of the sins of the world.

The voice of the narrator switches constantly as Wilson re-imagines the moment of colonization and creates a confrontation between the colonizer and the colonized. In order to give voices to the multiple narratives, he dispenses with conventional modes of storytelling and creates a world of poetry and myth. His descriptions of the jungle are lyrical and of an overwhelming density.

In one episode, the boat crashes and the crew members are forced to make their way to the top of a waterfall, where an epiphany of sorts takes place. The crew members are journeying to the heart of their own beings, and Wilson is seeking to take the reader back to the beginning of Creation.

Through his evocation of dreams, myths and traditions, Wilson has written an important novel that breaks many literary conventions.

This is the first of *The Guyana Quartet*, the other volumes being *The Far Journey of Oudin* (1961), *The Whole Armour* (1962), and *The Secret Ladder* (1963).

## ☺Read ons

*Bethany Bettany*, Fred D'Aguiar
The five-year-old girl of the title lives with abusive relatives in a rambling house in a small town. She learns to make herself invisible and then discovers the truth behind her parents' disappearance.

*The Ventriloquist's Tale*, Pauline Melville
Two illicit love affairs collide in Georgetown, one in the 1920s, featuring two mixed-race siblings, and the second in the present day, concerning an extra-marital affair. As the past is unravelled, incest, superstition and ignorance are all revealed in this witty, brilliant novel.

*The Counting House*, David Dabydeen
An Indian couple go to colonial Guyana at the end of the nineteenth century, hoping to begin a new life, but the tension between the different immigrants sparks off tragic events.

*Buxton Spice*, Oonya Kempadoo
A coming-of-age novel about four girls who live in the fictional town of Tamarind Grove. Against a backdrop of political upheaval in the country, they become aware of boys, their bodies and sex.

*The Murderer*, Roy Heath
A psychological study of a man's descent into madness as he deals with the guilt of his wife's murder and the attitude of those around him.

## MOTION STUDIES – PEDALS, WINGS, RAILS

*Southern Mail/Night Flight*, Antoine de Saint Exupery
Two vivid stories based on the author's own experiences. The first is an adventure of airmail pilots flying from France to North Africa; the second, along similar lines, is set above the clouds of South America.

*Leaving Earth*, Helen Humphreys
Grace, a Canadian aviatrix, attempts to break the world flight-endurance record in the 1930s with a female co-pilot. Battling the elements, convention, and her sabotaging husband, they form a deep friendship, and ultimately fall in love.

*Cassada*, James Salter
A spare, moving novel of US Air Force pilots stationed in Cold War Germany, vying with each other for flying superiority, with tragic consequences.

*No Highway*, Nevil Shute
An engineer is sent to Canada to investigate the unexplained crash of a recently designed plane. At some risk to his own safety, he flies out in an air-craft of the same type. Shute, once an aeronautical engineer, is renowned for his aviation stories.

*The Rider*, Tim Krabbé
An account of an amateur cycle race in France, this is also a meditation on cycling and life that is so atmospheric and pacey you feel as if you are in the saddle yourself.

*The Memory of Running*, Ron McLarty
A fat, friendless loser sets off on an unintended bike ride across America to claim his sister's remains and rediscovers what it means to live.

*Murder On the Orient Express*, Agatha Christie
Belgian super sleuth, Hercule Poirot, dusts off his little grey cells to solve another murder, this time aboard the most glamorous train of all, the Orient Express.

*The Necropolis Railway*, Andrew Martin
The first in a series of historical mysteries, set at the turn of the twentieth century, featuring Jim Stringer, a railway worker turned 'steam detective'.

*Moscow Stations*, Venedikt Yerofeev
A highly regarded but not widely known autobiographical novel that traces the main character's drunken and dreamlike journey across a corrupt and declining Russia, reflecting on life and his fellow passengers on the way.

*Stamboul Train*, Graham Greene
A spy thriller in which various characters with shady pasts wend their way across Europe on board the Orient Express to Istanbul.

*Closely Observed Trains*, Bohumil Hrabal
A young railway employee in Bohemia, towards the end of the Second World War, becomes involved in a plan to blow up one of the trains bound for the Eastern Front. A small masterpiece of Czech literature.

# THE CARIBBEAN

**KEY**TITLES

*A House for Mr Biswas*, V S Naipaul (Trinidad)
*Wide Sargasso Sea*, Jean Rhys (Domincan Republic)
*Annie John*, Jamaica Kincaid (Antigua)

## A HOUSE FOR MR BISWAS (1961)
V S Naipaul

Set in the Hindu community in postcolonial Trinidad, this is the life story of Mohun Biswas, a man who only ever wanted a home to call his own. It begins with his death, aged 46, at the point when he is finally ensconced in the house he always desired, in Port of Spain, with this wife and four children. It then recounts his life in a series of episodes from his birth onwards. He is born 'the wrong way' into a blatantly miserable and unloving family among whom he is seen as an omen of bad luck. When he misses his vocation to be a holy man, he becomes a sign painter, then a journalist and, through articles he writes about the poor, an outreach worker. After his father's death by drowning, for which he was inadvertently responsible, he transfers from one residence to another until he is tricked into marrying Shama Tulsi, whereupon he moves in with her large domineering family. They have little respect for or faith in him, and his wife continually takes their side over his. For his part, he complains about them constantly, disliking their ignorance and their vulgarity. Mr Biswas – as he is referred to throughout the book – becomes disagreeable, irritated and generally frustrated at his life and his inability to live in peace with his wife and children.

Full of the vivid life and unique character of Trinidad, this delightful comic novel reveals the multicultural background of the island and its attempts to incorporate different beliefs and customs. Mr Biswas' father was a contracted labourer who came from India to work in the sugarcane fields in Trinidad and Tobago, but Mr Biswas feels no connection to his Indian heritage and attempts to carve out his own identity.

Mr Biswas is something of an Everyman and the Trinidad setting is emblematic of the attempts of all postcolonial states to shake off repression and establish a new independent identity.

*V S Naipaul was awarded the Nobel Prize for Literature in 2001. His other books set in the Caribbean include* The Mystic Masseur *(1957).*

# WIDE SARGASSO SEA (1966)
## Jean Rhys

Taking as its starting point Charlotte Brontë's original mad woman in the attic in *Jane Eyre*, this novel sees Jean Rhys going back to her own roots as a Creole in the Caribbean. Always haunted by the untold story of the first Mrs Rochester, she decided to fictionalise the road to madness that Bertha took before she came to be locked up in Thornfield Hall.

The *Wide Sargasso Sea* is set in 1830s Jamaica. Creole heiress Antoinette Cosway meets a dashing young Englishman who is struck by her blend of sensuality and innocence. He is initially reluctant to involve himself with her, but is under pressure from his father to find himself a wife. He is finally persuaded by Antoinette's brother, and the lure of a large dowry, and they are quickly married.

After the wedding, they move out of the city to Granbois and then rumours begin to circulate. A man who claims to be Antoinette's half-brother appears, reporting that Antoinette's mother is still alive but insane. The young groom's mind is soon poisoned against his bride and he begins to treat her badly.

It is the inherent racism of those around her that prevents Antoinette from having a good life. Unlike Jane Eyre, she is not in the fortunate position of being able to reject love and security in the knowledge that society will always find a place for her. Antoinette is the daughter of the white plantation owner and, as a white Creole, she is accepted by neither community. Alone and distressed, Antoinette descends into madness.

The narrative voice switches between Antoinette and her (unnamed) husband, of whom a portrait is painted of a proud and arrogant man displaying the colonialist attitudes and double standards of the period. The story sees him sleeping with their black maid and, in a final act of proprietorial spite, changes his wife's name to 'Bertha'.

# ANNIE JOHN (1985)

Jamaica Kincaid

A classic Caribbean coming-of-age tale about a young girl growing up in Antigua. Her moral, psychological and intellectual development is set against her feelings for her mother, whom she initially adores but ends up hating.

At the outset, Annie John is alone at home with her mother, while her father is out at work. She dresses like her mother and helps her with the daily chores; she is happy and even calls her home a paradise. When the family moves to a house in the town, she has to mix with other children and her relationship with her mother begins to deteriorate, a process hastened by Annie's awkward transformation into a 'young lady'. One day she comes home from school and catches her parents making love: she feels rejected and isolated as a result of the incident and begins to answer her mother back almost in spite of herself.

Annie then begins to look for love outside the home. Firstly, she falls in love with Gwen, a school friend, to whom she declares her undying devotion and whose physical attention she enjoys in return. She subsequently meets another girl, called simply 'The Red Girl', a rather rough individual who lives a disordered life. Annie is captivated by this second girl and begins to steal money from her mother so she can buy the poorer girl presents. Annie's behaviour continues to deteriorate and, despite being the brightest in the class, she often finds herself in difficulties at school. This leads to trouble at home, especially with her mother, who screams at her and calls her a slut after seeing her talking to some boys in town, an accusation that prompts an uncharacteristically vulgar and impudent response from Annie.

This is a direct and honest account of a crucial passage in a young girl's life. Kincaid gives very colourful descriptions of the island of Antigua, with its variety of foodstuffs and abundant plant life, and shows how local spiritual traditions are kept alive despite the authoritarian presence of the British, as when a febrile and bedridden Annie is treated by obeah, a form of witchcraft using herbs, which effects Annie's final transformation to womanhood and her eventual emigration.

The novel was first serialised as a series of short stories in *The New Yorker* magazine.

## 🕮 Read ons

*The Oxford Book of Caribbean Short Stories*, Ed. Stewart Brown and John Wickham
Over fifty twentieth-century authors from Collymore to Danticat are included in this
sumptuous collection, highlighting the diversity and quality of Caribbean writing.

*Tar Baby*, Toni Morrison
Interracial love amid a host of colourful characters who come together in a
millionaire's mansion on an unnamed Caribbean island.

*Indigo*, Marina Warner
Old wrongs are put to right in this rewriting of *The Tempest*. It covers the seventeenth-century discovery of a Caribbean island and a modern-day celebration of
the event.

*The Polished Hoe*, Austin Clarke
A multi-prize-winning novel. It is 1952 and, as one woman confesses to murdering
a plantation owner, numerous previously unheard grievances emerge.

*In the Castle of My Skin*, George Lamming **(Barbados)**
A fatherless boy grows up in the 1930s to become a teacher, in this wonderfully
descriptive tale of village life. A classic of colonial Caribbean literature.

*Far Tortuga*, Peter Matthiessen **(Cayman Islands)**
With snippets of local dialect and beautifully rendered descriptions of the sea, this
is a tale of a reprobate crew that goes out turtle hunting in a sea fraught with
dangers.

*Texaco*, Patrick Chamoiseau **(Martinique)**
Using a blend of Creole fable, poetry and linguistic inventiveness, this novel tells
the story of 150 years of conflict and resolution throughout Martinique's troubled
history.

*Windward Heights*, Maryse Condé **(Guadeloupe)**
An intricate retelling of Emily Brontë's *Wuthering Heights* set in the late eighteenth
and early nineteenth century. When dark-skinned Razyé returns to his hometown,
his childhood love has married a rich white Creole.

*The Rum Diary*, Hunter S Thompson **(Puerto Rico)**
A hell-raising book that the author wrote when he was twenty-two, then lost. A young journalist drinks, loves and gets disillusioned in an unspoiled 1950s San Juan.

*A State of Independence*, Caryl Phillips **(St. Kitts)**
A man returns to the Caribbean after twenty years, feeling surprisingly isolated and lost as his homeland becomes independent and yet increasingly reliant on the USA.

# DOMINICAN REPUBLIC/HAITI

*Drown*, Junot Diaz **(Dominican Republic)**
An excellent collection of hard-hitting and lyrical short stories set in the barrios of the Dominican Republic and of Dominican immigrants' experiences of life in urban USA.

*The Feast of the Goat*, Mario Vargas Llosa **(Dominican Republic)**
A vivid recreation of the last days of the regime of dictator General Rafael Trujillo, leading up to his assassination in May 1961.

*The Farming of Bones*, Edwidge Danticat **(Haiti/Dominican Republic)**
A haunting novel about two Haitian lovers who find themselves caught up in the events of 1937, when the slaughter of all Haitians on Dominican land was ordered.

*The Comedians*, Graham Greene **(Haiti)**
Three men meet on a boat to Haiti. They learn to cope with the gradually increasing horror of their lives as 'Papa Doc' Duvalier's secret police terrorises a nation teetering on the brink of chaos.

*You, Darkness*, Mayra Montero **(Haiti)**
A biologist and an indigenous hunter go in search of a near-extinct blood frog, while zombies and the secret police stalk the jungle in a land where beauty and horror co-exist.

*Masters of the Dew*, Jacques Roumain **(Haiti)**
A beautifully evocative novel about a son who returns to his drought-stricken community in the 1930s. Considered Haiti's finest work of literature.

# TRINIDAD

*A Brighter Sun*, Samuel Selvon
A sixteen-year-old boy grows up quickly as he takes the responsibility of looking after his new wife and family. From one of the first generation of black British writers.

*Salt*, Earl Lovelace
An energetic and humorous look at the multi-ethnic make-up of an island still coming to terms with its own freedom, through the life story of a teacher who becomes involved in politics.

*Witchbroom*, Lawrence Scott
A wonderfully evocative novel. The last member of an old colonial family tells the history of the island with passion and romance.

*Carnival*, Robert Antoni
Hemingway's *The Sun Also Rises* is reset in the heat of the Caribbean. Three revellers look for meaning behind the partying and take to the mountains, but racially motivated violence invades their idyll.

# JAMAICA

*Summer Lightning and Other Stories*, Olive Senior
Children in conflict are the focus of each of these stories, all written in Jamaican dialect.

*Mint Tea and Other Stories*, Christine Craig
Stories of love, injustice and the emotional interior of women's lives set in superbly depicted lush surroundings, with occasional use of Creole.

*A High Wind in Jamaica*, Richard Hughes
A group of children put out to sea with a gang of manic pirates, in an attempt to return to England after a hurricane has flattened their land. A classic novel set in the Victorian period.

*Fruit of the Lemon*, Andrea Levy
A poignant and humorous novel set in the late 1970s. When her parents retire to Kingston, Faith Jackson makes her first visit to Jamaica and is regaled with stories of her ancestral past.

*A Kindness to the Children*, Joan Riley
In the tense climate of contemporary Jamaica, two women visit their family and friends and realise they are all struggling with a legacy of love, history and emotional despair.

*See also* **Guyana in South America**

# CUBA

KEYTITLE

*Three Trapped Tigers*, Guillermo Cabrera Infante

## THREE TRAPPED TIGERS (1965)
### Guillermo Cabrera Infante

This book is almost impossible to describe, featuring as it does a cacophony of voices and a non-existent plot. The novel begins with a series of seemingly unrelated tales the threads of which are expertly woven together in the final part. It is a wonderfully evocative and humorous portrait of Cuba in its Batista days.

Often hailed as a Cuban Ulysses, it presents a dead man's fond recollections of his youth and the country he left behind, a pre-Castro 1950s' Cuba. It is a wild, colourful, steamy, cabaret society full of characters living on the edge of a corrupt regime that is ripe for toppling. The novel is written in Cuban Spanish with puns galore, the title itself being the opening words of a Spanish tongue-twister: Tres Tristes Tigres. Infante is fluent in English and so is capable of inventing words and playing with language, not only in the original Spanish (or 'Spunnish', as Carlos Fuentes labelled it), but in English too. The translated version is almost forty pages longer than the original, owing to the author/translator's English wordgames.

The author plays not only linguistic games but also graphic games, including in the book blank pages, black pages, pages that are a mirror-image of a previous page, a playscript, some untranslated passages, dual-language pages, poetry, and a plethora of lists. Infante engages in endless parody and is capable of stylistic ventriloquism like no other author, mimicking writers from Shakespeare to Hemingway to Alejo Carpentier.

What the 'novel' lacks in conventional storytelling is more than made up for in the sense of place it evokes: the reader can almost taste the daiquiris and feel the joie de vivre that permeates the book.

*Exiled from Cuba from the mid-1960s, he also wrote* Infante's Inferno *(1979), a sort of Caribbean Don Juan.*

# 📖Read ons

*Dirty Havana Trilogy*, Pedro Juan Gutierrez
This novel could not be more aptly named. It is a sleazy and sexy trio of stories revolving around the main character Pedro Juan's sexual exploits in modern-day impoverished Cuba.

*Explosion in a Cathedral*, Alejo Carpentier
An important book from Cuba's most renowned writer, this is a historical novel about Victor Hugues, a revolutionary figure, set in the late eighteenth century, who recaptured the island of Guadeloupe from the English.

*Cuba and the Night*, Pico Iyer
From the pen of a travel writer comes a love story of modern Cuba in all its passionate contradictions, as a cynical American photojournalist falls for a Cuban woman who yearns for a better life.

*Our Man in Havana*, Graham Greene
A British vacuum-cleaner salesman unexpectedly finds himself becoming MI6's newest agent when he is unable to resist the money they offer him, money that he needs to finance his daughter's lavish lifestyle. As a thoroughly inept agent needing desperately to fulfil his brief, he fills his dispatches with fabricated events that begin to come worryingly true.

*Havana World Series*, José Latour
In 1958, a gang of Cuban criminals plan to rob a Havana casino, in this richly detailed and lively crime caper.

*Tango for a Torturer*, Daniel Chavarría
In this sexy thriller, a former revolutionary discovers a former torturer is hiding in the back streets of Havana. From an award-winning Uruguayan novelist.

*Havana Red*, Leonardo Padura
A murder mystery with a Cuban Philip Marlowe investigating the death of a transvestite in a country where everyone wears a mask in order to survive. Hot, sticky and steamy, this is the first of the Havana Quartet.

# CENTRAL AMERICA

## GENERAL CENTRAL AMERICA

*The Mosquito Coast*, Paul Theroux

## THE MOSQUITO COAST (1982)
Paul Theroux

Charlie Fox's dad, Allie, regards life in America with increasing disillusionment and, keen to relocate far away, he fabricates an imminent attack on America as a pretext for removing his wife and four children to the heart of Honduras. With the help of bemused locals, the family attempts to build a modern-day paradise in the jungle.

Allie is an ingenious man with a considerable degree of technological know-how, which he stresses is 'not magic, but science'. He manages to keep everyone alive and comfortable for quite a while, even building a machine capable of making ice, dubbed the 'Fat Boy'. Convinced of the universal appeal and importance of his invention, he journeys upstream to parade it to the indigenous people. However, he miscalculates the time the trip will take, and the ice melts. When Allie returns, he lies about the expedition and Charlie begins to see cracks in his dad's façade.

This is a fascinating, pacy, and at times extremely funny book that has at its heart the relationship between father and son. Based on a true story, it is seen through the eyes of the beleaguered Charlie. We watch him go from innocent acceptance to cynical rebellion. Ultimately, the Fox family's failure to make a new life for themselves in the jungle leads to catastrophe and it is Allie's inability to accept the truth that leads to the biggest tragedy of all.

Peter Weir's 1986 film of the book was well received, with Harrison Ford in the role of Allie.

## 📖Read ons

*And We Sold The Rain – Contemporary Fiction Of Central America*, Ed. Rosario Santos.
A classic collection, recently updated, that includes new and established authors from Costa Rica, Guatemala, El Salvador, Panama, Honduras and Nicaragua.

*A Flag for Sunrise*, Robert Stone
A highly political novel about an American anthropologist drawn into the maelstrom of a civil war in an unnamed Central American country.

*The Cyclone*, Miguel Angel Asturias **(Guatemala)**
From the pen of this Nobel laureate comes a groundbreaking, anti-big-business novel about the exploitation of workers on a banana plantation and their campaign to protect their rights. The first in his 'Banana Trilogy', of which the subsequent volumes are *The Green Pope* and *Eyes of the Interred*.

*The Divine Husband*, Francisco Goldman **(Guatemala)**
This sweeping history of South American politics is set at the turn of the last century, as an ex-nun has a series of lovers including true-life poet and hero of Cuban independence, Jose Marti.

*The Tailor of Panama*, John Le Carré **(Panama)**
An old Etonian is spying for his country and for his own greed. This is both a wonderful tour through the country and a satirical look at the events leading up to the handover of the Panama Canal.

*Two Serious Ladies*, Jane Bowles **(Panama)**
An extraordinary bittersweet novel about a honeymoon couple who split up when the wife prefers the company of a prostitute to that of her new husband. Based in part on her life with writer Paul Bowles.

*Desperadoes*, Joseph O'Connor **(Nicaragua)**
In the summer of 1985, two parents leave Ireland for Nicaragua to pick up the body of their son who has got caught up in the fighting. Described with almost photo-graphic realism and acute emotional dissection.

*Beka Lamb*, Zee Edgell **(Belize)**
A compelling portrayal of family life centred around compulsive liar, Beka, who seeks to change her ways when her best friend is expelled from school for becoming pregnant.

*Port Mungo*, Patrick McGrath **(Honduras)**
Set in New York and Honduras, it centres on the destructive relationship of two selfish painters who forgo family and convention in order to be together.

# MEXICO

## KEYTITLES

*Pedro Páramo*, Juan Rulfo
*The Years with Laura Díaz*, Carlos Fuentes

## PEDRO PÁRAMO (1955)
Juan Rulfo

Fulfilling the deathbed wish of his mother, Juan Preciado goes in search of his missing father, Pedro Páramo. The search takes him to the desert plains of Mexico and the town of Comala, where he finds that Pedro Páramo is dead. So, it seems, is everyone else. Souls that are not pure enough to enter heaven wander the streets, telling their tales of life and misery. Preciado, like the reader, is unsure what or who is real and he begins to suspect that he too may be dead.

The ghosts reveal Pedro Páramo's life story, in particular his love for Susana San Juan and his loneliness when she moves away after her father dies. Pedro ruthlessly builds an empire and marries the daughter of his biggest creditor, Juan's mother, Dolores. Pedro sends her away soon after the marriage. Years go by and Pedro sires many illegitimate children. Susana returns and Pedro unsuccessfully attempts to win her over, and this pursuit causes her to take refuge in madness and she dies unhappily. Pedro is later killed by one of his children, Abundio, in a drunken rage.

The narrative thread is often difficult to hold onto, as there are frequent switches between the first and third persons, interspersed with snippets of overheard conversations and stories told directly to Juan.

It is a classic of Latin American literature which defined the style that became Mexican modernist gothic. *Pedro Páramo* illustrates the social change in Mexico in the late nineteenth and early twentieth centuries, when mass migration to the cities left a huge number of ghost towns all around the country. It highlights the effect on the people of the Mexican Revolution of 1910-1920 and the depopulation of the countryside that followed.

*The idea for the book came to Juan Rulfo following a trip to his hometown after a thirty-year absence, when he found that its seven thousand inhabitants had been reduced to one hundred and fifty. This is an astonishing novel that requires close reading but rewards such efforts sumptuously. A film has been made, with a screenplay by Gabriel García Marquez.*

# THE YEARS WITH LAURA DÍAZ (1999)
## Carlos Fuentes

The novel is narrated by Laura Díaz's great-grandson, who sees an unknown woman in a mural by Diego Rivera and realises that it is his great-grandmother. Her German grandparents settle in Mexico in the 1880s and she is born on the coffee plantation of her grandfather, Don Felipe, at Catemaco in 1898. She lives with her mother and maiden aunts while her father works as a bank manager, living in Veracruz with his son, Santiago, from an earlier marriage. The family does not move to Veracruz until Laura is twelve years old. Her meeting with Santiago opens her eyes to a wider world, especially when he is shot for being a revolutionary.

Laura marries Juan Francisco Lopez Greene, a sombre working-class hero, and moves to Mexico City, where they have two sons. Their marriage is an unhappy one, however, and she eventually leaves him. Throughout the book, she has many lovers and much heartache, especially with the death of one of her sons. Nevertheless, she eventually becomes a politically committed photographer, encouraged by Diego Rivera and Frida Kahlo. Her fame establishes her identity and gives her a sense of fulfilment, a feeling of having contributed to her country's history.

In chronicling Laura's life throughout the twentieth century, in this protracted and diversionary book, Fuentes maps out the years of Mexico's development in the process. While she could be viewed as an Everywoman, Laura's tale is full of individual depth and feeling. The author is incapable of writing a dull line and historical anecdotes abound amid the dramatic and turbulent scenes of heartbreak and triumph. Mexico is brought to life in all its colour and sensuousness, its sights and smells vividly described by a literary master.

*The Years with Laura Díaz* is a more positive counterpart to Fuentes's *The Death of Artemio Cruz* (1962). In the earlier novel, Artemio Cruz is a revolutionary who becomes a capitalist and his story symbolises the triumph of greed over morality.

## 📖Read ons

*The Labyrinth of Solitude*, Octavio Paz
First published in 1950, these nine novelistic essays are a brilliant reflection on the Mexican psyche and the quest for identity, as seen by the Nobel-Prize-winning author.

*Caramelo*, Sandra Cisneros
A rich, vibrant novel that intricately embroiders tales of love and life for many generations of a Mexican family.

*The Power and the Glory*, Graham Greene
Widely considered Greene's best book, this novel vividly evokes the landscape of Mexico, describing a drunken Catholic priest's attempts to flee an anti-clerical purge.

*Under the Volcano*, Malcolm Lowry
On the Day of the Dead, an alcoholic consul's wife arrives to save him and their marriage, in this classic novel set in Mexico before the Second World War. *See also Dark as the Grave Wherein My Friend is Laid*.

*The Ultimate Good Luck*, Richard Ford
Harry and his girlfriend go to Oaxaca to secure her brother's release from jail and free him from the clutches of a particularly unpleasant drug dealer.

*Mexica*, Norman Spinrad
The epic story of Cortes and his conquistadors and their quest for gold and glory for Spain at the expense of the Aztecs and Montezuma.

*Like Water for Chocolate*, Laura Esquivel – *see* **READ ON A THEME: KITCHEN CONFIDENTIALS – FOOD AND DRINK**

READON A THEME

## KITCHEN CONFIDENTIALS – FOOD AND DRINK

*Like Water for Chocolate*, Laura Esquivel
An entertaining and highly charged romantic novel about a daughter condemned by tradition to look after her mother. She finds a voice for the thwarted love of her brother-in-law through the magic of cooking.

*The Debt to Pleasure*, John Lanchester
Tarquin Winot, gourmet and snob, takes a culinary journey from Portsmouth to Provence, recounting tales of his life. However, among the delicious recipes lurks something more sinister.

*The Devil's Larder*, Jim Crace
Sixty-four short fictions of quite breathtaking beauty make up this bizarre, erotic 'novel' whose pages are haunted by wonderful images and gastronomic obsessions.

*Les Liaisons Culinaires*, Andreas Staïkos
Two Athenian suitors vie for the love of a woman through cooking, each one attempting to outdo the other with increasingly mouthwatering dishes. A fun, slim read with recipes included.

*The Mistress of Spices*, Chitra Banerjee Divakaruni
A beautifully written story of the immigrant Indian owner of a spice shop in Oakland, California, who dispenses wisdom with her spices. We discover what happens one day when a lonely American enters her store.

*Cooking with Fernet Branca*, James Hamilton-Paterson
A comic farce, set in rural Tuscany, about a writer and foodie with bizarre tastes whose idyll is shattered when a new neighbour arrives.

*The Coffee Trader*, David Liss
A lively evocation of seventeenth-century Amsterdam. A persecuted Jew thinks coffee trading will make him rich and help him become respectable in society.

*Sideways*, Rex Pickett
Two friends, one about to get married, the other recovering from divorce, head into the Californian hills for a week of wine-tasting and womanising. A funny and touching novel of friendship and wine.

*The Vintner's Luck*, Elizabeth Knox
A young vintner in Burgundy in 1808 meets an angel who changes his fortunes and those of his wines, as they develop a long-running and complex relationship.

*Boogaloo on 2nd Avenue*, Mark Kurlansky
Acclaimed writer Kurlansky's fictional debut is set in New York in the 1980s and tells of a multicultural neighbourhood in transition, and one man's obsession with a German pastry chef. It also includes a selection of recipes.

# UNITED STATES OF AMERICA

## GENERAL USA

**KEY**TITLES

*USA*, John Dos Passos
*'Rabbit'* Series, John Updike

## USA (1930–1936)
### John Dos Passos

The novel covers the first thirty years of twentieth-century America, relating the lives of a dozen main characters, and hundreds of minor characters, from childhood onwards. Dos Passos intersperses these character studies with newspaper clippings of the time and short autobiographical ramblings. There is no continuous plot – rather a series of finely written sketches showing each character seeking to find his or her place in a world rapidly turning sour. The author also includes short biographical sketches of famous people of the day, including Thomas Edison, Henry Ford and Emma Goldberg.

Modernist technician though he may be, Dos Passos is also a first-rate storyteller who perfectly captures the voices of ordinary folk in a work that takes in the growth of the cities and the decline of the countryside, the formation of the unions and the resistance to them. From New York to Seattle, he covers the whole of this vast terrain. Historically, we see the impact the Mexican and Russian Revolutions had, the initial indifference to the First World War, the rise of Hollywood, and the slide into Depression. Jean Paul Sartre regarded Dos Passos, a committed socialist, as 'the greatest writer of our time', admiring his politics as much as his prose.

What Dos Passos offers here is a gritty portrait, rooted in reality, of an America sacrificing its ideals at the altar of capitalism. The book is essential reading for anyone interested in American history and it is an astonishing accomplishment, a work that in many estimations is a serious contender for the prize of The Great American Novel.

The book comprises three novels: *The 42nd Parallel* (1930), *1919* (1932), and *The Big Money* (1936). They were first published in a single volume in 1938.

# 'RABBIT' SERIES (1960–1990)
## John Updike

Harry 'Rabbit' Angstrom is an Everyman American who finds it difficult to mature into a responsible and contented adult. Over the course of the four novels, and the four decades they cover, this feckless and troubled man encounters numerous disappointments and tragedies, and finally dies a very discontented individual. It is a personal journey that mirrors the changes wrought in American society during this period.

Harry, a former school basketball hero, lives in the fictional town of Brewer, Pennsylvania. In the first novel, *Rabbit Run*, he is a young man suffocating in a dead-end job and living in a one-roomed apartment in a poor district, with his pregnant wife, Janice, and their two-year-old son, Nelson. Janice has started drinking heavily and Harry embarks on an affair with a part-time prostitute, more out of boredom than desire. The ensuing tragedy does nothing to foster responsibility and conscientiousness in Harry, and the novel ends unresolved.

*Rabbit Redux* captures the spirit and optimism of the 1960s. The novel finds Harry on the verge of middle age. His wife has walked out on him and he is trying to cope with the demands of his son, Nelson, now twelve years old. The novel captures the spirit and optimism of the 1960s.

By the time the 1980s come along, *Rabbit is Rich* sees Harry as a successful used car salesman in Reagan's America, wrestling with his libido, as well as with his fatherly duties as Nelson approaches marriage.

In the final volume, *Rabbit at Rest*, Harry and Janice finally leave Brewer and retire to Florida. Harry himself has become dangerously obese and depressed, while Nelson is now a drug addict attempting to take control of his own life.

Harry is insensitive and selfish, and yet his constant search for the happiness and fulfilment that elude make him a strangely endearing figure. Updike's writing is brutally realistic, caustically humorous and full of widsom. This series is an extraordinary accomplishment and a comprehensive picture of America in the latter half of the twentieth century.

The four 'Rabbit' novels are *Rabbit, Run* (1960), *Rabbit, Redux* (1971), *Rabbit is Rich* (1981), and *Rabbit at Rest* (1990). A novella, *Rabbit Remembered*, appears in the short story collection, *Licks of Love* (2001). For the 1995 Everyman four-volume edition, Updike reinstated sexually explicit passages that were edited out of the original, and added an informative introduction.

## Read ons

*The Granta Book of the American Short Story*, Ed. Richard Ford
Over forty stories make up this weighty compendium of the best of post-war American fiction. It is a personal selection that eschews the obvious and delights at every turn.

*Underworld*, Don DeLillo
A novel that moves back and forth in time and tells the stories of numerous characters, many of them from real life, with the object of revealing the garbage at the heart of American society.

*Beloved*, Toni Morrison
This Pulitzer-Prize-winning novel is a complex, powerful study of slavery, set in the wake of the Civil War. It deals with the ghost of a dead baby who comes back to haunt its mother.

*Accordion Crimes*, E Annie Proulx
Spanning the entire twentieth century, these are brutal tales of poverty and prejudice. The history of the land of the free is told through the connections that various immigrant families have with a green accordion.

*What We Talk About When We Talk About Love*, Raymond Carver
Stories that lay bare the human soul. Various characters speak of love, in the stark unsettling world of Carver's unique prose.

*Invisible Man*, Ralph Ellison
This contemporary classic tells of a black man's journey through 1950s' America, from the Southern states to New York, searching for meaning and identity in a land in which he is racially invisible.

### *American Pastoral*, Philip Roth
When a young woman blows up her local post office in protest at the Vietnam War, her father's carefully constructed life starts to unravel. An incisive examination of all that America stands for.

### *Blonde*, Joyce Carol Oates
A fictional biography of Marilyn Monroe that explores the interior life of an icon who has come to symbolise the American Dream.

### *Narratives of Empire Series*, Gore Vidal
Seven novels that span the history of the United States from the Revolution to the post-war years: *Burr, Lincoln, 1876, Washington DC, Empire, Hollywood: a Novel of the Twenties*, and *The Golden Age*.

### *Birds of America*, Lorrie Moore
Short stories by one of America's masters of the genre. Keen observations and portraits of modern American life, written in intelligent and witty prose.

### *Mason and Dixon*, Thomas Pynchon
A tale of the lives and loves of the two eighteenth-century English surveyors whose famous boundary line separates the American North from the American South to this day.

### *Tracks*, Louise Erdich
The gripping opening line, 'We started dying before the snow, and like the snow, we continued to fall', sets the tone for this moving novel of the Chippewa, Native Americans of North Dakota who are gradually being wiped out by disease and the loss of their land to white settlers.

### *The Chosen*, Chaim Potok
Two Jewish boys from differing families – one a strict Hasidic, the other orthodox – become spiritual brothers in the 1940s and survive a lifetime of threats to their friendship.

# EAST COAST

## KEY TITLES

*Dinner at the Homesick Restaurant*, Anne Tyler
*Revolutionary Road*, Richard Yates
*The Stories of John Cheever*, John Cheever

## DINNER AT THE HOMESICK RESTAURANT (1982)
Anne Tyler

Pearl Tull is dying and looking back on her life in Baltimore. She had to bring up three children single-handedly when her travelling salesman husband, Beck, left her in 1944. Her three children are now adults and each chapter presents the reader with a different perspective of life in the family home.

Cody, the eldest boy, is a vindictive, paranoid bully. He is jealous of the attention given to his younger brother, Ezra, and does all he can to disrupt his life, even to the extent of robbing him of his one true chance for happiness.

Then there is hapless, shy, accepting Ezra himself. The only one who really loves their mother, he is also the one in whom she is disappointed. He fails to go to college to become a teacher, instead settling for the life of a restaurant-owner. He lives with Pearl until her death, caring for her and becoming her eyes when she eventually goes blind.

Jenny, a paediatrician, is the youngest. On her third marriage, she strides obliviously through life, determined to avoid emotional scrutiny or suffering.

Pearl's pride and fear of outside interference force the family to live a closeted life in which outsiders are viewed as unwelcome aliens and homeliness is absent. Ezra makes repeated vain attempts to bring the family together round the dinner table, and he even changes the name of his restaurant to 'Homesick' as an attempt to create a homely feel for his diners that was so evidently lacking in his own.

*Each of Anne Tyler's books is a masterclass in writing. Other novels include* The Accidental Tourist *(1985), which was made into a successful film,* Breathing Lessons *(1988) and* Back When We Were Grownups *(2001). Both Roddy Doyle* and Nick Hornby have described her as 'the greatest living novelist writing in English'.

# REVOLUTIONARY ROAD (1961)
Richard Yates

On the surface, Frank and April Wheeler have everything: they are good-looking, young, intelligent, reasonably well off, and they have two beautiful children. However, they feel trapped in a suburban cul-de-sac that embodies values they despise and is far removed from the European intellectual and cultural haven to which they claim to aspire. Unsure how they came to be so ensnared, they seek to remedy their situation and save their lives.

Although imbued with a post-war optimism that leads them to believe they can achieve anything they want, they unfortunately do not know what they want, other than to escape the hellish blandness of their present life.

April suggests that the way out of this empty existence is to leave their Connecticut home and move to Paris. The plan is for her to earn money while Frank 'finds himself', an ambition he has nurtured for years but the reality of which suddenly terrifies him. What if there is nothing to find?

They set the wheels in motion, all the while nursing the fear that they are chronically unsuited not only to the lifestyle they are pursuing but also to each other. As a result, they unwittingly begin a psychological game of subversion that threatens their marriage.

Yates reveals the speciousness of the American Dream with confidence, and the disintegration of a relationship is revealed not just through the piercing dialogue, but also the poignant remnants of that which is unspoken. This is a well-constructed novel that is unsentimental yet emotionally profound.

*Criminally neglected as an author in his own lifetime, Richard Yates saw his novels go out of print before he died. Recently, they have been enjoying something of a renaissance, with various eminent writers trumpeting his rediscovery and the reissue of this and many of his earlier novels. See also* The Easter Parade *(1976) and* Spring Harbour *(1986)*

# THE STORIES OF JOHN CHEEVER (1979)
John Cheever

John Cheever is a genius who has been called 'the Chekhov of the suburbs'. Many of his stories are set in Shady Hill, a fictional suburb in New York State, where his characters inhabit largely recognisable worlds. Cheever takes the reader beneath the surface to view the turbulent undercurrents with a perfect line of poetic beauty that sums up a place, a feeling, or the emotional totality of a situation.

There are sixty stories in this superb collection, spanning thirty years of writing. They expose the fragile nature of people's lives, of a spiritual emptiness that money or status can rarely compensate for. There is joy here, as well, and pathos, but there's also much excessive drinking behind closed doors, extra-maritial affairs, broken dreams and shattered illusions. The people are unerringly real and Cheever's humanity stands out.

As well as famous stories such as *Goodbye My Brother*, *The Enormous Radio* and *The Swimmer*, this collection includes *The Sutton Place Story*, in which a child goes missing, and *Torch Song*, a portrait of a woman's fractured life that has a breathtaking finale. In addition, *The Five Forty-Eight* sees a jilted lover following a man back to his cosy neighbourhood with a gun and a plan for humiliation, and *The Scarlet Moving Van* tells the story of a couple continuously forced to move house because of the husband's recidivist drinking.

This collection won the Pulitzer Prize for Fiction and the National Book Award.

*Cheever's novels include the* The Wapshot Chronicle *(1958),* The Wapshot Scandal *(1964) and* Bullet Park *(1969).*

## ᕤRead ons

*Sea Glass*, Anita Shreve (New Hampshire)
A year in the life of a newly married couple as they move to a New England coastal community as the Depression approaches.

*Wonder Boys*, Michael Chabon (Pittsburgh)
A weekend in the life of a novelist whose life is a mess. He has a brilliant but troubled student, a pregnant mistress and a wife who has just left him.

*The Sportswriter*, Richard Ford (New Jersey)
A classic novel of modern America, full of subtle observations on life and love and the problems they throw up. Frank Bascombe's story is continued in *Independence Day* and *The Lay of the Land*.

*The Wedding*, Dorothy West (Massachusetts)
A slim novel about the black bourgeoisie in the Martha's Vineyard of the 1950s. Stories of past loves are revealed when a black heiress opts to marry a poor white musician.

*Blackbird House*, Alice Hoffman (Massachusetts)
A novel in the shape of twelve interlaced short stories, all set in the same Cape Cod farmhouse, from the time of the American Revolution to the present day.

*The Secret History*, Donna Tartt (New England)
A psychological and literary thriller that sees a group of classics students caught up in murders in a high-class Vermont school.

*Peyton Place*, Grace Metalious (New England)
A look at the lives of three women in a picturesque pre-war town where secrets are buried deep. A groundbreaking look at sex and poverty that shocked a nation.

*Empire Falls*, Richard Russo (Maine)
Three different families are traced through several generations, as small-town America is laid bare in this poignant and compelling portrait of ordinary lives.

*The Cider House Rules*, John Irving **(Maine)**
A rambling, complex novel about a boy raised in an orphanage and his relationships with those he loves. Set between 1930 and 1950.

*The Great Gatsby*, F Scott Fitzgerald **(Long Island)**
During one summer in the mid 1920s, a man chronicles the glitzy life of his intriguing and enigmatic neighbour as he watches the idle rich at play.

*Light Years*, James Salter **(New York State)**
An astonishingly beautiful meditation on love, marriage, families and the melancholy passing of time. Nedra and Viri, a golden couple living in the Hamptons, appear to have everything but find happiness elusive.

# NEW YORK

## THE AGE OF INNOCENCE (1920)
Edith Wharton

Edith Wharton returned to the Old New York society of the 1870s for this, her Pulitzer-Prize-winning classic. Newland Archer is a young lawyer and socialite. His fiancée, May Welland, is well bred and much respected. They announce their engagement at a time when May's cousin, Ellen Olenska, returns from Europe amid rumours that she has left her brutal husband and run off with his secretary. Newland initially regards Ellen with distaste, but comes to feel sympathy for her plight. She is something of a free spirit, unfettered by the strict conventions that Newland has never previously questioned, and this spirit attracts him. As they become more entangled, Newland is forced to choose between following his heart and playing by the conventional rules of a society that has served him very well. When Ellen talks of divorcing her husband, New York society is appalled and Newland is instructed to disabuse her of the idea. Affairs are accepted, even expected, but divorce is a disgrace too far.

Wharton places the hypocrisy and snobbery of the upper echelons of American society under the microscope and her words glide over the page like a well-danced waltz. Her detailed descriptions of society life – the food, the furnishings and the fashions – are exquisitely realised, as is the poignancy of the doomed love and the personal dilemma at the centre of the story.

New York is the setting for many of her novels, including *The House of Mirth* (1905) and the *Old New York* quartet of novels (1924).

# WHAT I LOVED (2003)
Siri Hustvedt

Leo Hertzberg is an art historian looking back on his life, from the time he strikes up what proves to be a lifelong friendship with experimental artist Bill Wechsler, in the mid 1970s, to the turn of the century.

Bill is married to a fragile poet, Lucille, while Leo's wife Erica is an academic. They become fathers of boys within a short time of each other and by the time Bill moves in upstairs from the Hertzbergs, he has fallen for his muse, Violet, and is now in a relationship with her. She is carrying out research into nineteenth-century hysterics.

This is a book about art, the rarefied milieu of SoHo galleries, and academic interpretations. It is also a book about perception – what we see, and what we think we see – and about how we love. Hints of tragedy to come hold the reader's interest through the long descriptions of Wechsler's art that hold up particularly the earlier parts of the story. When a death occurs, we shift from the cerebral to the physical.

Bill's child, Mark, becomes a powerful force in the novel and a character whose nature and behaviour are difficult to analyse. Is he psychologically damaged, or is he simply an emblem of a generation of young people out of reach of their parents? He becomes something of a sociopath, sliding into a club subculture and developing a taste for 'Horror Art'. He befriends the main exponent of this violent and disreputable style, enfant terrible Teddy Giles, and, fuelled by drugs and crime, the pair embark on an odyssey that leads ultimately to murder.

*Hustvedt has a flair for taking the reader into the hearts and minds of characters and exploring them in detail. As an art critic, she is particularly interested in the creative impulse and in seeking out meaning in people's lives. This is her third novel and it received widespread critical acclaim. The previous two,* The Blindfold *(1992) and* The Enchantment of Lily Dahl *(1996), are also set in New York.*

# LAST EXIT TO BROOKLYN (1964)

Hubert Selby Jnr

This is Selby's best-known book – six visceral stories that together form a loosely structured novel about life in a Brooklyn neighbourhood. They are tales of prostitutes, transsexuals, drug addicts and hoodlums. Selby claims to have written simply what he saw out of his window in 1950s' New York, but the stories read rather like conversations in a poolroom or bar, as though a customer leans over and whispers in the reader's ear. With almost non-existent punctuation, this is initially a difficult narrative to follow but ultimately rewarding.

The taboo nature of the subjects Selby deals with, and his stark way of portraying them, attracted controversy when some of the individual stories were published. They contain much violence, drug-taking, profanity and homosexual activity, and feature a colourful cast of down-and-outs and deadbeats: the transsexual Georgette, with absurd aspirations; Harry, who uses time off during an industrial strike to cruise the gay bars and discover his real sexuality; Tralala, who robs drunken sailors and gets her comeuppance in the most brutal of fashions; and Abraham, the 'cool ass' stud with the starving family at home.

It is an intense portrait of the underclass, painted before such a label existed. Selby's talent is to make the reader interested in these powerless unfortunates, using language and narrative structures that defy convention as much as do the lives of the individuals they describe.

The novel has had a troubled history. It was once banned in Italy and it became the subject of two court cases in the UK in the late 1960s. A film was made in 1989, which re-ignited interest in Selby's work.

## 📖 Read ons

*Bright Lights, Big City*, Jay McInerney
Cleverly told in the second person, this book charts a frantic week in the life of a young Manhattan highflier, as his life collapses all around him.

*The Catcher in the Rye*, J D Salinger
Classic 1950s' coming-of-age novel about Holden Caulfield's twenty-four hours in the Big Apple, talking to locals, avoiding phonies and coming to terms with his troubled life.

*Ragtime*, E L Doctorow
The story of three very different immigrant families in New York in the first two decades of the 1900s, interwoven with real-life characters and events.

*A Tree Grows in Brooklyn*, Betty Smith
A classic tale of a poor Irish-German girl growing up with a domineering mother and an alcoholic husband on the eve of the First World War.

*Ladies' Man*, Richard Price
With hints both of Jay McInerney and Woody Allen, this enthralling novel charts a desperate but hilarious week in the life of Kenny, who loses his girlfriend, his job and the illusion that he has any real friends.

*The Fortress of Solitude*, Jonathan Lethem
Steeped in popular culture, this is a story of friendship between two boys – one white and one black – in the 1970s, by an author who has been dubbed the 'Poet of Brooklyn'.

*Jazz*, Toni Morrison
Reading like a solo from one of the jazz greats, this story follows Joe and Violet Trace through love, death and hard times in Harlem from the 1920s to the present day.

*Another Country*, James Baldwin
Baldwin highlights the difference between bohemian Greenwich Village and underprivileged Harlem in this tale of a suicidal black musician in 1950s' New York.

### The Collected Stories, Grace Paley
All of her classic stories from over thirty years of writing are collected here. These loosely connected tales of the city prove her to be one of the great exponents of the art of the short story.

### New York Trilogy, Paul Auster
In three seemingly unrelated novellas that ultimately come together, Paul Auster redefines the detective novel and produces a neat piece of metafiction in the process. Imbued with themes of identity and language, this is endlessly fascinating cerebral chewing gum.

### A Rage in Harlem, Chester Himes
A fast-paced sardonic thriller with elements of the grotesque sees a hapless young man enlist his streetwise twin brother to rescue his shady girlfriend. The first of Himes' series of crime novels set in Harlem.

### Extremely Loud and Incredibly Close, Jonathan Safran Foer
An enchanting novel about a nine-year-old boy, Oskar, who searches all five boroughs of the city for the lock to the key his father left him when he was killed in the 9/11 attacks.

### The Bonfire of the Vanities, Tom Wolfe
Dickensian in size and scope, Wolfe's debut novel deftly dissects New York society in the 1980s. A Wall Street yuppie's life spirals out of control after he is involved in a hit-and-run incident.

# AMERICAN SOUTH

## KEY TITLES

*Wise Blood*, Flannery O'Connor
*Absalom, Absalom*, William Faulkner
*A Confederacy of Dunces*, John Kennedy Toole

## WISE BLOOD (1952)
Flannery O'Connor

Flannery O'Connor was born in Savannah, Georgia, to the only Catholic family in a 'Christ-haunted', fanatically Protestant area, and her work deals with individuals tormented by issues of faith. In her twenties, she was diagnosed with the fatal lupus disease, the same illness that took her father's life. This awareness of her own impending death doubtless contributed to the dark tone of her work. She died in 1964 at the age of thirty-nine.

*Wise Blood* was her first novel, extended from a short story. It is the tragic-comic story of Hazel Motes, a soldier returning from the Second World War with religion on his mind. His grandfather was a wandering preacher who fed Hazel with images of Jesus. Hazel tries to avoid Jesus by avoiding sin, but, disillusioned by his wartime experiences, he feels tormented by the Son of God, whom he grows to hate, at one point stating 'Jesus was a liar'. He attempts to establish his own 'Church without Christ' and he stands on street corners preaching his twisted gospel. He encounters Asa Hawkes, a preacher who feigns blindness, and his degenerate fifteen-year-old daughter, Sabbath, whom Hazel steals away for his own pleasures.

O'Connor is interested in the violent turnings of the mind and her work is dark and full of Gothic sensibilities. Although there is a subtle humour throughout, the novel has a chilling conclusion. A 1979 film by John Huston has attained cult status.

*O'Connor was an expert short-story writer and her collection* A Good Man is Hard to Find, *or 'Nine stories of original sin', as she called them, is exceptional, as is her only other novel,* The Violent Bear it Away *(1962), in which a boy struggles with his destiny as a prophet and with his atheist father, a teacher who seeks to cure him of his faith.*

# ABSALOM, ABSALOM! (1936)

William Faulkner

This is an epic family drama about the life of Thomas Sutpen, as told by five different narrators. Born into a peasant family in Appalachia, Sutpen has the will to rise above his station and proclaim his name to the world. After a brief time in Haiti, where he marries and has a son, he turns up alone in Jefferson, Mississippi, in 1833.

He builds a huge mansion with his bare hands, on a hundred-acre site that he swindles from a Chickasaw Indian. The house comes to be stained with the sins of the South. Sutpen becomes very rich but remains unpopular. He marries a local trader's daughter and they have two children, Henry and Judith. Henry goes to university and meets Charles Bon, whom Judith falls in love with and wishes to marry.

Charles is Sutpen's abandoned son from his Haitian wife, and when the father tells Henry this, Henry refuses to accept it and leaves the family home. The Civil War begins and when Sutpen and Henry meet up again after four years of fighting, the father tells the son that Charles has Negro blood in him, a fact that explains why Sutpen deserted Charles's Haitian mother. Henry is outraged and sets about preventing the marriage, in the end killing Charles and subsequently fleeing.

Sutpen comes back from the war to a ruined family and a ravaged plantation, but not to the end of the story. The novel is full of dark imagery and passionate tragedy. It highlights the South's mixed feelings about its own past, and underlines the tragic consequences of slavery.

Faulkner's story shows how damaging it can be to cling to the past and especially to the idea of purity of blood. He questions the notion of objective truth and makes the novel intentionally ambiguous, imposing on the reader a kind of false memory that mirrors the selective memory of the protagonists as seen in the crucially incomplete or contradictory versions of events they present.

*All of Faulkner's novels are set in the Deep South, and they include* As I Lay Dying *(1930) and* Light in August *(1932).*

# A CONFEDERACY OF DUNCES (1980)

John Kennedy Toole

A behemoth of a character, Ignatius J Reilly is a confirmed wastrel who plays the lute and rails against the declining morals of the world at large, and New Orleans in particular. Yet although outwardly slothful, Ignatius has a very sharp mind. Intelligent and acute, he is continually committing his thoughts to paper, filling notepads that he scatters around the back bedroom of the house he shares with his long-suffering mother.

He has avoided work for nearly thirty years, but is finally forced into looking for a suitable occupation, doubting that such a thing exists. Working his way through several jobs and leaving a trail of destruction behind him, he finally becomes a hotdog vendor, much to his mother's embarrassment. Unsurprisingly, he is dismissed after eating all of his stock.

Ignatius subsequently has various adventures around town and inadvertently mixes with lowlifes of all sorts, a seeming magnet for the oddballs of a fabulously seedy New Orleans, including his girlfriend Myrna Minkoff, who believes the answer to his problems may lie in matters sexual.

The book is an anti-paean to the declining grandeur of a once-glorious city, not simply a comic rant against the world, in all it excess, its weaknesses and its humanity, but also a book of heartbreaking sadness, much of it evinced by the grotesque Ignatius himself.

*The author committed suicide in 1969, at the age of thirty-one, destroyed by the endless stream of rejections from publishers. The novel was finally published posthumously fifteen years after it was written, and ironically won the Pulitzer Prize the following year. Another book,* The Neon Bible*, written when Toole was just sixteen, is a novel piece of juvenilia.*

## 📖Read ons

*To Kill a Mockingbird*, Harper Lee **(Deep South)**
A heart-warming and captivating book about a child's view of racial tension and small-town prejudice in the 1930s. It won the Pulitzer Prize and remains her only novel.

*The Ballad of the Sad Café*, Carson McCullers **(Deep South)**
A haunting, Gothic tale of a love triangle involving three misfits in the swamplands of Georgia.

*The Color Purple*, Alice Walker **(Deep South)**
A classic story of a black woman's struggle for empowerment. Although the victim of great hardship and prolonged abuse, Celie finds that love triumphs and ultimately redeems.

*Delta Wedding*, Eudora Welty **(Deep South)**
This novel describes how a tightly knit well-to-do Southern family copes with the impending marriage of one of its members to an undesirable outsider.

*Property*, Valerie Martin **(Deep South)**
Against a background of slave rebellion and unrest in the nineteenth century, Manon Gaudet has to endure her unhappy marriage to a philandering Louisiana sugar-plantation owner.

*A Walk on the Wild Side*, Nelson Algren **(New Orleans)**
A story of the trials of a country boy as he leaves Texas for New Orleans in the Depression era, keeping company with various deadbeats and lowlifes.

*The Moviegoer*, Walker Percy **(New Orleans)**
The novel takes place during Mardi Gras celebrations in 1950, when 'Binx' Bollins decides to do something with his empty life.

*The Awakening*, Kate Chopin **(Louisiana/New Orleans)**
A young woman is destroyed by the conventions of her time as she attempts to find her own sexual and emotional identity. Scandalous for its time.

### *Modern Baptists*, James Wilcox **(Louisiana)**
When Bobby Picken's handsome half-brother turns up, various misunderstandings and dramas ensue in this comic novel about the quirky goings-on in a fictional town.

### *A Gathering of Old Men*, Ernest J Gaines **(Louisiana)**
A compelling portrait of racial conflict, in which a group of elderly black men confess to the murder of a white farmer on a sugar plantation.

### *Tourist Season*, Carl Hiaasen **(Florida)**
A dark, comic thriller about a private eye who becomes involved in a series of odd crimes involving reptiles, committed by Florida based eco-terrorists.

### *Prodigal Summer*, Barbara Kingsolver **(Alabama)**
A sensuous hymn to nature that weaves together the lives of three of the inhabitants of the forested mountains of southern Appalachia, over the course of one hot summer.

### *Look Homeward, Angel*, Thomas Wolfe **(South Carolina)**
Written in unashamedly romantic prose, this is an epic tale of desire and longing, revealing the despair and loss of innocence that can ensue when a person grows up and leaves the family home.

# MIDWEST/GREAT LAKES STATES

## KEY TITLES

*A Thousand Acres*, Jane Smiley
*So Long, See You Tomorrow*, William Maxwell
*Herzog*, Saul Bellow
*Winesberg, Ohio*, Sherwood Anderson

## A THOUSAND ACRES (1991)

Jane Smiley

This is a retelling of King Lear in modern-day Iowa. When Larry Cook gives away the family farm to his three grown-up daughters and their husbands, everyone is shocked. This unexpected act of generosity is uncharacteristic of the patriarchal Cook and some of his neighbours suspect undue pressure has been exerted. All hell breaks loose when Larry decides he wants the farm back. With no wife and mother to hold things together, family loyalties are stretched to the limit and Larry becomes a physical and emotional wreck.

Unlike Shakespeare's play, this story presents the women's perspective on events, and it is Ginny, the eldest daughter, who has to contend with the problems that arise from her father's decisions. In a male-dominated environment, she is torn between what feels right and what she has been taught to believe is right.

*A Thousand Acres* is expertly written in delicious prose that contains passages so deftly crafted they often leave the reader breathless. The relationship between character and landscape is keenly explored and the work builds to an astonishingly powerful and effective climax. Smiley captures perfectly the unquestioning and narrowminded facets of the redneck mind.

A Thousand Acres *has won both of America's highest literary awards: the Pulitzer Prize for Fiction and the National Book Critics' Circle Award. Of her other novels,* The All-True Travels and Adventures of Lidie Newton *(1998) is set in Kansas.*

# SO LONG, SEE YOU TOMORROW (1980)
## William Maxwell

A man recalls his childhood in 1920s' Lincoln, Illinois, when an incident came between him and his best friend. Fifty years on, he finds the incident impossible to forget.

The unnamed narrator and Cletus Smith are two lonely teenagers. The narrator has never fully recovered from his mother's death, during the flu pandemic of 1918, and after a period of intense grief, his father has remarried. Cletus lives on a nearby farm with his parents. When his mother, Fern becomes tragically involved with a local farmer, Lloyd Wilson, his life is blown off course. The resulting murder breaks the bond between the boys.

Maxwell recreates the killing with the aid of newspaper cuttings, placing the reader at the heart of the drama. Written in economical prose, this short novel is a masterpiece of understated radiance. It begins with a pistol shot and the killing of Lloyd Wilson, apparently by Cletus's father, who we are told cut off the dead man's ear before killing himself. Feeling that the event has tainted his friend, the narrator ignores him at school. As an old man, he regrets his failure to express the sympathy he felt at the time and he laments the ending of their friendship.

*Maxwell is an elegant stylist whose stripped-down prose still manages to capture the wheatfields of the Mid-West and the wasteland of a young boy's heart. He was born in Lincoln, Illinois, a town he has returned to often in his fiction, as he does in the novels* They Came Like Swallows *(1937) and* Time Will Darken It *(1948).*

# HERZOG (1964)

## Saul Bellow

Moses Herzog is going mad, or so his second ex-wife, Madeleine, tells everyone. She has even warned the local police against him. He holes up alone in his country home in the Berkshires, writing letters to anyone he can think of, including dead philosophers. Rejecting accusations of madness, he decides that what he needs is a holiday.

He dashes to New York, where he was once a professor of some repute, to spend the night with his lover, Ramona. He then decides to go to Chicago to fight for the custody of his daughter, June, and perhaps murder Madeleine and her lover, his former best friend, Valentine. Taking his dead father's gun, he spies on the two lovers through the window. When he is jailed by the police, his brother, Will suggests some time in a psychiatric home would not go amiss.

While Herzog rummages around in his own past looking for clues as to how he has ended up in this situation, he shows us much of the Jewish cultural life of Chicago and tells the poignant tale of his father, a man who failed. Herzog is disappointed in himself and in the stable but ultimately dull life provided for him, until, through vigorous self-analysis, he begins to see how life can be better.

In typical energetic and witty style, Bellow dissects Herzog's mind and, in the process, takes the reader on a life-affirming journey.

*Saul Bellow was born in Canada but raised in Chicago and it is the Windy City that provides the setting for many of his novels, including* The Dangling Man *(1944) and* Humboldt's Gift *(1975). He won the Nobel Prize in 1976.*

# WINESBURG, OHIO (1919)

## Sherwood Anderson

This is an exceptional cycle of twenty-five stories, all set in Winesburg, Ohio, a fictional representation of the small town of Clyde, where the author was raised. George Willard is the author's alter ego, a young newspaper reporter keen to escape small-town life.

The townsfolk go to George with their stories, as if their lives will somehow be dignified in print. George himself hopes that his own life will be ennobled in the telling of these tales. But these are tales of 'grotesques', and their stories are 'as delicious as the twisted apples that grow in the orchard in Winesburg.' Anderson reveals in the prologue the view that the label 'grotesque' can rightly be applied to those who have discovered a truth about life and then made it the centre of their existence, in turn twisting the truth into a lie.

We see numerous characters warped and buffeted by life: a woman driven by loneliness to run naked through the rain into the arms of the first man she sees; a doctor who believes he will be crucified because 'we are all Christ'; a taciturn farmhand forced to quit his teaching job in another town on account of his roving hands. These are exquisite and poignant tales.

Initially dismissed as morbid and sleaze-ridden, Anderson's realistic mode of writing was a revelation at the time, this book was a huge influence on a generation of writers, including Hemingway and Faulkner.

## 📖Read ons

*A Boy's Own Story*, Edmund White
A beautifully written, semi-autobiographical coming-of-age novel about growing up gay in the American Midwest of the 1950s.

*Pigs in Heaven*, Barbara Kingsolver
When Cherokees arrive to claim their daughter, her adoptive mother takes her on the run. A moving, intelligent sequel to *The Bean Trees*.

*Love Medicine*, Louise Erdich (**North Dakota**)
Stories are told through the voices of various Chippewa men and women, spanning fifty years from 1934 to 1984. Other novels are *The Beet Queen*, *Tracks* and *The Bingo Palace*.

*My Antonia*, Willa Cather (**Nebraska**)
A wonderfully told classic tale of immigrant life on the plains of Nebraska in the nineteenth century. Cather also wrote *O, Pioneers*, which covers the same territory.

*The Road Home*, Jim Harrison (**Nebraska**)
A family saga that spans three generations, this wonderfully descriptive book recounts the life of the Lakota Sioux. A companion piece to the superb *Dalva*.

*Paradise*, Toni Morrison (**Oklahoma**)
A complex blend of flashback and memory tells the tale of Ruby, an exclusively black farming community founded by freed slaves.

*Sister Carrie*, Theodore Dreiser (**Chicago**)
A classic tale of a country girl moving to the big city to make good, made extraordinary by Dreiser's naturalistic style.

*Main Street*, Sinclair Lewis (**Minnesota**)
A riveting account of an educated city woman who marries a doctor and moves to a small town. Her attempts to introduce culture to the lives of her neighbours are met by prejudice and ignorance.

*Lake Wobegon Days*, Garrison Keillor **(Minnesota)**
A series of vignettes set in a fictional town that find humour and poignancy in the little things in life. The first of many novels in this best-selling series.

*Winter's Bone*, Daniel Woodrell **(Ozarks)**
A bleak realistic and gritty saga set among the dispossessed, as a seventeen-year-old girl tries to keep her family together against all the odds.

*The Virgin Suicides*, Jeffrey Eugenides **(Michigan)**
They were adored by all the local boys, but one by one, the five beautiful Lisbon sisters all inexplicably committed suicide. A touching novel full of black humour.

## IN THE DRIVER'S SEAT – ROAD NOVELS

*On the Road*, Jack Kerouac
The daddy of all road novels and one that epitomises the Beat generation of 1950s America. Sal Paradise and Dean Moriarty take drugs, live life on the edge, and look for kicks as they speed across America.

*Not Fade Away*, Jim Dodge
A rollicking rock 'n' roll road trip. Floorboard George takes a white '59 Cadillac, originally intended for the Big Bopper, and heads for the singing star's place of premature death. Crazy characters litter the route, with cops and gangsters giving chase.

*Travelling With Djinns*, Jamal Mahjoub
Yasin and his son, Leo travel through Europe in their run-down Peugeot, unsure of where they are heading. A compelling novel about the search for cultural identity.

*Foreign Parts*, Janice Galloway
Two Scotswomen go on a driving holiday together in France. As they motor through the Gallic countryside, visiting a succession of guidebook-recommended sights, their dysfunctional friendship is put to the test.

*Vibrator*, Mari Akasaka
A young, troubled female journalist impulsively decides to take off with a truck driver she meets at a petrol station. Through him, she reassesses her life and an unusual love affair develops. An engaging road novel set in modern Japan.

*Europa*, Tim Parks
Jerry Marlow, stuck in a midlife crisis, takes a claustrophobic three-day coach trip from Italy to Strasbourg to protest at the European parliament. We delve deep into his troubled mind, the dilemmas of his life, and the state of Europe.

*Zen and the Art of Motorcycle Maintenance*, Robert M Pirsig
First published in 1974, this novelistic odyssey charts the journey by motorcycle of the narrator and his son, from Minnesota to California, with philosophical and psychological insights along the way.

*Even Cowgirls Get the Blues*, Tom Robbins
Sissy Hankshaw, with her unfeasibly large thumbs, hitchhikes across America in this characteristically quirky novel from Robbins, featuring a whole host of bizarre goings-on.

*Under the Skin*, Michel Faber
A woman drives alone through the Scottish Highlands looking for lone, hunky hitchhikers to pick up, with unusual motives. A dark, compelling tale that confounds the reader's expectations.

*The New Life*, Orhan Pamuk
Part road novel, part metaphysical mystery. A university student reads a book that transforms his life. He embarks on a coach journey round Turkey, in search of truth.

# TEXAS/AMERICAN WEST

**KEY**TITLES

*Blood Meridian*, Cormac McCarthy
*Death Comes for the Archbishop*, Willa Cather
*Angle of Repose*, Wallace Stegner

## BLOOD MERIDIAN (1985)
### Cormac McCarthy

This is a masterpiece of poetic ghoulishness, based on true events and historical characters. In the late 1840s, an unnamed boy simply called 'The Kid' runs away from home and becomes involved with the Glanton Gang whose job is to clear the borderlands between Mexico and Texas of 'Indians'.

They come across Judge Holden who effectively leads the gang from then on. He is an erudite, yet crazed albino, a monstrous figure and one of the great creations in literature. As they go about their business the death count get higher and the vicious bloodletting, as men are killed, scalped and in various ways tortured, is phenomenal. Judge Holden declares war divine, telling his gang it is the only reason for being.

The descriptions of the landscape are elegiac, and the images McCarthy leaves in the reader's head are gothic, biblical in tone and yet stunning and truly unforgettable. The violence is never gratuitous and has a vitality of its own. The whole book debunks the myths of heroism and the macho behaviour of men. The Indians are as bad as the Mexicans, who are as bad as the white folk.

Thirty years on, when all the gang are dead, and yet the Judge seems no older, he claims immortality for himself and seems less man and more guiding principle. He may even be the devil himself. When The Kid and the Judge meet up again the latter accuses the kid of betrayal, just because he held a measure of clemency in his heart. McCarthy has indeed written a macabre masterpiece.

*His other novels include the acclaimed* Border Trilogy*, comprising* All the Pretty Horse *(1992),* The Crossing *(1993) and* Cities of the Plain *(1998).*

# DEATH COMES FOR THE ARCHBISHOP (1927)
## Willa Cather

In the summer of 1848 two Catholic missionaries are sent to New Mexico to introduce Christianity. Bishop Jean Marie Latour and Father Valient are old friends and have known each other since their days at the seminary. The two are very different in temperament, but similarly devout. While the rustic Father is happy to involve himself with the natives, advancing into areas that have not seen a Catholic priest in years, the bourgeois Bishop is more contemplative in nature.

Their mission is to set up a parish and a diocese in the wilds of New Mexico. This episodic and charming book covers several decades and Cather herself describes it not as a novel, but as a narrative. Written in her characteristically leisurely style, it gives equal weight to its themes of food, death and landscape. The two characters travel extensively and the topography of the area is brought vividly to life.

The title is somewhat misleading, as the death in question is just one in a whole series of events, events that give the reader the impression of viewing a series of paintings in whose frozen images a slice of life is portrayed.

The faith of the two missionaries never wavers and it is testimony to Willa Cather's guile as a writer that the story is not heavy with religion but retains a calmness that is quietly captivating. She portrays events and characters entirely without judgement, presenting the different ethnic groups in New Mexico – the Native Americans, the Whites and the Mexicans – as separate entities, each with its own individual culture. There is a tacit acknowledgment that the European mind cannot – and should not – attempt to fathom the customs and beliefs of the native, that some things should remain unknowable.

This is a more reflective novel than her previous books, which deal with the experiences of pioneers and settlers in the plains of Nebraska. *See* the **Midwest** section for a listing.

# ANGLE OF REPOSE (1971)

## Wallace Stegner

Wallace Stegner is generally regarded as the greatest writer of the American West and this is the book he said he was born to write. Lyman Ward, a retired historian, returns to his ancestral home of Grass Valley, California, in the Sierra Nevada. He has a degenerative bone disease and is confined to a wheelchair. He plans to spend his remaining years editing the papers of his grandmother, a writer and illustrator in the nineteenth century. Over a hundred years ago, she made the arduous journey west. In the process of editing these papers, Lyman finds himself examining his own life and that of his family.

It emerges from the papers that his grandmother, Susan Burling Ward, was a highly intelligent, educated artist who married Oliver Ward and moved to the 'Wild West'. She endured life with her new husband, a handsome, earnest, but not very sophisticated engineer. Deprived of art and culture, Susan learnt to appreciate the beauty of the landscape around her and managed to build a home for their family. The West of her account is not a land of opportunity established by fearless pioneers: it is a harsh, unforgiving terrain that becomes the lethal foe of anyone trying to set up home. The differences in the Wards' temperaments and horizons are exacerbated by the landscape, and Susan's emotional and intellectual voyage is sensitively portrayed.

There are parallels between the Ward family history and Lyman's current predicament. He is looking for that 'angle of repose' into which he can peacefully ease, but he too is at odds with life in the 1970s. His disillusionment with his estranged wife, Ellen, and his only son, Rodman, highlight his anxiety. As he trawls through his ancestors' lives and follows his grandmother's journey, he is forced into making an emotional journey of his own.

Controversially based on the life of nineteenth-century writer and illustrator, Mary Hallock Foote, this quiet American classic is rich in detail and description, and debunks many of the myths of the American West. It won the 1972 Pulitzer Prize for Fiction.

## Read ons

*Little Big Man*, Thomas Berger
An amusing tale of an old white man recounting the early part of his life, spent living with the Cheyenne. Along the way he meets many of the Wild West's famous names, including General George Custer.

*Lonesome Dove*, Larry McMurtry
A complex web of subplots develops as two cowboys drive cattle from Texas to Montana. An intelligent, prize-winning novel that spawned two prequels and a sequel.

*On the Night Plain*, J Robert Lennon
A terse, bleak tale of a man left to tend the family ranch alone in the 1940s, until his brother arrives with his girlfriend.

*The Miracle Life of Edgar Mint*, Brady Udall (Arizona and Utah)
An inventive coming-of-age tale about the misadventures of half-Apache Edgar, whose constant misfortunes do nothing to dent his tireless optimism.

*Naked Pueblo*, Mark Poirier (Arizona)
Twelve short stories that are plaintive, comical and unsentimental in nature. All of human life is here among the trailer parks and disaffected youth of Tucson.

*Plainsong*, Kent Haruf (Colorado)
A simple but effective character-driven novel centred around the lives of seven lonely people in rural Colorado.

*St. Agnes' Stand*, Thomas Eidson (New Mexico)
Pleasurable hokum about a man on the run who comes to the aid of a nun and seven orphans he finds stranded in the desert and praying for salvation.

*Riders of the Purple Sage*, Zane Grey (Utah)
A classic western about a lone gunman arriving on the horizon to save a beautiful rancher whom the local Mormon Church is harassing in an attempt to secure her land.

### *Vernon God Little*, D B C Pierre (Texas)

A quirky, satirical Booker-Prize-winning novel about a young man blamed for a Columbine-style massacre of his schoolmates. Humorous and edgy, but not for everyone.

### *Pop. 1280*, Jim Thompson (Texas)

A seemingly lazy and incompetent sheriff begins to take revenge on all those who have ever pushed him around. Darkly humorous. *See also The Killer Inside Me*.

# SOUTH WEST

KEYTITLES

*The 'California Novels'*, John Steinbeck
*The Tortilla Curtain*, T C Boyle
*Tales of the City*, Armistead Maupin

## THE 'CALIFORNIA NOVELS' (1933 – 1954)
John Steinbeck

To single out just one of Steinbeck's California novels is almost impossible. All are near masterpieces and each evokes superbly the territory around the Salinas Valley, Monterey, and the San Joaquin Valley.

They begin with *To a God Unknown* (1933), a novel full of mythological and biblical undertones. It is the tale of a farmer who fulfils his father's dream of running a flourishing farm in Southern California. He believes that a magnificent oak tree houses his dead father's spirit and brings him good fortune. However, when his Christian brother, disapproving of such pagan beliefs, destroys the tree, the result is disease and ruin.

*Tortilla Flat* (1935) is a light-hearted novel about a stretch of land beyond Monterey. A Spanish settler inherits two houses and decides that fun is more important than money. He opens their doors to a variety of unconventional layabouts who proceed to live a wild life.

His most studied and most famous novel is *Of Mice and Men* (1937), a simple but effective tale of two itinerant workers who find employment on a ranch in the Salinas Valley. George and his simple-minded companion, Lennie, a giant of a man with the mentality of a child, dream of owning a farm themselves one day, but fate intervenes in the shape of the rancher's wife.

*The Grapes of Wrath* (1938) is an iconic novel that looks deep into the heart of America. It concerns the Joad family, tenant farmers in Oklahoma, who are driven from their land by dust storms. They are forced to join thousands of others in a quest for work in California.

After the war, Steinbeck produced *Cannery Row* (1945). This series of vignettes tells the tale of a group of people living near a sardine factory who try to throw a party for a good friend, Doc Chong, only to ruin his house in the process. It is an upbeat novel with fully realised characters and numerous amusing incidents.

*Steinbeck drew from the first biblical family and his own re-imagined ancestral kin for* East of Eden *(1952), a tempestuous tale of two interlinked families as they love and feud in the rich farmlands of Salinas Valley.*

*Two years later, he returned to* Cannery Row *territory with* Sweet Thursday *(1954), a book that follows events after the Second World War. Doc Chong is depressed and looking for love.*

# THE TORTILLA CURTAIN (1995)
T Coraghessan Boyle

This is a conscious nod to John Steinbeck's *Grapes of Wrath*, from which the title itself is a quotation. In the foothills of Southern California's Topanga Canyon, two couples live in close proximity. Nature writer Delaney Mossbacher and his wife, real estate agent Kyra, live in an exclusive, secluded housing development with her son, Jordan. Mexican Cándido Rincón camps out in the bushes at the bottom of the ravine with his pregnant seventeen-year-old wife, ironically named América. They are illegal immigrants desperate for work and on the edge of starvation. Delaney accidentally knocks down Cándido while driving to the recycling plant one day. He gives Cándido $20 when he refuses medical help. Cándido's injuries are so severe as to prevent him from working, so his pregnant wife has to look for a job.

The novel cleverly switches between the two protagonists, showing their contrasting fears and dilemmas. The Rincóns are portrayed as honest people, and their history and earlier life in Mexico are sympathetically chronicled. They cling to their vision of the American Dream, a dream that eludes their grasp at every turn. The Mossbachers are trendy liberals interested in living close to nature. However, their local residents committee has just voted to put up an electric fence round the compound, to keep the immigrants out.

This novel highlights Americans' fear of strangers, portraying this fear as a low-level but all-pervasive racism and American society as one in which WASPs protect their own and use the system to cheat and lie their way to the top. As misfortunes befall both couples, the Rincóns are forced to live like the wild coyotes Delaney admires so much. In turn, Delaney becomes increasingly self-protective and prejudiced, blaming the influx of immigrants for everything. The concentric circles of their very different lives move closer together until the inevitable climax occurs.

Alternately comic and harrowing, this novel nevertheless recounts with poignancy the aspirations of those striving to live the American Dream and those seeking to protect it.


# TALES OF THE CITY (1978)
## Armistead Maupin

This is the first novel in a popular series centring on an apartment house at 28 Barbary Lane. The landlady is the enigmatic and maternal Anna Madrigal, whose main hobby aside from growing cannabis seems to be interfering in her lodgers' often untidy lives. In this opening novel, a naïve young secretary, Mary Ann Singleton, moves from Cleveland to San Francisco. She meets a host of colourful characters, including Michael 'Mouse' Tolliver, a droll man continuously looking for Mr Right; Mona Ramsey, a bisexual ex-hippie; and an evasive roof tenant, Norman Williams.

The book is a warm, gentle evocation of life in the 1970s (the series itself progresses to the end of the 1980s) with enough 'outrageous' characters to keep the reader interested. The unexpected crossing of different plot lines may be too much for some, and the whole has something of the tone of a soap opera. Nevertheless, the high-spirited series takes a delight in human differences, and Maupin can be both amusing and touching.

Originally published in serial form in the *San Francisco Chronicle*, the book retains a journal's refreshing immediacy. It had its finger on the pulse of the social climate and was one of the first novels to talk seriously about AIDS.

So popular was the serial that it furnished six volumes. The full list is: *Tales of the City* (1978), *More Tales of the City* (1980), *Further Tales of the City* (1982), *Babycakes* (1984), *Significant Others* (1987) and *Sure of You* (1989). Although not officially the seventh book in the series, *Michael Tolliver Lives* (2007) is about 'Mouse' in his fifties. Some characters from the series also make minor appearances in Maupin's later novels, *Maybe the Moon* (1993) and *The Night Listener* (2000).

## 📖 Read ons

*Play It As It Lays*, Joan Didion (California)
An acerbic dissection of the shallow world of show business as we watch a young woman's life disintegrate through drink and drugs.

*House of Sand and Fog*, Andre Dubus III (California)
An Iranian ex-colonel, in search of a new life, is pitted against an alcoholic house-cleaner. Both attempt to lay moral and legal claim to a bungalow in San Francisco.

*Big Sur*, Jack Kerouac (California)
These are sad and beautiful drunken ramblings in which Kerouac seeks to withdraw from the fame his writing has brought him, holing up in a cabin down by the Pacific Ocean.

*A Confederate General from Big Sur*, Richard Brautigan (California)
A comic and surreal send-up of the sixties following the misadventures of two couples who move into a house with glass walls. The book has six endings.

*The Crying of Lot 49*, Thomas Pynchon (California)
A woman is bequeathed a legacy that sets her on a curious quest. A surreal comedy of paranoia and puzzlement satirising, amongst other things, 1960s' hippies.

*The Postman Always Rings Twice*, James M Cain (California)
A short psychological thriller about a drifter and his lover who murder her husband and make it look like an accident.

*Fup*, Jim Dodge (California)
A duck called Fup comes into the lives of Tiny and his Grandaddy Jake and begins to impose order on their chaotic lives. A perfectly formed little tale set in the hills of northern California.

*Carter Beats the Devil*, Glen David Gold (San Francisco)
San Francisco's development over the early twentieth century is lovingly told in this richly detailed and well-researched story of a real-life magician and his involvement in the sudden death of a president.

*Fear and Loathing in Las Vegas*, Hunter S Thompson **(Las Vegas)**
Dated but hilarious drug-tour extravaganza, as a journalist and his attorney take a long weekend off in search of the American Dream.

# LOS ANGELES

KEYTITLES

*Less Than Zero*, Bret Easton Ellis
*The Big Sleep*, Raymond Chandler

## LESS THAN ZERO (1985)
Bret Easton Ellis

This is an acerbic examination of the American Dream fulfilled and taken to its logical conclusion, testing the notion that a person has the right to reach out and take whatever he or she wants.

Easton Ellis's novel follows Clay on his return to Los Angeles in his winter break from college. He meets up with some old friends, including ex-girlfriend Blair, who is still interested in continuing their relationship.

Clay and his affluent, amoral, late-teens friends hang around in bars, do drugs and go to parties. Not realising how bored they are, they watch films they do not know the names of and have sex with people they cannot even recall.

The author's prose is stark yet significant, highlighting the emptiness of their lives. The hero's slow disintegration is all the more chilling for its disconnectedness. His emotionally detached relationships with his family, his friends and his analyst are very well portrayed.

This was Easton Ellis's first book, published when he was barely out of his teens. It is a powerful depiction both of a lost generation of people who have everything except something to lose, and of the acquistive Reagan era, a time when to have was to be.

*The novel established the author as something of a spokesperson for this blank generation. A disappointing, if unsurprisingly stylish film appeared in 1987.*

# THE BIG SLEEP (1939)
## Raymond Chandler

No one does Chandler like Chandler. The author who spawned a thousand parodies is, however, more than just a writer of wisecracking detective fiction. His main character, Philip Marlowe, has the familiar human emotions of longing, desire and despair, and Chandler makes the pain hurt and makes the places real, in writing that fairly crackles.

In this, the first Marlowe novel, we find the private eye summoned to General Sternwood's mansion and commissioned to discover who is blackmailing the dying General over his wayward youngest daughter, Carmen, a schizoid nymphomaniac who steps out of line as easily as she slips out of a dress.

Marlowe finds himself involved in pornography, extortion, kidnapping and, of course, murder, and he has time to fall in love along the way.

All of Chandler's novels cover the same terrain, both psychologically and geographically. The area around the Hollywood hills becomes a character itself, with Los Angeles portrayed as a dark, sprawling city teeming with criminals and possessed of a violent underworld. However, like a romantic knight of old, Marlowe makes a valiant attempt to hold on to his humanity.

*Readers return to Chandler for the sensational plotlines almost as much as they do for his remarkable metaphors. He wrote six other Marlowe novels, including* Farewell My Lovely *(1940) and* The Long Goodbye *(1953). The Big Sleep was made into an iconic film with Humphrey Bogart and Lauren Bacall, in 1946. Scripted by William Faulkner, and excellent though it was, it could only hint at the darkness that really dwells in these pages.*

## 🕮 Read ons

*Ham on Rye*, Charles Bukowski
This is a coarse and coruscating autobiographical account of the early life of a writer, as close to a literary dust-up as it gets, by a man once dubbed 'America's greatest poet'.

*Ask the Dust*, John Fante
A gutsy tale, set in 1930s' Los Angeles, of a young man who abandons his home town in order to write. He begins an affair with a Mexican waitress that ends in madness and disaster.

*White Oleander*, Janet Fitch
When her poet mother kills her ex-lover, a teenage girl finds herself in a string of foster homes, each one more testing than the last.

*Devil in a Blue Dress*, Walter Mosley
A black veteran of the Second World War is hired to track down a woman and finds himself patrolling the mean streets of South Central Los Angeles. The first in a number of Easy Rawlins novels.

*L A Confidential*, James Ellroy
A stylish, brutal novel with a labyrinthine plot about corruption and criminality within the Los Angeles Police Department in the 1950s. It forms one part of Ellroy's *L A Quartet*, which also includes *The Black Dahlia*.

*The Killing of the Saints*, Alex Abella
Witchcraft and the supernatural are interwoven in this riveting courtroom drama concerning two members of a Cuban cult accused of murder.

## READ ON A THEME

## ADVENTURES IN THE SCREEN TRADE – HOLLYWOOD/MOVIES

*Postcards from the Edge*, Carrie Fisher
A wickedly funny satire about the lifestyles of the rich and famous, following Susan Vale through drug addiction and rehab.

*Hollywood*, Charles Bukowski
An irreverent fictional account of the making of the film *Barfly*, which was based on Bukowski's own early life. The author takes no prisoners and many film figures find themselves portrayed wearing only the thinnest of disguises.

*The Last Tycoon*, F Scott Fitzgerald
Completed by an editor after the author's death, this novel portrays Hollywood in its heyday and concerns the love affair of a young movie mogul and an 'outsider'.

*Blue Movie*, Terry Southern
A profane look at the sleazy side of filmmaking, as a serious director attempts to make a big-budget adult movie.

*The Day of the Locust*, Nathanael West
An excellent, savage tale of a set designer who becomes involved with a cavalcade of Hollywood hopefuls living and loving on the fringes of Tinseltown.

*I, Fatty*, Jerry Stahl
A fictionalised account of the strange and scandalous life of silent movie star Roscoe 'Fatty' Arbuckle.

*The Comedy Writer*, Peter Farrelly
Henry Hollaran quits a dead-end job and heads for Los Angeles to try to hit the big-time as a Hollywood scriptwriter. A raucous novel from the co-writer/director of the film *There's Something about Mary*.

*Get Shorty*, Elmore Leonard
Chasing an unpaid debt to Holloywood, a loan shark falls in with the big boys. Complex, snappy and mean, it is one of the finest novels of its genre.

*Inside Daisy Clover*, Gavin Lambert
Already jaded by her mid-twenties, a former child star fights her way back to the top in this excellent portrayal of the 1950s' dream factory.

*The Book of Illusions*, Paul Auster
In a quest to discover the fate of a silent movie star who disappeared in 1929, a literature professor begins to reconnect with real life again following the death of his wife and child.

# NORTH WEST/ALASKA/HAWAII

**KEY**TITLES

*Housekeeping*, Marilynne Robinson
*Snow Falling on Cedars*, David Guterson

## HOUSEKEEPING (1980)
Marilynne Robinson

This is a carefully crafted novel that demands to be read slowly. Ruth narrates the tale of her own troubled life and that of her younger sibling, Lucille, in the fictional town of Fingerbone, Idaho, set on the shores of a mountain lake, where their grandfather died in a spectacular train accident years ago. The landscape is hard and unforgiving, and people live at the mercy of the freezing winters and floods.

One day, after dropping the two girls at their grandmother's house, Ruth and Lucille's mother drives off a cliff. The girls stay with their grandmother until her death, half a dozen years later. Her two elderly maiden sisters, Lily and Nona, come to look after the girls but they are ill equipped for the task. They decide to send for the girls' aunt, the enigmatic Sylvie, who abandons her life as a transient to raise them.

Sylvie is revealed to be absent-minded and emotionally remote, to the extent that the girls are never sure that she will stay. Isolated to the point of invisibility, the girls yearn for some connection, but the sisters' differing attitudes towards their eccentric aunt signal their divergent paths. While Lucille is appalled at Sylvie's unorthodox housekeeping style, Ruth is quietly intrigued. With such a history of abandonment behind them, the girls take emotional nourishment from wherever they can and Ruth's natural allegiance to her aunt is both sad and haunting. When Lucille wishes to move out to her schoolteacher's home, Ruth is unwilling to join her. It is then that Sylvie's lack of parental skills is brought to the notice of the townsfolk. On the eve of a meeting to decide Ruth's fate, she and Sylvie take action to protect their unconventional union.

A masterpiece of elegance, *Housekeeping* was highly acclaimed upon publication and was recently included in *The Observer's 100 Greatest Novels of All Time*. A lyrical film was made in 1987 by Scottish director Bill Forsyth.

## SNOW FALLING ON CEDARS (1994)
David Guterson

The action takes place on the fictional island of San Piedro, in Puget Sound, off the coast of Washington State. It is only a few years since the end of the Second World War and a Japanese man, Kabuo Miyamoto, is on trial for the murder of a local fisherman, Carl Heine.

The narrative moves back and forth in time to reveal the hostility the locals have for the Japanese, even those, like Kabuo, who were born in America and fought on the side of the Allies. However, the Japanese have their brooding resentments, too. They see their whole community being either interned or exiled while erstwhile friends and neighbours sit back and do nothing. Kabuo and his wife, Hatsue see themselves robbed of the land Kabuo's father worked on and paid for.

The local newspaperman is Ishmael Chambers. An embittered war veteran, he lost an arm fighting in Tarawa. He lives alone and still has feelings for Kabuo's wife, Hatsue, his childhood sweetheart. If Kabuo is convicted of the fisherman's murder, he sees a chance to be together again with Hatsue. However, he finds information that could point to Kabuo's innocence, forcing him to wrestle with his conscience.

Guterson paints the imaginary town of San Piedro with an artist's eye and the smell and feel of a fishing community is sharply brought to life in this multi-layered work.

Snow Falling on Cedars *was made into a highly successful film in 1999. Guterson's other books are* East of the Mountains *(1999) and* Our Lady of the Forest *(2003).*

## 📖Read ons

*Close Range – Brokeback Mountain and Other Stories*, E Annie Proulx **(Wyoming)**
Proulx is an original and this collection of stories about hardship and heartache, set against the backdrop of an unforgiving landscape, confirms her genius.

*The Horse Whisperer*, Nicholas Evans **(Montana)**
A guilty mother enlists the help of a man to help tame her daughter's unruly horse, but his presence in their fractured lives threatens to do more harm than good.

*Wildlife*, Richard Ford **(Montana)**
A poignant tale of a teenage boy in 1950s' Montana who records the failure of his parents' marriage that ensues when his father loses his job as a golf professional and his mother embarks on an affair.

*Ten Little Indians*, Sherman Alexie **(Seattle)**
Nine haunting, lyrical short stories about Spokane Indians, with flashes of linguistic brilliance.

*Surveillance*, Jonathan Raban **(Seattle)**
This novel artfully explores modern-day paranoia and the quest for truth via technology. It is the second in Raban's trilogy of novels based in Seattle. *See also Waxwings*.

*The Coast of Good Intentions*, Michael Byers **(Seattle)**
A collection of beautifully crafted short stories set in Seattle and the surrounding cities. They are wonderfully evocative of the Pacific Northwest landscape.

*The Seal Wife*, Kathryn Harrison **(Alaska)**
In 1915 a government scientist is sent to the magnificently rendered wilds of Alaska to establish a weather station. His isolation and loneliness drive him into the arms of two very different women.

*The Call of the Wild*, Jack London **(Alaska)**
A classic tale of a dog kidnapped and taken to Alaska to work. Although treated harshly, he survives to find love again, but is ultimately unable to deny his animal nature.

*Hotel Honolulu*, Paul Theroux **(Hawaii)**
An autobiographical story of a writer recounting amusing tales of the strange guests in the hotel he runs on a Hawaiian island.

*Paradise News*, David Lodge **(Hawaii)**
A serio-comic novel about an ex-priest who travels, with his cantankerous father, to see a dying relative. Hitherto living a directionless and celibate life, he finally meets a woman.

## READ ON A THEME

### PRIDE AND PREJUDICE – BLACK IN AMERICA

*Breaking Ice: An Anthology of Contemporary African-American Fiction*,
Ed. Terry McMillan
Short stories and excerpts from novels by a wide variety of established and emerging African-American authors.

*Go Tell It on the Mountain*, James Baldwin
A groundbreaking novel that tells the story of Johnny Grimes, his awakening to the world around him, his hatred for his preacher father, and his family's harsh times in Depression-era Harlem.

*Native Son*, Richard Wright
In 1930s' Chicago, a young black man from the slums accidentally kills a white girl and is executed for his crime. A compelling and iconic book about racial prejudice in the twentieth century.

*Their Eyes Were Watching God*, Zora Neale Hurston
First published in 1937, this classic novel, written in the African-American vernacular of the time, deals with a woman's search for personal fulfilment.

*The Autobiography of an Ex-Colored Man*, James Weldon Johnson
A light-skinned narrator of mixed race is caught between two worlds as he gives his reasons for his decision to take the easier but regrettable option of living life as a white man.

*A Lesson Before Dying*, Ernest J Gaines
A young innocent black man is sentenced to death and the local school-teacher is given the task of educating him, to allow him to die with dignity. A powerful and award-winning story set in 1940s' Louisiana.

*The Salt Eaters*, Toni Cade Bambara
A novel of spiritual renewal, faith healing and social change, set in the imaginary Southern town of Claybourne and centred on the predicament of a suicidal woman.

*The Interruption of Everything*, Terry McMillan
A sassy and humorous story about a woman whose routine life is turned upside down when she discovers she is pregnant again at the age of forty-four. *See also* **Disappearing Acts** and **Waiting to Exhal**e.

*Friends and Lovers*, Eric Jerome Dickey
A heartfelt novel of love and friendship with finely observed characters. The relationships of two couples from Los Angeles take very different paths to happiness.

*Invisible Man*, Ralph Ellison, *see* USA: General America
*Beloved*, Toni Morrison, *see* USA: General America
*The Color Purple*, Alice Walker, *see* USA: American South
*The Wedding*, Dorothy West, *see* USA: East Coast

## READONATHEME

## TYPICAL AMERICANS – THE ASIAN/LATINO IN AMERICA

*The House on Mango Street*, Sandra Cisneros
In this series of short, touching vignettes, Esperanza, a young Mexican-American girl, describes her struggles and aspirations growing up in the Hispanic quarter of Chicago.

*Drown*, Junot Diaz
An excellent collection of hard-hitting and lyrical short stories telling of Dominican immigrants' experiences of life in the urban United States.

*The Mambo Kings Play Songs of Love*, Oscar Hijuelos
A colourful and sensual depiction of Cuban exiles in the United States. Two brothers travel to New York, form their own band and enjoy moderate success in the mambo craze of the 1950s.

*Loving Che*, Ana Menendez
A young woman, raised by her Cuban grandfather in Miami, receives a package that reveals her estranged mother's past and her affair with Che Guevara in the 1950s.

*Soledad*, Angie Cruz
When her mother falls ill, Soledad is forced to return to her Dominican family and old New York neighbourhood to help care for her. An inspiring story of a woman straddling two cultures and looking for contentment.

*The Killing of the Saints*, Alex Abella, *see* **USA: Los Angeles**

*The Namesake*, Jhumpa Lahiri
Lahiri's debut novel tells the story of a family of Bengali Indians in America. The son, Gogol, deals with conflicting loyalties and searches for his place in the world.

*The Mistress of Spices*, Chitra Banerjee Divakaruni
A beautifully written story of the immigrant Indian owner of a spice shop in Oakland, California, who dispenses wisdom with her spices. We discover what happens one day when a lonely American enters her store.

*Jasmine*, Bharati Mukherjee
Widowed at seventeen, Jasmine leaves her Indian village and heads for a new life in America. Torn between assimilation and tradition, she travels around, changing her name frequently, and relying on her indomitable spirit to see her through.

*The Perfect Man*, Naeem Murr
In the 1940s, a young Anglo-Indian boy is brought up by his uncle's mistress in a small town where he learns to fit in. However, the townspeople have a terrible secret.

*The Joy Luck Club*, Amy Tan
Tan's acclaimed and moving first novel deals with mother-daughter relationships, Chinese tradition versus American lifestyles, and the correlation between past and the present. Set in China and San Francisco.

*Eating Chinese Food Naked*, Mei Ng
A novel of love, sex, food and family about a Chinese-American girl who, after graduating, returns to her parents home in New York and is forced to confront her emotions and the past.

*Comfort Woman*, Nora Okja Keller
A harrowing story of a Korean woman forced to be a sex slave for Japanese soldiers during the Second World War, and of the price she pays for keeping the truth hidden from her daughter.

*When the Emperor Was Divine*, Julie Otsuka
This spare and poignant story tells of a Japanese-American family sent to an internment camp after Pearl Harbour, and of their return, years later, to try to rebuild their shattered lives.

*A Gesture Life*, Chang-Rae Lee
A retired suburban doctor struggles with the remorse he feels for his role in supervising 'comfort women' for Japanese soldiers in the Second World War.

*Typical American*, Gish Jen
Three Chinese immigrants, forced to leave China after it succumbed to Communism, set out to achieve the American Dream. In the process, they become everything they were once critical of in American society.

## NOVELS ABOUT NATIVE AMERICANS:

*Love Medicine*, Louise Erdrich, *see* General USA section
*Tracks*, Louise Erdrich (Nth. Dakota), *see* Midwest/Great Lakes States section
*The Road Home*, Jim Harrison (Nebraska), *see* Midwest/Great Lakes States section
*Ten Little Indians*, Sherman Alexie, *see* North West/Alaska/Hawaii section
*Little Big Man*, Thomas Berger, *see* Texas/American West section
*River Thieves*, Michael Crummey, *see* Canada
*Black Robe*, Brian Moore, *see* Canada

# CANADA

## SELECTED STORIES (1997)
Alice Munro

Alice Munro is widely regarded as a master of the short story craft and is often referred to as Canada's Chekhov. Her tales are mostly set around the farmlands in Ontario, around Lake Huron, and further to the west in British Colombia.

This anthology includes twenty-three stories from seven collections that span thirty years. She writes about ordinary folk and everyday life and the fears and desires that bubble beneath the surface. The majority of her stories feature vigorous and strong-willed young women who are apt to push at boundaries, and older women who have maintained a degree of sensitivity while cultivating the inner strength necessary to survive.

The farming areas she portrays are a throwback to earlier times, stagnant and laced with the kind of ignorance that breeds casual prejudice. She is fond of juxtaposition: light and dark, landscapes that are both intimidating and magnificent, and the search for joy and hope in a difficult life.

In *Walker Brothers Cowboy*, a young girl compares the happiness that her father's old girlfriend feels at seeing him again with the disappointment her mother feels at having married him. *Something I've Been Meaning to Tell You* sees the return of a childhood sweetheart upsetting the lives of two older women who thought they had accepted their lot. In *Lichen*, a long-divorced couple have stayed friends but while she accepts getting older with good grace, he finds young girls with whom to furnish his 'willed but terrible transformations'.

*This anthology is a fitting testimony to Munro's extraordinary talent. Her individual collections are:* Lives of Girls and Women *(1971)*, Something I've Been Meaning to Tell You *(1974)*, Who Do you Think You Are? *(1978)*, The Moons of Jupiter *(1982)*, The Progress of Love *(1986)*, Friend of My Youth *(1990)*, Open Secrets *(1994)*, The Love of a Good Woman *(1998)*, Hateship, Friendship, Courtship, Loveship, Marriage *(2001)*, No Love Lost *(2003)*, Runaway *(2004)*, *and* The View From Castle Rock *(2006)*.

# THE BLIND ASSASSIN (2000)

## Margaret Atwood

In this tale within a tale, set against almost a century of Canadian history, Iris Chase Griffen relates her life story before she dies. Now in her eighties, she belonged to a once-wealthy family of prominent industrialists in her hometown of Port Ticonderoga. Her younger sister, Laura Chase, died in her mid-twenties, in 1945, when her car went off a bridge. Laura had written a novel, *The Blind Assassin*, which Iris managed to publish, bringing Laura posthumous and long-lasting fame.

Laura's novel is about two unnamed lovers – one a Marxist agitator (who resembles a young radical the sisters harboured and both fell in love with), the other a privileged rich girl – who meet up in squalid back-street rooms. He writes pulp science fiction stories for her, set on the planet Zycron, a land where babies are blinded and then trained to be killers. His stories become surreal metaphors for the lives and loves of the two Chase sisters.

Iris writes her memoirs for her estranged granddaughter, Sabrina, in an attempt to explain their estrangement. The memoirs centre on her life in the 1930s and 1940s. She tells of her marriage, at eighteen, to scheming bully and budding politician, Richard Griffen, a marriage arranged as part of a deal to save her financially embarrassed father. She tells of the period when Laura reluctantly came to live with them after their father died, and of the day her younger sister was, quite without warning, committed to an insane asylum, and of how Iris was unable to visit her, causing a rift in the family that no amount of time could heal.

The novel is a heady mixture of styles and includes newspaper clippings and letters, and Atwood has the reader's attention oscillating between the two 'novels'. With the author's precise prose and gift for storytelling, balanced by the sheer weight of her imagination, this is both a beautifully detailed family saga and a complex and subtle feminist meditation on the constraints of women.

The Blind Assassin *won the 2000 Booker Prize. Her other Canada-based novels are* Surfacing *(1972) and* Alias Grace *(1996).*


# THE REPUBLIC OF LOVE (1992)
## Carol Shields

This is a clever and engaging novel about all aspects of love. Set in a close-knit community in Winnipeg, the chapters alternate between the two protagonists, Fay McLeod and Tom Avery. Both are approaching forty and both are unhappy. Fay has never married, while Tom has a hat trick of failed legal couplings behind him.

They do not actually meet each other until half-way through the book. Before that coup de foudre, we see Fay splitting up with her newest partner, an Englishman called Peter, whom she works with at the Folklore Centre. She also meets her seemingly happily married father regularly for breakfast and is making plans for a month-long trip to Europe to research a book on mermaids. In the meantime, Tom is a late-night DJ who goes to singles groups and to friends' houses for Sunday lunch. He is bored by children and ill at ease with his single status.

Fay has come to regard love as a teasing malady but, being a romantic, she nevertheless believes that she may still find a truly loving relationship. When she meets Tom at a children's party, on the eve of her European trip, she finds herself profoundly touched by the meeting. A rash declaration of love binds them together before they have time to consider whether they are ready for commitment, before Fay has properly taken account of Tom's failed marriages, and before Tom has had the chance properly to assess his feeling that this relationship will be different.

Shields is a consummate writer and the polished prose and ironic tone immerse the reader fully in the situation she creates for her likeable and very forgivable characters.

A film was made of *The Republic of Love* in 2003. Despite not moving to Canada until she was in her twenties, Shields chooses a Canadian setting for most of her novels, including *Unless* (2002).

# THE SHIPPING NEWS (1993)

E Annie Proulx

Quoyle, is something of a misfit, large and ungainly with a prodigious chin. He has no self-esteem and very little talent, and finds it impossible to hold down a job as a journalist. Living in New York he marries a wildcat called Petal Bear and they manage to have two daughters, although Petal Bear seems to lose interest in Quoyle almost immediately. She has numerous boyfriends, treats Quoyle with open hostility, and ignores the children to the point of denying their existence. When she leaves him, she takes the children with the intention of selling them to a child pornographer. Somehow Quoyle manages to rescue them, but almost simultaneously his wife dies in a car crash and his parents kill themselves in a suicide pact.

Quoyle's aunt, Agnis Hamm, arrives on the scene and suggests they leave New York for the ancestral homeland of Newfoundland. With nothing to tie him to the Big Apple, and with the offer of a job writing the shipping news in a local Newfoundland newspaper, Quoyle takes his family and they settle down into an odd kind of bliss. In his new life, Quoyle gets along with everyone, gaining respect and even finding love.

Proulx's writing style is short, verb-less sentences that are rhythmic and punchy. Her humour is harsh and her characters border on the eccentric. There is a great sense of place in this book. Newfoundland is at the mercy of the sea, and water is a defining factor in the lives of its inhabitants, as is the bleak climate, with its six-month-long winters.

The theme of redemption and the notion that love comes in many forms are central to the book, which won a host of prizes including the Pulitzer Prize for Fiction and the National Book Award. A film was made in 2001, with the slight and personable Kevin Spacey curiously cast as the ugly giant, Quoyle.

## 📖Read ons

*The Tenderness of Wolves*, Stef Penney
In this atmospheric debut novel, the search for a missing teenager, following a brutal murder, brings a host of opportunists and unwanted publicity to a remote Canadian settlement in 1867. The novel won the 2006 Costa Book of the Year Award.

*In the Skin of a Lion*, Michael Ondaatje
A series of beautifully realised, interrelated stories about the immigrants who helped build the city of Toronto in the 1920s.

*The Bird Artist*, Howard Norman
This is the first book in his Canadian trilogy, set at the turn of the last century in a remote fishing village in Newfoundland, about an artist who confesses to the murder of a lighthouse keeper. The remaining volumes are *The Haunting of L* and *The Museum Guard*.

*A Map of Glass*, Jane Urquhart
The book is set both in present-day Toronto and in nineteenth-century rural Ontario. An artist discovers a dead body, a discovery that takes him on a quest for meaning in his own life and in Canada's past.

*Black Robe*, Brian Moore
A realistic and brutal look at the attempt of two Jesuit priests to convert the Algonquin Indians to Christianity in seventeenth-century French Canada.

*The Cure for Death by Lightning*, Gail Anderson Dargatz
A coming-of-age tale replete with recipes, advice and Indian legends, about a fifteen-year-old girl trying her best to survive her hard life on a frontier farm in British Colombia in the 1940s.

*Fifth Business*, Robertson Davies
Dunstan Ramsey, a retiring teacher, writes a letter to the principal of the school where he taught to explain how relevant his life has been. The dazzling first part of *The Deptford Trilogy*.

*The Romantic*, Barbara Gowdy
This updated version of Abelard and Heloise tells the tragic story of Louise and her lover Abel, who grow up together in a Toronto neighbourhood.

*River Thieves*, Michael Crummey
A debut novel by a renowned poet, set in the early nineteenth century, about the last days of the Beothuk Indians of Newfoundland and their encounters with European settlers.

*Girlfriend in a Coma*, Douglas Coupland
In Vancouver, in 1979, just hours after losing her virginity, a teenager inexplicably falls into a coma. Two decades later, she awakes to a changed world, a daughter and impending apocalypse.

*The Apprenticeship of Duddy Kravitz*, Mordecai Richler
A hilarious novel that focuses on the young life of a poor Jewish boy raised in Montreal as he attempts to get on in the world.

*Next Episode*, Hubert Aquin
In this largely autobiographical novel, first published in 1965, a Quebec nationalist writes a novel about a terrorist while in the psychiatric ward of a Montreal prison. In 2003, it was chosen as the Canadian novel for all Canadians to read.

*The Stone Angel*, Margaret Laurence
Nearly a hundred years old, Hagar Shipley recalls her troubled life and her sometimes misguided quest for independence, in the best-known of the author's series of novels set in the fictional town of Manawaka, Manitoba.

*Fugitive Pieces*, Ann Michaels
The story of a young Polish boy who escapes the fate of his family in the holocaust and of his son's coming to terms with these events. A moving, poetic novel set in both Canada and Greece.

*No Great Mischief*, Alistair MacLeod
An orthodontist meets up with his alcoholic brother and the two discuss the history of the MacDonald clan, going back to their Scottish roots and their ancestors' arrival in Cape Breton in 1779.

## READ ON A THEME

## SHIPPING NEWS – NAUTICAL NOVELS

*The Oxford Book of Sea Stories*, Ed. Tony Tanner
An excellent and diverse anthology of tales of life at sea, featuring all the authors famous for the genre, including Joseph Conrad and Jack London, plus a few surprises, for example H G Wells and Edgar Allan Poe.

*Lord Jim*, Joseph Conrad
Conrad has been described as the greatest writer of the sea. Here, he tells of a crewman on a ship who is unable to forgive himself for abandoning his vessel and leaving its passengers to drown.

*The Sea-Wolf*, Jack London
A gripping yarn of good battling against evil, set aboard a seal-hunting ship sailing from San Francisco Bay into the Pacific Ocean and featuring a classic seafaring villain, Captain Wolf Larsen.

*The Nautical Chart*, Arturo Perez-Reverte
An exciting maritime adventure about a sailor and an enchanting naval museum worker who search for a Jesuit galleon that sank with a mysterious cargo off the coast of Spain in the seventeenth century.

*Long John Silver*, Bjorn Larsson
The prince of pirates recounts his life before and after his appearance in *Treasure Island*. This is a brilliantly written novel full of swashbuckling adventure and life on the open seas.

*Every Man for Himself*, Beryl Bainbridge
This is a meticulously researched novel set aboard the Titanic and recounting the days leading up to its appointment with destiny.

*Star of the Sea*, Joseph O'Connor
An impressive novel that describes the journey taken in 1847 by hundreds of Irish refugees across the Atlantic to New York.

*The Voyage Home*, Jane Rogers
A woman is returning to England by boat from Nigeria, after the death of her father. His revealing diaries, the presence of two desperate stowaways, and a sexual encounter with a crew member make for an eventful journey.

*No Signposts in the Sea*, Vita Sackville-West
A terminally ill journalist leaves his job and takes a cruise. The abundance of free time, and his unrequited love for a beautiful fellow passenger, cause him to reassess his life and values.

*Outerbridge Reach*, Robert Stone
Owen Browne sets out on a solo round–the-world yacht race, but the solitude and his inadequacies as a sailor lead him into a nightmare. Meanwhile, his wife falls in love with another man.

*Debatable Land*, Candia McWilliam
Six oddly assorted characters sail by yacht across the Pacific, from Tahiti to New Zealand, reminiscing and analysing their lives as they go.

*To the Ends of the Earth: A Sea Trilogy*, William Golding
Golding's acclaimed sea trilogy tells the story of a ship's difficult and tense journey to Australia in the early nineteenth century. Comprises *Rites of Passage*, *Close Quarters* and *Fire Down Below*,

# AUSTRALASIA

## AUSTRALIA

**KEY**TITLES

*The True History of the Kelly Gang*, Peter Carey
*Eucalyptus*, Murray Bail
*The Idea of Perfection*, Kate Grenville
*Remembering Babylon*, David Malouf

## TRUE HISTORY OF THE KELLY GANG (2000)

Peter Carey

Ned Kelly is the most famous outlaw in Australian history. This first-person retelling of his story, in stream-of-consciousness prose marked by an absence of punctuation, captures perfectly the flavour of life in nineteenth-century Australia, with all its violence, depravity and rough justice.

Kelly was hanged at the age of twenty-six and he writes this version of events for the daughter he will never see. One senses that Carey is having a good time, playing literary father to an Australian folk hero. His sympathies are obviously with the downtrodden Kelly, yet they are conveyed quite without sentimentality.

Kelly's father is gone by the time he is twelve and although he tries to be a good boy and help his beloved and beleaguered mother, events constantly conspire to force him off the straight and narrow. When he is apprenticed to a legendary bushwhacker, Harry Power, his criminal days begin in earnest, although he remains a fundamentally decent man whose good intentions are defeated by circumstances and he finds himself marginalised in world of colonial self-interest, corrupt authority and prejudice.

The romance of Ned and Mary, the mother of his daughter, is touchingly relayed against a backdrop of violence and doom. The bleakness of existence is reflected in the arid deserts, the ramshackle homes and the decimated lives. Modern Australia was born in the dust and fire of that period and Ned Kelly's story is relevant for anyone interested in the birth of this nation.

*Peter Carey's other Australian novels are* Illywhacker *(1985) and* Oscar and Lucinda *(1988).*

# EUCALYPTUS (1998)
Murray Bail

Holland is a man obsessed with eucalyptus trees and over many years he plants hundreds of different species on his remote farm in New South Wales. He is a widower who, when his only child – the beautiful and languorous Ellen – comes of age, lets it be known that he will give her hand in marriage to the first man who can name all the trees on his estate.

One by one suitors arrive, attracted by rumours of Ellen's astonishing beauty. However, it seems that no man is equal to the task her father has set them, and Ellen begins to worry that she may be destined to waste her best years in idle contemplation. Finally, an expert from Adelaide – Mr Cave – arrives to take up the challenge. He is rumoured to have personally inspected every single eucalyptus in the state of South Australia.

The days pass and the rather indifferent Mr Cave is making progress towards the prize. However, one day an unnamed stranger appears in the grounds and begins to tell Ellen stories, testing her father's earlier injunction to 'Beware of any man who deliberately tells a story'.

There begins a contest of sorts between the clinical and scientific Mr Cave and the wild and imaginative stranger. Just as the plants have two names, the Latin or scientific and the commonplace, so there are two ways of viewing the world: as a mere repository of objects and facts, or as a place of innumerable wonders to be interpreted and delighted in.

The stranger does not name the trees but gives each one a life. He regales Ellen with tales of lonely women too shy to voice their feelings, hairdressers, spinsters, piano teachers and bird breeders, all lovers who have missed their chance to love. As Ellen hears his tales, she is prompted to examine her real feelings.

The eucalyptus is Australia's national tree and each chapter has a eucalyptus heading. The book is very evocative of the landscape and is rich in folklore and charming observations about nature and art. Although set in modern-day Australia, it has a delightful fairytale quality and is a thoroughly seductive read.

*Murray Bail's other novels include* Holden's Performance *(1987).*

# THE IDEA OF PERFECTION (1999)
## Kate Grenville

This novel begins with a quotation from Leonardo da Vinci – 'an arch is two weaknesses which together make a strength' – summarising a plot in which two weak people build a bridge to each other and to themselves.

The people are Harley Savage, a tall, dowdy woman who has already lost three husbands, the last to suicide, and Douglas Cheesman, a socially inept engineer with one failed marriage behind him. Both are outsiders in the small town of Karakarook in New South Wales. Douglas has the task of demolishing a bridge known locally as 'Bent Bridge', while Harley works for a heritage organisation campaigning to preserve the structure as a tourist attraction. Karakarook is in danger of being passed by: the highway goes somewhere else, the only bank in town is on the verge of closure, and all major industries have long since departed.

The bleak landscape of the outback is the backdrop against which two lonely souls from the big city learn to see their country through fresh eyes. Grenville captures the spirit of small-town Australia perfectly, with subtlety and wit. The romance between the two misfits is finely tuned and neatly paced.

*The novel won the Orange Prize in 2001. Grenville's other novels include* The Secret River *(2005), a historical novel about an English thief sent to Australia and the tragic confrontation between the aboriginal people and the white settlers.*

# REMEMBERING BABYLON (1993)

David Malouf

In the 1840s in Northern Australia, a white English boy, Gemmy Fairley, is washed ashore after being thrown overboard by the ship's crew and is taken in by Aborigines.

Sixteen years later, with memories of his original life and language fading, he emerges from the bush with the desire to rediscover his past. He is found by newly arrived white settlers in an unnamed outpost in Queensland and is taken in by a Scottish family, the McIvors.

Initially it is hoped he can live a normal life among them. However, the settlers' fears and anxieties militate against this hope. Some see him as a spy sent by an aboriginal people intent on massacring all white people. Others are unnerved by his presence: by the smell of mud that emanates from him, by his stammering, inarticulate English, and by his natural twitchiness.

Malouf presents Gemmy as a lost opportunity for Australian peoples to integrate, describing him with irony, through the words of a religious minister, as 'a true child of the place as it will one day be'. That is how it could have been, had the white European settlers and the native black Aborigines learnt to integrate. However, this may well be at the root of the settlers' apprehension, the notion that they could so easily assimilate and lose the very essence of themselves. They call him the 'blackfeller' and even after a year, they still don't trust him. When he is seen openly talking with some Aborigines the consequences are swift and brutal.

The McIvors, however, learn to love him as he teaches them a more natural way of living, an experience that has a profound and lasting effect on the family and sees them increasingly alienated from the rest of the settlement.

Based on a true incident, and written by a poet, this outstanding novel depicts the natural world of the outback in rich and loving detail.

*David Malouf has published several other novels, including* Harland's Half Acre *(1984), a family saga set in rural Australia.*

## 🐚Read ons

*A Fringe of Leaves*, Patrick White
A ship travelling to England in the 1840s is wrecked off the coast of Queensland and two survivors are taken to live with a tribe of aboriginal people.

*The Playmaker*, Thomas Keneally
It is 1789 and the inmates of Australia's first-ever penal colony stage a play in celebration of the King's birthday. Based on a true incident.

*Cloudstreet*, Tim Winton
Follow the fortunes of two very different families as their lives are pitched together in Western Australia, in the period between the Second World War and the mid 1960s.

*My Brilliant Career*, Miles Franklin
Written in 1901, this is a classic novel about a young girl craving life and love in the outback. The author refused to allow the book to be reprinted after it came to be regarded as autobiographical.

*Picnic at Hanging Rock*, Joan Lindsay
An intriguing novel that deals with the aftermath of a mysterious incident in which a group of schoolgirls go on a picnic and three of them, along with a teacher, disappear.

*A Town Called Alice*, Nevil Shute
A woman survives her time as a Japanese prisoner of war and looks to make good with her inherited fortune. She goes into the outback in search of a soldier punished for helping her during the war.

*Oyster*, Janette Turner Hospital
A fake messiah by the name of Oyster sets up his end-of-the-millennium cult in Queensland in this sensuous, provocative novel.

*Everyman's Rules for Scientific Living*, Carrie Tiffany
An award-winning novel, set in the 1930s, that follows a seamstress touring the country teaching better farming methods. She finally settles down in an inhospitable region to put her own methods to the test.

*Three Dollars*, Elliot Perlman
In Melbourne, a chemical engineer examines his life and wonders how he has come to lose his money, his beautiful wife and his comfortable suburban lifestyle.

*Gould's Book of Fish*, Richard Flanagan **(Tasmania)**
An imaginative and audacious novel about a convict in a Tasmanian penal colony in the nineteenth century who is ordered to keep a journal and paint pictures of the local fish for scientific study.

*The Hunter*, Julia Leigh **(Tasmania)**
This impressive novel, set in the wilds of Tasmania, deals with a man searching for a Tasmanian tiger, a dog-like carnivorous marsupial thought to be extinct.

*English Passengers*, Matthew Kneale **(Tasmania)**
A humorous tale of a historical expedition to Tasmania and of how the Tasmanian aborigines fought against colonialism. Winner of the Whitbread Prize.

# NEW ZEALAND

## KEYTITLES

*The Bone People*, Keri Hulme
*Owls Do Cry*, Janet Frame

## THE BONE PEOPLE (1985)
### Keri Hulme

Three damaged lives come together on the beaches of New Zealand's South Island. Part-Maori artist, Kerewin Holmes, builds herself a large tower by the sea, so she can isolate herself from other people. However, her solitude is disturbed one day when Simon Peter, a mute child of indeterminate age, breaks in. She subsequently becomes involved in his life and with his adoptive father, Joe Gillayley, a local Maori labourer and a drunk with a bad temper and his own sad history.

We discover that Simon was washed up on the beach three years earlier, following a boating accident that claimed the lives of both of his parents. Joe and his pregnant wife, Hana, took Simon in but, less than a year later, Hana and their eight-month-old son, Timote, died of flu, leaving Simon alone with Joe, a volatile man with a disturbing approach to parenting. Meanwhile, Kerewin is exploring her own painful familial past and discovering why she is so keen to live in isolation.

The novel is a complex mix of Maori mythology, poetry and passion, with a story told from the perspectives of multiple narrators. It is written with humour, vitality and a raw savagery that is occasionally disturbing. However, this is ultimately a tale of redemption and of how our craving for perfection in love can blind us to the good. It won the Booker Prize in 1985 and remains Keri Hulme's only novel.

# OWLS DO CRY (1957)

## Janet Frame

All of Janet Frame's novels draw on her own experiences. This novel, her first, is about the Withers children – Toby, Daphne, Francie and Teresa, known as Chicks – growing up in the town of Waimaru (a fictionalised Oamaru, the author's home town), halfway between the South Pole and the equator.

The Withers are poor in monetary terms but rich in 'wonder currency'. What they lack in material goods, they make up for in words, play and dreams, spending their days rummaging through the rubbish dump, where imagination turns tat into treasure. The children use words like magic spells, to wrestle the miraculous from the world of reality. Their exhausted parents do their inadequate best to bring them up, but the children grow to become isolated and damaged individuals, grasping onto 'the wrong magic and the wrong fairy tale'. When Francie dies at the rubbish dump, her death has profound effects on her siblings for the rest of their lives.

The second part of the novel sees the three children as adults: Daphne has had a breakdown and is in an institution, Toby still lives at home, and Chicks has opted for marital normality. Their ultimate destiny is heartbreakingly sad.

Frame's writing is intense. The poetry in her prose fairly shimmers on the page and her descriptions of nature and the landscape are illuminating and insightful.

*Owls Do Cry* is the first of a loose trilogy and is followed by the extraordinary *Faces in the Water* (1961), about her experiences in a New Zealand mental asylum, while *The Edge of the Alphabet* (1962) completes the series.

*Janet Frame gained international recognition when Jane Campion turned the second volume of her autobiography* An Angel at My Table *(1984) into a successful film in 1990.*

## 🕮Read ons

*The Garden Party and Other Stories*, Katherine Mansfield
Fifteen stories that are typical of the author's understated style. They are sensitive and accurate glimpses into the complex relationships of people's everyday lives.

*The Whale Rider*, Witi Ihimaera
Kahu, an eight-year-old Maori girl, battles against her family and tradition to become next in line to be chief of her tribe, a position that traditionally follows the male line. A moving novel of modern Maori life.

*The Singing Whakapapa*, C K Stead
A modern-day descendant of pakeha pioneers tries to find meaning in his life while researching the life of an eighteenth-century missionary in New Zealand.

*Plumb*, Maurice Gee
A classic novel about George Plumb, a Presbyterian minister living in the provinces who is attempting to reconcile a complex private life with religious integrity. The first of a trilogy that continues with *Meg* and *Sole Survivor*.

*Baby No Eyes*, Patricia Grace
Several stories are woven together in this lush Maori tale of family ghosts that highlights how present-day struggles are echoes of past actions.

*The House Guest*, Barbara Anderson
Secrets and mysteries are revealed when, following the death of his wife, a professor begins to investigate the life of a writer, once a houseguest of a childhood friend.

*Rain*, Kirsty Gunn
A beautifully descriptive and languid novella about a young woman recalling the summers spent with her neglectful alcoholic parents and younger brother in a holiday cottage by a lake.

*Once Were Warriors*, Alan Duff
A controversial take on urban life amongst the Maoris. A couple living in poverty leave their children prey to drugs and violence. The book is written in a mixture of vicious slang and raw prose. There is a sequel, *What Becomes of the Broken Hearted*.

*The Colour*, Rose Tremain
A man takes his wife and mother to New Zealand and falls victim to gold fever in this meticulously written tale set in the mid nineteenth century.

# PACIFIC ISLANDS

## ⚋Read ons

*The Moon and Sixpence*, W Somerset Maugham (Tahiti)
Loosely based on the life of Paul Gauguin, this novel sees an Englishman desert his conventional life for an artistic one on a South Pacific island. First published in 1919.

*Frangipani*, Célestine Hitiura (Tahiti)
A colourful and vibrant story of difficulties in the relationship between mother and daughter as the daughter reaches adulthood, highlighting how traditional Tahitian ways are adapting to modern life.

*They Who Do Not Grieve*, Sía Figiel (Samoa)
The stories of three generations of Samoan women are told in poetic and dream-like detail.

*Stevenson Under the Palm Trees*, Alberto Manguel (Samoa)
Robert Louis Stevenson is living out his final years in Samoa, when a strange missionary appears and tragic events ensue.

*Henderson's Spear*, Ronald Wright (South Sea Islands)
A Canadian filmmaker, in jail in Tahiti, is writing a letter to the daughter she gave up for adoption twenty years earlier, detailing her own and her ancestors' colourful lives.

*Mr Fortune's Maggot*, Sylvia Townsend Warner (South Sea Islands)
A South Sea Island missionary learns about love from his feelings for a native boy, in this beautifully realised novel.

*Easter Island*, Jennifer Vanderbes (Easter Island)
Two parallel stories of love and betrayal, set sixty years apart, illuminate the lives of two women and the quest to discover the origins of the famous giant statues on Easter Island.

## PARADISE LOST – UTOPIAN NIGHTMARES

*Lord of the Flies*, William Golding
A group of schoolboys are left to fend for themselves on a desert island after a plane crash. At first they have an idyllic existence, but they soon descend into anarchy and brutality.

*Foe*, J M Coetzee
A clever postmodern retelling of **Robinson Crusoe**. Susan Barton, marooned on Crusoe's island, returns to England and prevails upon author Daniel Foe to tell her story. He does, but with some minor revisions.

*Island*, Aldous Huxley
A utopian island in the Pacific, where technology is fused with Eastern philosophy, prospers until Western capitalism destroys the idyll.

*Rushing to Paradise*, J G Ballard
Wildlife crusader, Dr Barbara Rafferty, turns an island in the Pacific into a sanctuary for endangered species, but her actions have lethal consequences.

*Jurassic Park*, Michael Crichton
An eccentric entrepreneur creates a theme park populated by real dinosaurs, genetically produced from fossilised DNA. Things go horribly awry when, as a result of industrial espionage, the dinosaurs break free.

*The Mosquito Coast*, Paul Theroux, *see* **Central America**
*The Beach*, Alex Garland, *see* **Thailand**

# ASIA

## SOUTH-EAST ASIA

## THE HARMONY SILK FACTORY (2005)
Tash Aw

This debut novel, set in a tumultuous and lushly described Malaysia of the 1940s, tells the tale of Johnny Lim, a Chinese-Malayan, through three distinct voices, those of his son, his wife and a devoted friend. In the first section, Johnny's son, Jasper, tells of his father's wickedness and his reputation as the most feared man in the neighbourhood. Johnny died a drug smuggler and a thief, running his various criminal operations from his house, The Harmony Silk Factory, but we learn that he began life as a lowly peasant working in a British-owned tin mine. An altercation with a racist foreman, whom he kills, alters his life and his exiled wanderings lead him to become a top salesman for the Tiger Brand Trading Company, a firm that secretly funds communist guerrillas in their resistance to the forthcoming Japanese occupation. After the sudden death of the company's kindly owner, Lim becomes head of the company and betrays his comrades to the Japanese secret police. He marries the most beautiful woman in the Kinta valley, Snow Soong, who happens to be the daughter of the richest man. She dies giving birth to Jasper.

The second part of the novel tells of the relationship between Johnny and Snow Soong through her diaries. She recounts their belated honeymoon to the Seven Maiden Islands in 1941, a journey they undertook with a Japanese professor, Mamoru Kunichika, and a British aesthete, Peter Wormwood. It is the latter's fond reminiscences thirty years later, from an eastern nursing home, that close the book.

Aw offers an interesting perspective on this part of the world in a fascinating and endearing tale that highlights the complexity of human character and motive. *The Harmony Silk Factory* won the Whitbread First Novel Award in 2005.

## ⌇Read ons
*Foreign Bodies*, Hwee Hwee Tan (Singapore)
A culture clash is at the heart of this fast-paced debut novel, as three friends are caught up in a corrupt legal system and must move fast to find a way to free themselves.

*The Singapore Grip*, J G Farrell (Singapore)
On the eve of the Second World War, Singapore is about to fall into the hands of the Japanese in this tragicomic love story. It completes Farrell's *Empire Trilogy*, a series that begins with *Troubles*, followed by the Booker-Prize-winning *Siege of Krishnapur*.

*The Malayan Trilogy*, Anthony Burgess (Malaysia)
Written in the mid 1950s, these three novels chronicle the adventures of an English history teacher in the last days of British colonial rule. The trilogy is also known as *The Long Day Wanes*.

*The Rice Mother*, Rani Manicka (Malaysia)
This multigenerational saga is cloaked in exotic magic realism and spans a hundred years of Malaysian history as seen through the eyes of Lakshmi and her family.

*Highways to a War*, Christopher Koch (Cambodia)
A boyhood friend pieces together a portrait of a legendary war photographer who went missing in Cambodia in 1976.

*The King's Last Song*, Geoff Ryman (Cambodia)
Two friends set out to rescue a twelfth-century book containing the writings of one of Cambodia's greatest kings. An evocative novel that interweaves the country's tragic distant and recent past.

### *The Coroner's Lunch*, Colin Cotterill (Laos)

A retired doctor is appointed coroner in post-revolutionary Laos and resorts to supernatural methods to deal with the sudden appearance of the bodies of Vietnamese soldiers. The first in a series of Dr Siri Paiboun mysteries.

### *The Blue Afternoon*, William Boyd (Philippines)

An architect meets a doctor who claims to be her father. He proceeds to tell her his life story.

# INDONESIA

*Buru Quartet*, Pramoedya Ananta Toer
Four novels that cover the early twentieth-century history of Indonesia in the form of a love story, as a naïve student becomes involved with a leading Javanese family. The author was imprisoned for his writings.

*The Year of Living Dangerously*, Christopher Koch
This once-banned novel was the inspiration for a famous film. It follows a group of journalists in Jakarta as a communist coup is attempted in 1965.

*The Redundancy of Courage*, Timothy Mo
A Chinese businessman is caught up in the Indonesian invasion of East Timor in 1975.

# THAILAND

*Sightseeing*, Rattawut Lapcharoensap
A keenly observed debut collection of short stories that bring the country to life and show it as more than just a beautiful playground for tourists.

*Bangkok 8*, John Burdett
A Buddhist police officer investigates the death of a US marine in the back streets and brothels of Bangkok. The first in a series of crime novels featuring Detective Sonchai Jitpleecheep.

*The Beach*, Alex Garland
A backpacker heads for a mythical, paradisiacal beach and finds a secluded society of like-minded people living there. Utopian ideals evaporate quickly as a power struggle ensues.

# BURMA/MYANMAR

*Saving Fish From Drowning*, Amy Tan
A holiday along the Burma Road goes horribly wrong for a group of Americans when they are kidnapped and held in a jungle-covered mountain.

*The Piano Tuner*, Daniel Mason
In the late nineteenth century, the British War Office sends a diffident piano tuner from London to the jungles of Burma to tune a rare piano belonging to an eccentric but influential sergeant major. Haunting and erotic.

*Burmese Days*, George Orwell
Orwell's first novel, based on his own experiences, focuses on the corruption of colonial rule and the lives of expatriates in Burma towards the end of the British Empire.

*The Glass Palace*, Amitav Ghosh
A breathtaking journey through Burma, Malaya and India over a century of history, beginning with the exile of the Ming of Burma.

# VIETNAM

*The Sorrow of War*, Bao Ninh

## THE SORROW OF WAR (1991)
Bao Ninh

This is the best-known novel about the Vietnam War by a Vietnamese author. Bao Ninh served in the Glorious 27th Youth Brigade and wrote this extraordinary, semi-autobiographical novel ten years after the events it describes. This complex narrative graphically portrays the grim reality of fighting for the ordinary Vietnamese soldier, its chaotic structure suggestive of the tortured mental state of its narrator, Kien, a North Vietnamese soldier who spent a decade fighting in the South. He embarks on the writing as an act of therapy, and his account reflects the despair felt in the post-war period by many ex-combatants attempting to assimilate into ordinary life, men for whom the reality of slaughter mocks the propaganda they were fed on the righteousness and glory of the War. This slim novel tells many gruesome stories of atrocities on both sides and recounts the bravery of individual soldiers.

It is a story not only of horror and brutality but also of heartbreaking personal loss. During a grim episode in which he is ordered to bury the bodies of his slain comrades, Kien remembers his pre-war life, in particular his romance with Phuong, his first and only love, who accompanies him on the journey to join his platoon, only to become separated from him. Later, Kien learns of the brutal attack she suffered at the hands of soldiers.

This powerful and, in parts, beautiful book is already regarded as a classic. It remains the author's only book, although he is rumoured to have written a second novel, *Steppe*, which he has been reluctant to submit for publication.

**Read ons**

*Beyond Illusions*, Duong Thu Huong
A woman has to choose between love and pragmatism when both her husband and her lover are forced to compromise their ideals in order to survive in post-war Hanoi.

*The Tapestries*, Kien Nguyen
A fairytale account of the life of a tapestry-maker in the court of the last king of Vietnam in the early 1900s.

*The Lover*, Marguerite Duras
Set in 1930s' Saigon, this slim novel is the story of a love affair between a French girl and a Chinese man. Philosophical and tender.

*The Things They Carried*, Tim O'Brien
This skilful blend of memoir, novel and short story recounts the experiences of soldiers involved in the Vietnam War.

*The Quiet American*, Graham Greene
An embittered English journalist, his emblematic Vietnamese girlfriend, and an enthusiastic American diplomat find themselves at odds in war-torn Indochina in the 1950s.

# FAREAST

## JAPAN

### KEYTITLES

*The Wind-up Bird Chronicle*, Haruki Murakami
*The Makioka Sisters*, Junichiro Tanizaki
*The Silent Cry*, Kenzaburo Oe
*Memoirs of a Geisha*, Arthur Golden

## THE WIND-UP BIRD CHRONICLE (1997)
### Haruki Murakami

Toru Okada gives up his job and spends his time pottering around the house. Then his life takes a decidedly odd turn: his cat goes missing, one night his wife fails to come home, and he begins to receive erotic phone calls from a stranger.

When he befriends a morbidly cheery teenage girl who shows him a dried-up well, he decides to spend a few days at the bottom of it, where he meditates on his life.

Toru's determined attempts to find his wife, despite her wish not to be found, bring him into contact with many bizarre characters whose interventions serve only to take Toru deeper into a mystery he cannot solve, a mystery that seems to reflect the moral ambiguity of modern Japanese history, taking in as it does Japan's occupation of Manchuria and the harsh treatment meted out to Japanese prisoners in Siberian coalmines.

Toru endures numerous and varied trials that signal the alienation and dislocation of modern man, whose nameless fears become objectified, one as the wind-up bird of the title. Murakami's rather flat and detached prose takes us into a world that is often confusing and unresolved, but always engrossing.

*Haruki Murakami is currently the most popular Japanese novelist, both in his own country and in the West. His other, less surreal novels include* Norwegian Wood *(1987) and* South of the Border, West of the Sun *(1992).*

# THE MAKIOKA SISTERS (1943–48)
Junichiro Tanizaki

The four Makioka sisters are descendants of a noble Japanese family, now fallen on hard times but still eager to maintain their dignity. The two eldest sisters, Tsuruko and Sachiko, are married. The book recounts their attempts to find a suitable husband for the third eldest sister, Yukio. The youngest sister, Taeko, must wait for her sister to be married off before she can find a husband of her own.

Yukio is quiet and shy but also stubborn, refusing to accept the many choices of husband her sisters offer her and showing herself to be unimpressed with mere wealth or status. The sisters are continually forced to lower their standards, but one major obstacle still stands in their way. The youngest sister, Taeko, disgraced the family years ago when she attempted to elope with her lover. A newspaper ran the story of this aborted elopement, but mistakenly identified Yukio as the sister at the centre of the scandal, a mistake which, although rectified to an extent by a small and tardy retraction, has left a permanent stain on Yukio's reputation.

This elegant book depicts the fading splendour of Osaka in the 1930s and the sorrow and disgrace of a once-prominent family. Taeko is the only sister in touch with the modern world, renting a studio and running her own successful doll-making business. Much of her behaviour is frowned upon by her sisters, and she finds herself constantly pushing against the boundaries they impose. The other sisters remain frozen in time, clinging onto the traditions that sustained their forebears, while modern Japan encroaches all around them. *The Makioka Sisters* is a triumph of the particular: the quotidian worries of the family are skilfully articulated and intimate details are worked into dramatic episodes, as the world outside moves inexorably and ominously towards war. With perfect characterisation and supreme skill, Tanizaki has written a modern masterpiece.

*His other novels include* Some Prefer Nettles *(1929) and the erotic classic* The Key *(1956).*

# THE SILENT CRY (1967)

Kenzaburo Oe

Though a dark and complex read, *The Silent Cry* is regarded as one of the great post-war Japanese novels, winning the Tanizaki Prize, one of Japan's highest literary awards. It tells the story of two brothers and their attempt to start a new life, an attempt stifled by confrontation and the existence of dark family secrets.

 Mitsu is a depressed scholar with an alcoholic wife, Natsumi, and a disabled child in an institution. His younger brother, Takashi, returns from America obsessed by family history, especially that of their grandfather's younger brother, the leader of a peasant revolt a hundred years earlier. Takashi suggests to Mitsu that they return to the village of their childhood to sell some family property and start their lives anew.

 However, back in the ancestral home, Mitsu's life falls apart even more when his wife becomes estranged and eventually his brother's lover. Takashi, meanwhile, stirs the villagers to revolt against a modern-day emperor – the Korean owner of a local supermarket – after having also secretly agreed to sell the family estate to him. Mirroring the events of a hundred years ago, the villagers become disenchanted with the revolt. Unpleasant revelations about the family's past also surface, including the murder of their elder brother and the suicide of their mentally disabled sister, an incident in which Takashi is somehow implicated.

 Stylistically obtuse, *The Silent Cry* is a metaphor for the conflict between tradition and modernity, illusion and truth. The author won the Nobel Prize for Literature in 1994.

# MEMOIRS OF A GEISHA (1997)

Arthur Golden

Sayuri tells her life story from an elegant suite in the Waldorf Astoria. The story begins with the death of her mother, in 1929, and her fisherman father's decision to sell nine-year-old Sayuri to an okiya or geisha house in Kyoto. With her stunning blue-grey eyes and undeniable charm, she soon arouses the jealousies of the other girls, especially the primary geisha, Hatsumomo. Protected by an older girl, Sayuri learns the disciplined arts of the geisha: how to apply the elaborate make-up, how to arrange her hair correctly, how to pour saké, and how to beguile powerful men.

The customary auction of her virginity to the highest bidder takes place and a record amount is paid for her mizuage. A sugar daddy is found for her and she eventually becomes the new head of the okiya. However, the advent of the Second World War brings her fortunes once again to a nadir. She secretly pines for the true love of her life, a man she knows simply as 'The Chairman', who showed her kindness in the past. After many hardships and desperate times, she effectively becomes his mistress. He helps her move to New York in later life and she opens a teahouse.

*Arthur Golden is a Japanese scholar whose meticulous research is evident throughout this fascinating look at an exotic and mysterious culture. He was sued by a retired geisha, Mineko Iwasaki, for citing her as a reference source for the book, thereby breaking the geisha code of secrecy. Iwasaki's own memoir,* Geisha of Gion, *is itself an interesting read.*

*Memoirs of a Geisha* was made into a hugely successful film in 2005.

## 📖 Read ons

*The Oxford Book of Japanese Short Stories*, Ed. Theodore W Goosen
Taking stories from over a hundred years of Japanese literature, these tales include many new translations and two from Nobel Prize winners.

*The Sailor Who Fell From Grace With The Sea*, Yukio Mishima
A young sociopathic teenager observes his mother's relationship with a prospective stepfather and moves from hero worship to notions of revenge.

*Silence*, Shusaku Endo
A thought-provoking book about the attempt of two Portuguese priests to spread the gospel in sixteenth-century Japan, while across the country Christians are being persecuted and killed.

*Musashi*, Eiji Yoshikawa
Written in the 1930s, this novel details the astonishing life of the legendary seventeenth-century Samurai, Miyamoto Musashi, author of the classic *The Book of Five Rings*.

*Rashomon*, Ryunosuke Akutagawa
A collection of short stories from the turn of the last century, famously adapted by Japanese filmmaker Akira Kurosawa.

*Ring*, Koji Suzuki
A journalist investigates the mysterious deaths of his niece and four other students after watching a videotape. The book spawned a series of cult films and launched a new literary star.

*The Master of Go*, Yasunari Kawabata
Based on true events, an old grand master plays a young pretender in the game of go in this classic novel about the state of Japan following defeat in the Second World War.

*Woman in the Dunes*, Kobo Abe
A clever and beautiful book about a teacher on holiday in a remote village. He is held captive with a female outcast in her home at the bottom of a pit.

### *The Tale of Murasaki*, Liza Dalby
This fascinating novel tells of a young woman observing the exotic court life that surrounds her, and of Murasaki's writing of *The Tale of Genji*, an eleventh-century classic of Japanese literature.

### *Silk*, Alessandro Baricco
A touching, poetic novella about a young French merchant in the 1860s, who is sent to Japan to obtain eggs for the breeding of silkworms. Though happily married, he falls in love with a concubine and a secret love affair develops.

### *Fear and Trembling*, Amélie Nothomb
An impressive comic novella about a young Belgian woman grappling with cultural differences between East and West.

### *Shogun*, James Clavell
A famous epic set in sixteenth-century Japan. When a Dutch trading ship is wrecked off the coast of Japan, its crew is taken prisoner and its captain slowly becomes bewitched by the country's culture and embroiled in its feudal politics.

### *I Am a Cat*, Natsume Soseki
An episodic and whimsical novel, written in 1906, about a disdainful cat describing the bourgeois lives of all those he comes across.

# TOKYO

TOKYO

---

## KEYTITLES

*Kitchen*, Banana Yoshimoto
*Number9Dream*, David Mitchell

## KITCHEN (1987)

Banana Yoshimoto

When young Mikage's grandmother dies, she is left all alone in the world. However, Yuichi, a boy from a florist's patronised by her grandmother, suggests that Mikage come to live with him and his mother. Yuichi's beautiful mother turns out to be his father, Eriko, in a dress. Eriko runs a nightclub and is rarely home in the evenings. In spite of this unconventionality, Mikage moves in, pleased to have found a new family, however curious.

So begins this quirky and engaging novella about love, death and survival. When Eriko is killed, the two youngsters are left to deal with their feelings for each other and responses to the tragedies they have experienced. Mikage drops out of school and takes a job in a cookery college, expressing herself through her culinary skills. Meanwhile, emotionally distant Yuichi is slowly realising that in order to develop as an adult he must learn to express his feelings.

Contemporary Japanese culture combines with Western influence to reveal a repressed nation expressing its emotions in oblique ways. Mikage's mood swings and adolescent obsessions are accurately presented and she has worthwhile and poetic observations to make, in spite of her tender years. Some subtleties are lost in translation, nuances are submerged, and metaphors are sometimes strained, nevertheless, this remains a charming novella.

The UK edition presents two novellas in a single volume. The second extended short story, *Moonlight Shadow*, explores similar themes to those of the first, but in a rather more ethereal way. Yoshimoto's later novels include *Goodbye Tsugumi* (1989) and *Lizard* (1993).

# NUMBER9DREAM (2001)

## David Mitchell

A young student, Eiji Miyake, arrives in Tokyo from his small island home determined to find the father he has never met. He is naïve and resilient and yet fully unprepared for the furiously kinetic capital city.

As he sits in a café opposite the office of his father's lawyer he imagines his way into the building and then plays out the scene differently in his head each time. The scene is thus set as Eiji imagines and fantasises his way through the novel, for the ground constantly moves from beneath the reader's feet. Mitchell's literary ventriloquism is highly tuned and he writes all genres well, whether it be cyberpunk games, shocking violence or gripping family saga. There are especially tender reminisces of Eiji's childhood with his now deceased twin sister, Anju, and the problems with their alcoholic mother, which are handled effectively.

Eiji rents a capsule room above a video shop and stays in Tokyo for a couple of months, working to get by and meeting an array of odd characters. Following his father's trail brings him into contact with big-time gangsters and Eiji finds himself in possession of a computer disk with vital information that people are prepared to kill for.

Because so much in this book takes place inside Eiji's head, the reader is often left wondering what is real and what is fantasy. Mitchell's precise and poetic prose makes the mundane fascinating and the fantastical real, and his energetic style and playful humour make the eminently likeable Eiji's quest an adventure worth pursuing. With unashamed borrowings from other writers, and from manga comics and films, this is an episodic, multi-layered adventure that reveals the surreal nature of modern Japan alongside its ancient counterpart and, like the city itself, it's probably not for everyone.

### ☙Read ons

*Strangers*, Taichi Yamada

A clever modern ghost story about a lonely man who meets a strange woman and two people who could be his dead parents. As he inveigles his way into their lives, he begins to lose sight of his own.

*Norwegian Wood*, Haruki Murakami
A middle-aged businessman recalls his early loves, including his first, the schizophrenic and suicidal girlfriend of his best friend. A touching book, and rooted more in reality than much of Murakami's work.

*Out*, Natsuo Kirino
When a woman strangles her husband in a fit of rage, she enlists the help of her colleagues to dispose of the body. A dark and gritty urban thriller that pulls no punches.

*Snakes and Earrings*, Hitomi Kanehara
This is a raunchy, violent tale of a trio of tattooed and pierced Japanese youngsters whose drug-fuelled and sexually promiscuous lifestyle leads to their being wanted for murder. A bestseller and cult classic in Japan.

*In the Miso Soup*, Ryu Murakami
A macabre but entertaining story of a Japanese guide showing Tokyo's nightlife to an odd American tourist who turns out to be a psychopathic killer. A cross between Haruki Murakami and Bret Easton Ellis.

*Audrey Hepburn's Neck*, Alan Brown
An amusing take on cultural difference and the elusiveness of love. A Japanese animator is obsessed with American women, while his gay American friend has a penchant for Japanese men.

*The Earthquake Bird*, Susanna Jones,
An unusual crime thriller in which an English woman is arrested for murder. The reader is taken through the mean streets of Tokyo and the backstreets of the woman's past in an effort to discover why.

*Mr Foreigner*, Matthew Kneale
An EFL teacher has a relationship with one of his students, becoming embroiled in a nightmare in which her family demands that he marry her.

## READON A THEME

## ROOMS WITH A VIEW – HOTEL NOVELS

*Hotel Honolulu*, Paul Theroux
An autobiographical tale of a writer who tells amusing stories about some of the strange people who stay in the hotel he runs on a Hawaiian island.

*Hotel Savoy*, Joseph Roth
A POW from the First World War is returning home. He arrives in an unnamed town in Eastern Europe and stays in the Hotel Savoy. The guests are strange, the town is in flux and Europe is on the brink of Fascism.

*Hotel World*, Ali Smith
An inventive novel in which five female characters describe one night at the Global Hotel, where their lives all interconnect after a chambermaid dies in an accident with the dumbwaiter.

*Finbar's Hotel*, Dermot Bolger (Editor)
The story of this famous Dublin establishment, as told in interconnected short stories by seven Irish authors, including Roddy Doyle and Colm Tóibín. A sequel, *Ladies' Night at Finbar's Hotel*, is also available.

*A Nice Change*, Nina Bawden
A breezy novel that recounts the tragedies and love affairs that afflict a group of holidaymakers in the Hotel Parthenon in a Greek resort.

*Mrs Palfry at the Claremont*, Elizabeth Taylor
An elderly, disillusioned, independently minded widow moves to the Claremont Hotel, an establishment in which most residents are living out their final days. She meets a young aspiring writer and a beautiful friendship develops.

*The Hotel*, Elizabeth Bowen
A superbly crafted period drama set in the 1920s about several English guests whiling away their holiday at a smart hotel on the Italian Riviera.

*The Hotel New Hampshire*, John Irving
An entertaining saga that centres on an unconventional family and the
father's attempts to run a hotel, firstly in New Hampshire, then in Vienna.

# CHINA

*Empress Orchid*, Anchee Min
*Shanghai Baby*, Wei Hui
*Soul Mountain*, Gao Xingjian

## EMPRESS ORCHID (2004)
Anchee Min

Anchee Min's story of Tzu Hsi, China's longest-reigning female ruler and its last Empress, is the author's attempt at correcting the record books. For decades, Tzu Hsi was declared 'a mastermind of pure evil and intrigue' in Chinese textbooks, for her role in the decline of the Ch'ing Dynasty in the late nineteenth century. With smuggled documents and new information, Anchee Min has discovered a powerful, strong-minded, beautiful woman who used her talents to become the Emperor's lover and confidante.

'Orchid', as she is known, comes from a noble but penniless family in Anhwei, the poorest province in China. At the age of seventeen she goes to Peking to bury her father and, in order to avoid marrying an ill-favoured cousin, she enters a contest to become one of Emperor Hsien Feng's seven wives or three thousand concubines. She is initially chosen as a low-ranking concubine, which gives her entry to the Forbidden City. Once inside, however, she soon begins to feel bored and frustrated, despite the opulence and beauty of her new surroundings. Thousands of women vie for the young Emperor's attention, and every day Orchid makes herself beautiful in the hope that the Emperor will choose her. After months of waiting, and with the help of her eunuch, she finally comes to his notice.

She is intelligent and beautiful enough to become favoured by him and she eventually gives birth to his only son, Tung Chih, in 1856. When the Emperor dies five years later, he names her as the Empress Dowager, aged only twenty-six, much to the displeasure of regents and advisors, who at one point kidnap her and her son in an effort to depose her.

*Anchee Min has written a fascinating and detailed account of the life of a remarkable woman. This is the first of an intended trilogy; the subsequent novels will cover Orchid's forty-six-year rule. Min's previous novels include* Becoming Madame Mao, *(2001).*

## SHANGHAI BABY (1999)
Wei Hui

Coco works as a waitress in a café in Shanghai. There she meets Tian Tian and almost immediately moves in with him. An artist supported by his estranged mother in Spain, Tian Tian encourages Coco to write a novel – she is already a published author with a collection of short stories in circulation. Although the two love each other very much, Tian Tian is sexually impotent, which leaves Coco frustrated. When she meets Mark, a suave German businessman with a wife, a young child, and a penchant for sadomasochism, a sexual relationship begins that leads to Coco falling in love.

Coco's emotional dilemma is examined in the discussion of the novel she is writing, a novel that not only mirrors the life she is leading but also the life of the book's author, Wei Hui. This is a technique that explores the notions of truth and identity, in the process taking the reader on a dazzling tour of Shanghai's fashionable hotspots. What might have been nothing more than a sleazy foray into the glitzy lives of rather unlikeable people is in fact a serious and emotionally honest account of Coco's sexual awakening and Tian Tian's degeneration into drug abuse.

It was famously banned in China, and publicly burnt by parents fearing it would encourage dissolution in their own daughters.

*Wei Hui's second novel,* Marrying Buddha *(2005), also features Coco, but this time in New York, where the author now lives.*

# SOUL MOUNTAIN (1990)
## Gao Xingjian

When the author's misdiagnosis with lung cancer was corrected, he went on a ten-month journey along the Yangtze River and in the forests of Sichuan Province. Along the way, he collected folktales, Daoist songs and stories from the people he met. This long, formless 'novel' is the result. *Soul Mountain* is both a journey and a dialogue with the self. Alternate chapters are, curiously, written in the second person.

Stories are what keep a culture alive and the people in these pages live out stories of of love, comedy, sex and violence in a land where, Xingjian tells us, the soul of the individual is under threat from the imposition of uniformity and the stranglehold of bureaucracy and oppression.

It has been argued that this book's modernist approach and existential philosophy make it more Western than Eastern. The author's time in Paris will perhaps account for the existential influence, and while it may not be a typically Asian novel in its structure and formlessness, nor in its terrain of the conflict between the meditative and the physical, the corporeal and the spiritual, its collection of folktales and legends nevertheless places it in a very specific Chinese context.

*Soul Mountain* was begun in Beijing in 1982 and finally published in Taiwan in 1990. It was expertly translated into English by Mabel Lee in 2000. Gao Xingjian was awarded the Nobel Prize for Literature in the same year.

## Read ons

*Waiting*, Ha Jin
Each summer a doctor asks his wife for a divorce so he can marry the woman he loves. Each summer she agrees, then changes her mind. One summer he decides he cannot wait any longer and takes matters into his own hands.

*Balzac and the little Chinese Seamstress*, Dai Sijie
Two sons of dissidents are sent to a remote village to be 're-educated' under Mao's Cultural Revolution in the 1970s. However, when they encounter Western literature and a beautiful girl, their real re-education begins.

*The Noodle Maker*, Ma Jian
A collection of loosely connected, witty stories related by a propagandist. The stories show how modern China changed over the latter part of the twentieth century.

*Farewell My Concubine*, Lilian Lee
A love triangle set in the glamorous world of Chinese opera, about the unrequited love of one student for another and the beautiful concubine that comes between them.

*The Garlic Ballads*, Mo Yan
In the late 1980s, a bumper crop of garlic means the farmers are unable to sell their goods and they feel forced to confront corrupt government officials. From China's most popular author.

*When We Were Orphans*, Kazuo Ishiguro
A renowned detective in London in the 1930s returns to Shanghai, the city where his parents vanished when he was a boy, to investigate the unsolved mystery of their disappearance.

*Empire of the Sun*, J G Ballard
A fictionalised account of the author's childhood during the Second World War, when he was taken away from his parents and imprisoned in a labour camp in Shanghai.

*Fortress Besieged*, Qian Zhongshu
Originally published in 1947, this is a classic novel set in the 1930s about a rather bumbling opportunist who, after receiving his education overseas, returns to make a disastrous marriage.

*Snow Flower and the Secret Fan*, Lisa See
This fascinating novel traces the life-long friendship of two girls in rural China in the nineteenth century.

*The Bonesetter's Daughter*, Amy Tan
A modern-day American woman learns about the hardships her mother suffered in China as she translates her mother's journal.

*The Girl Who Played Go*, Shan Sa
When a young Chinese girl in Japanese-occupied Manchuria beats all opponents in go, one adversary, a Japanese officer, begins to find himself intrigued by her.

*Raise the Red Lantern*, Su Tong
A young student becomes the fourth wife in the Chen household, in 1930s' provincial China, and finds herself competing with the other concubines for the sexual attentions of their master.

*A Thousand Years of Good Prayers*, Yiyun Li
An award-winning collection of stories, mainly set in rural China, that show how the country is coping with the modern world.

# HONG KONG/KOREA/TAIWAN/TIBET

*The Monkey King*, Timothy Mo

## THE MONKEY KING (1978)
Timothy Mo

A wickedly funny novel, set in 1950s' Hong Kong. A Macanese man, Wallace Nolasco, makes a marriage of convenience to May Ling Poon, the daughter of the rich but parsimonious Mr Poon's second concubine. Wallace moves into the family home, a dilapidated townhouse called Robinson Path, in one of the oldest parts of Hong Kong Island.

Also living there are Mrs Poon; the eldest son, Ah Lung, and his ill-treated and suicidal wife, Fong; two spinster sisters once molested by Japanese officers; and a team of resentful servants. The new arrangement forces the amahs to sleep on the floor. Disgusted, they surreptitiously take their revenge by treating Wallace badly.

Wallace's presence in the house gradually incites antipathy from all quarters and he finds himself constantly in the face of a battle. He is determined to undermine Mr Poon's power and assert his own. However, Wallace's antics only lead to trouble, especially when, after securing a job in a government office, certain indiscretions lead to his being quietly sent away.

*The Monkey King* was Mo's debut novel and it is a wonderfully evocative exposition of Chinese culture and the traditions of family life. It also highlights the anomalies of Hong Kong itself and the difficulties of adapting to the modern world. It is generally regarded as the best novel about the territory.

The Monkey King *of the title is an iconic character of Asian literature who is a disruptive and mischievous influence. Timothy Mo was born in Hong Kong in 1950 to a Cantonese father and an English mother.*

## 📖 Read ons

*Fragrant Harbour*, John Lanchester (**Hong Kong**)
A richly detailed Hong Kong and its complex twentieth-century history are seen from the 1930s onwards, through the eyes of three residents: a hotel manager, a journalist and an entrepreneur.

*History's Fiction*, Xu Xi (**Hong Kong**)
This collection of short tales of everyday lives takes the reader through four decades of troubled times from the 1960s to the 1990s, from one of Hong Kong's foremost contemporary English-language novelists.

*White Ghost Girls*, Alice Greenway (**Hong Kong**)
This lush and sensuous novel describes the lives of two American high school girls growing up in late 1960s' Hong Kong.

*The Poet,* Yi Mun-yol (**Korea**)
A fascinating insight into Korean culture that recounts the life of a celebrated nineteenth-century Korean poet and his transition from a comfortable and wealthy existence to the life of a wandering wordsmith and outcast.

*Fox Girl*, Nora Okja Keller (**Korea**)
This novel captures perfectly the unfortunate lives of three Korean girls, children of American GIs, disowned by their community and forced to work as prostitutes in post-war Korea.

*The Shadow Walker*, Michael Walters (**Mongolia**)
A crime novel set in the Mongolian capital and the wilds of the Gobi desert. The culture and scenery are eloquently described as we follow ex-policeman Nergui on the trail of a murderer.

*The Butcher's Wife*, Li Ang (**Taiwan**)
Based on a true-life murder, this is a short but graphic account of the abuse a woman suffers from her husband until she decides to take matters into her own hands.

*Red Poppies: A Novel of Tibet*, Alai (**Tibet**)
A brutal epic chronicling the rise and fall of a Tibetan chieftain, set in the early part of the twentieth century. The first of an intended trilogy.

*Stick Out Your Tongue*, Ma Jian (Tibet)
A loose collection of stories told by a Chinese man as he wanders around Tibet, meeting its people and learning about the ancient culture and modern-day privations. It was banned in China.

READONATHEME

## ADVENTURES IN WONDERLANDS – IMAGINARY PLACES

*Lost Horizon*, James Hilton
A plane crashes in the remote mountains of Tibet and the survivors are taken to a mythical, utopian village called Shangri-La, not marked on any map. Here they find a peaceful alternative to the busy Western style of life. But is there also a dark secret at its core?

*Three to See the King*, Magnus Mills
A humorous fable about a man living in a tin house who sees his few neighbours disappear to follow the charismatic Michael, a messianic figure building a community of tin houses in a canyon.

*A Modern Utopia*, H G Wells
Two walkers trekking in the Swiss Alps stumble into a space-warp and find themselves in a utopian parallel earth where socialism and equality reign.

*Speak for England*, James Hawes
A contestant in a reality-TV show is left alone in the jungle when the entire TV crew is killed in an accident. He finds himself in a mysterious place that looks exactly like 1950s' England.

*In the Country of Last Things*, Paul Auster
An epistolary novel, set in the near-future, about a woman searching for her brother who has disappeared. She comes to an unnamed and disintegrating city where civilisation has almost disappeared.

*Six*, Jim Crace
Set in an imaginary European city, this novel follows the exploits of hyperfertile actor Felix Dern and his relationships with six different women, all of whom he has made instantly pregnant.

*Sweet Dreams*, Michael Frayn
A slick satire on modern notions of happiness, in which Howard Baker dies in a car accident and goes to Heaven. He finds it to be a congenial, middle-class society that caters to everyone's needs.

*The Unusual Life of Tristan Smith*, Peter Carey
This book follows the adventures of severely afflicted Tristan Smith, citizen of a parallel earth. He travels from his third-world homeland Efica to oppressive superpower Voorstand, to find his fortune. A wonderful political satire.

*Hav*, Jan Morris
The author first wrote about the imaginary city-state of Hav in 1985. This new edition includes that earlier book and a recent 'revisit' in which she finds the place transformed and modernised. A fascinating blend of fiction and travel journal.

*The Paper Eater*, Liz Jensen
A utopian satire on large retail companies and consumerism, set on a man-made island called Atlantica. The place is run by computers and has a booming economy based on global waste-disposal.

# INDIANSUB-CONTINENT

## INDIA

**KEY**TITLES

*The God of Small Things*, Arundhati Roy
*The Home and the World*, Rabindranath Tagore
*A Suitable Boy*, Vikram Seth
*Midnight's Children*, Salman Rushdie

## THE GOD OF SMALL THINGS (1997)
Arundhati Roy

From its opening paragraph, rich with luscious prose, the sumptuous tone of this novel is set. You can almost smell the swaying coconut trees or hear the croak of the bush crickets. It is the late 1960s and we are in the company of Rahel and her twin brother, Estha, in the tiny river town of Ayemenem in Kerala, southern India. The twins' mother, Ammu, still a beautiful woman, has divorced their violent father to live with their blind grandmother, Mammachi, grand-aunt Baby, and uncle Chacko, a hopelessly inept Oxford-educated man. They run a pickle factory and are wealthy enough to feel aloof from the common people, unsympathetic of their needs and wilfully ignorant of their demands for equality and independence. When Chacko's English ex-wife, Margaret, visits after a long absence, the twins are especially excited, for she brings with her their cousin, Sophie, whom they are eager to get to know. However, things change forever in the course of the day.

The dark shadow of Communism hangs over the land and caste prejudices and class snobberies force events to a shuddering climax. Their lonely mother, Ammu's forbidden love for an Untouchable turns the poignant into the tragic. The narrative makes frequent switches in time, from the present day, with an adult Rahel returning to the decaying house in Ayemenem to meet Estha, now mute, back to the events that surrounded the tragic death at the centre of the story.

*Winner of the Booker Prize in 1997,* The God of Small Things *remains her only novel.*

# THE HOME AND THE WORLD (1915)
## Rabindranath Tagore

Nikhil is a wealthy landowner with modern ideas. He encourages his wife, Bimla, to come out of purdah so that she can be his social equal, an equality that will validate their love. At first, she is reluctant to leave the comfort of her traditional role, but she does eventually emerge.

They are visited by the suave Sandip, her husband's friend and a revolutionary, and Bimla is seduced by the visitor's passionate personality. Nikhil is aware of her attraction but refuses to send Sandip away, believing that his wife should be free to choose her own path.

Bimla's personal dilemma mirrors the plight of Bengal itself and the choice it faces between the safety of the old world and the transforming influence of the modern. The story is told from the perspective of the three protagonists, a modernist approach that works surprisingly well with Tagore's wonderfully ornate style.

In 1905, Bengal's boundaries were redrawn and it was divided into two provinces by the British, which provoked the Swadeshi protest movement, resulting in a protectionist trade policy and a boycott of British goods. Protests descended into riots, souring Tagore's initial enthusiasm for a movement which he came to see as detrimental to the Muslim poor. He wrote this novel as an illustration of his beliefs.

The translation by Tagore's nephew, Surendranath, is a worthy one that does, however, occasionally strike a slightly more formal tone than the original. The book provoked controversy both in India and abroad, but it remains a fascinating look at life in India at the beginning of the last century. Satyajit Ray made a sumptuous film in 1984.

# A SUITABLE BOY (1993)
Vikram Seth

This huge novel is set in 1951, four years after India achieved independence from Britain. It concerns a widow, Mrs Rupa Mehra, and her attempts to find a suitable marriage partner for her youngest daughter, Lata. In spite of the eminent suitability of her mother's choice – ambitious businessman, Haresh Khanna, owner of a shoe factory – the rebellious Lata is not persuaded. She has already fallen in love with a fellow student, the dashing Kabir. As a Muslim, he is dismissed by her family as an unsuitable match for Lata and, during the summer break, she is sent away to Calcutta to stay with the Chatterjis. Here she meets and befriends a sophisticated poet, Amit. His proposal of marriage places Lata in a dilemma.

Seth combines the personal and the political to reveal much about the relationship between the newly independent states of India and Pakistan and the influence that the politics of the period has on ordinary lives. He also communicates a vivid sense of place – brutal riots, sumptuous religious processions, heat, overpowering smells and exotic flora are all brought to life in succulent prose that keeps the reader enthralled throughout this 1400-page journey.

# MIDNIGHT'S CHILDREN (1980)
Salman Rushdie

The narrator of the novel, Saleem Sinai, is born at midnight on August 15th, 1947, the day of India's independence from British rule. All of the 1,001 babies born at this time find themselves with miraculous powers. Saleem's peculiar gift is the ability to mentally float freely into the minds of other people.

Now thirty years old, Saleem tells his life story, and with it the history of modern India, as his unusual gift allows him to see events through the eyes of such luminaries as Gandhi and Nehru, as well as through those of street beggars and little children.

It emerges that Saleem has an evil 'twin', Shiva, a motherless child of the streets with a capacity for malevolence. Using his gift, Saleem discovers that he and Shiva were switched at birth, and that he himself is the product of an illicit liaison between his Hindu mother and an Englishman.

Saleem's personal crisis is redolent of the political turmoil of the subcontinent at the time, and the events of his life are played out against a backdrop of the partition of Pakistan, the secession of Bangladesh and the eventual imposition of martial law.

This multi-layered book manages to be engaging on several levels: family saga, political document, and simple love story. Rushdie's magnificent prose is playful, erudite, fantastical and moving.

*Midnight's Children* won the Booker Prize, and also claimed the title of Booker of Booker's, for the best novel in the award's twenty-five-year history.

## Read ons

*A Malgudi Omnibus*, R K Narayan
Three novels from Narayan's series of books featuring the imaginary town of Malgudi, offering a wise and tender picture of rural life in south India for the past sixty years. A master at work.

*Clear Light of Day*, Anita Desai
Family conflicts ignite as two sisters come together after years apart in an India still feeling the pain of partition.

*The Hungry Tide*, Amitav Ghosh
Gorgeous settings and wonderful descriptions illuminate this novel about the search for dolphins off the Sunderban Islands in the Bay of Bengal.

*Untouchable*, Mulk Raj Anand
One day in the life of a low-caste Indian street cleaner. Written in the 1930s, Anand barely contains his indignation in this powerful and fiery short novel.

*A River Sutra*, Gita Mehta
A retired government official, living on the banks of the holy river Narmada, encounters numerous people who weave together a loosely connected thread of love stories in this richly romantic book.

*Freedom Song*, Amit Chaudhuri
Three beautifully wrought novellas that describe the modern postcolonial world of India in poetic detail. Set in Bombay, Oxford and Calcutta.

*Heat and Dust*, Ruth Prawer Jhabvala
An elegant tale of a woman journeying to India in the 1970s to discover the truth about the grandmother who scandalised society by eloping with an Indian prince fifty years earlier.

*A Passage to India*, E M Forster
An Indian doctor is accused of assaulting a young Englishwoman. The resulting trial causes an enormous rift in Anglo-Indian relations.

*Black Narcissus*, Rumer Godden
Nuns attempt to establish a convent in the ruins of an old palace high in the mountains, but the sensual and elemental power of paganism disrupts their plans.

*The Romantics*, Pankaj Mishra
A young Brahmin goes to Benares, India's holiest Hindu city, to discover the real India, but he is distracted by Europeans and falls in love with a French woman.

*The Blue Bedspread*, Raj Kamal Jha
Before his recently orphaned niece is adopted, an old man records their harrowing family history to pass on to her.

*Difficult Daughters*, Manju Kapur
An educated woman must choose between tradition and the modern way, as pursuing her love for a professor will see her rejected by her family.

*The Alchemy of Desire*, Tarun J Tepal
India is brought vividly to life in this erotic feast about a writer and his muse who make love and seek truth in Delhi and the Himalayan Mountains.

# MUMBAI

KEYTITLE

*A Fine Balance*, Rohinton Mistry

## A FINE BALANCE (1995)
Rohinton Mistry

This is a wonderful novel of Dickensian scope featuring four people who come together to form unlikely alliances. It is 1975 and a state of emergency has been declared by Indira Gandhi. Seamstress Dina Dalal, a Parsi widow in her early forties, is determined to maintain her financial independence and avoid a second marriage.

She rents out a room in her small flat to an old friend's student son, Maneck Kohlah, sent by his father to study for a college diploma, because the family shop is failing. Dina also employs two Hindu tailors, Ishvar Darji and his nephew, Omprakash, both untouchables who left their village after Omprakash's father was murdered for crossing caste boundaries.

Initially suspicious of each other, these four individuals develop friendships and allegiances, forming an ad hoc family. Through their stories of hardship, the reader is given a vivid sense of the tremendous effort needed simply to survive as a poor person in an astonishingly cruel India plagued by bureaucracy, endemic corruption, and bigotry. A black humour permeates the book, although this does little to prepare the reader for the harrowing denouement. Ultimately, this is a story of the misery of poverty and powerlessness, but it does carry an underlying message of hope.

*All of Rohinton Mistry's novels are set in India. His other works are* Such a Long Journey *(1991) and* Family Matters *(2002). He has also written a collection of short stories,* Tales from Firozsha Baag *(1987).*

## 📖 Read ons

*The Last Song of Dusk*, Siddharth Dhanvant Shanghvi
A beautifully written tale of love in a magical world, following the marriage of a couple whose seemingly perfect life is visited by tragedy.

*Love and Longing in Bombay*, Vikram Chandra
There is love, murder and supernatural shenanigans in this loose collection of tales about modern Bombay, all told in Chandra's lucid style.

*The Death of Vishnu*, Manil Suri
A captivating novel describing the lives of the inhabitants of a block of flats in a Bombay slum, and of Vishnu, the odd-job man who lies dying in the stairwell.

*Baumgartner's Bombay*, Anita Desai
An elderly German Jew lives alone with his cats in a seedy room off a back street in Bombay, reflecting on his life as an outsider.

*Shantaram*, Gregory David Roberts
A sensational autobiographical novel about an Australian drug addict escaping from prison and settling in Mumbai to work as a slum doctor.

*The Space Between Us*, Thrity Umrigar
A captivating tale of the interconnected lives of a middle-class Parsi widow and her Hindu maid, offering a view of the class/caste divide that exists in modern India.

*Beach Boy*, Ardashir Vakil
An upper-middle-class, pre-teen boy describes in vivid detail the world he sees around him in the early 1970s, as he obsesses about sex, food and films.

*Bombay Ice*, Leslie Forbes
A literary thriller set in Bollywood. A crime journalist is concerned for her sister's welfare and goes to Bombay to investigate. A clever debut novel by a Canadian journalist.

# PAKISTAN/SRI LANKA/ BANGLADESH

## KEYTITLES

*Kartography*, Kamila Shamsie **(Pakistan)**
*Reef*, Romesh Gunesekera **(Sri Lanka)**

## KARTOGRAPHY (2002)
Kamila Shamsie

Raheen returns to Karachi from New York University in the mid 1990s and tells of her childhood, in particular of her friendship with Karim, a friendship begun from the time they shared a crib, such was the closeness of the relationship between their parents. We learn that these parents swapped partners before marrying, for reasons that remain secret.

In 1986, Raheen and Karim were thirteen years old and living in Karachi, a city of tension and violent turmoil. When a car Karim is travelling in is shot at, his parents decide that the city is no longer safe and move to London, summarily ending the youngsters' friendship.

The bulk of the novel unravels past mysteries and, through flashbacks, takes the reader back to 1971, the time of the parents' strange pact and of the war that resulted in the formation of Bangladesh. Raheen seeks to understand why current talk of muhajirs (immigrants) should have any relevance to her own life.

Shamsie uses Karim's ambition to be a cartographer to map out the city of Karachi with affection and skill, conveying with considerable panache the blend of war, politics and heartbreak that pervades these lives. This is a touching love story about friendship and belonging.

# REEF (1994)

## Romesh Gunesekera

When Triton meets a compatriot later in London, his mind is brought back to the Sri Lanka of his youth. He tells his life story, of how from the age of eleven he is sent to work for Mister Salgado and from the moment he hears his master's rich voice he becomes completely devoted to him. When the drunken butler is dismissed and the cook retires, Triton is left in charge. He learns to become everything to his master, but takes particular pride and relish in his role as cook.

In a world of political turmoil, Triton keeps the Salgado household ticking along nicely. When a lady, Nili, comes to visit, she seems to find the key to Mister Salgado's heart, but it is Triton's love-cake and mutton patties that win her over.

Ranjan Salgado is a marine biologist researching the destruction of Sri Lanka's coral, an ecosystem with a fragility that has its counterpart in the Salgado household. When Miss Nili moves in and becomes the nona of the house, the arrangement initially runs smoothly, but the chaos outside encroaches upon their cosy world and Triton begins to question the life of servitude he has chosen. Political upheaval forces the household to decamp to London, where Triton eventually opens his own restaurant.

*A beautifully described novel full of the scent of the jungle, wild flowers and cool ocean breezes. This was Romesh Gunesekera's first novel and was short-listed for the Booker Prize. His earlier collection of short stories,* Monkfish Moon *(1992), also deals with Sri Lanka's political tensions.*

## ☜Read ons

*Season of the Rainbirds*, Nadeem Aslam **(Pakistan)**
An award-winning novel that sees the lives of the inhabitants of a rural Pakistani village disrupted when a judge dies and a mailbag that went missing nearly twenty years ago suddenly reappears, containing information that some would have preferred to remain secret.

*Shame*, Salman Rushdie **(Pakistan)**
A modern, exuberant fairy tale that gives the short history of Pakistan in allegorical form, highlighting the violence that is born out of shame.

*Hot Water Man*, Deborah Moggach **(Pakistan)**
An entertaining comedy of manners in which British expatriates mix with the locals and undergo unexpected transformations in the heat of Karachi.

*Moth Smoke*, Mohsin Hamid **(Pakistan)**
When Daru begins an affair with the wife of his childhood friend and benefactor, his life begins to fall apart. In desperation, he turns to crime and drugs. The novel is set in 1998 against a backdrop of nuclear testing and renewed tensions with India.

*Running in the Family*, Michael Ondaatje **(Sri Lanka)**
Different tales about the life and ancestry of the author are pieced together, along with poetry and travel writing.

*The Hamilton Case*, Michelle de Kretser **(Sri Lanka)**
A tale as lush as the ghostly jungles of Ceylon it evokes. An old Oxford-educated lawyer hears revelations that makes him question his whole life.

*A Golden Age*, Tahmima Anam **(Bangladesh)**
A mother struggles to keep her family together as the Bangladesh War of Liberation is about to begin.

*Galpa: Short Stories by Bangladeshi Women*, Ed. Niaz Zaman and Firdous Azim
An exciting and wide-ranging selection of stories from established and new authors covering everything from the War of Independence to family relationships.

## READONATHEME

### PILGRIMS' PROGRESS – SPIRITUAL JOURNEYS

*Siddartha*, Herman Hesse
Siddartha, son of a wealthy Brahmin, gives up his privileged life to begin a lifelong search for spiritual truth and enlightenment. A wonderful fable of Indian and Buddhist philosophy.

*Journey to Ithaca*, Anita Desai
Two newly wed Europeans, Matteo and Sophie, travel to India in Matteo's pursuit of enlightenment. When he falls under the spell of a holy woman, Sophie has to struggle to win her husband back.

*The Alchemist*, Paulo Coelho
A multi-million-selling fable about Santiago, an Andalusian shepherd boy who travels to North Africa on a journey of self-discovery. Coelho's other novels have similarly spiritual themes.

*Lila: An Inquiry Into Morals*, Robert M Pirsig
A sequel to Zen and the Art of Motorcycle Maintenance, exchanging the motorcycle for a boat. Further explorations of morality and the quality of life.

*One: A Novel*, Richard Bach
Bach and his wife journey to parallel universes to discover what would have happened if they had made different life choices.

*Mutant Message Down Under*, Marlo Morgan
A bestselling, fictionalised, and somewhat controversial account of the author's journey into the Australian outback and her time spent among aboriginal people.

*The Razor's Edge*, W Somerset Maugham
A young American veteran of the Great War leaves his life behind to find spirituality in India.

*Astonishing the Gods*, Ben Okri
A dream-like odyssey in which a boy enters an enchanted world and embarks on a journey of self-discovery. Told in Okri's inimitable lyrical prose.

*The Dharma Bums*, Jack Kerouac
Published a year after *On the Road*, this is an autobiographical novel about Zen Buddhism and the search for meaning, set in the Californian hills around San Francisco.

*Theo's Odyssey*, Catherine Clement
Fourteen-year-old Theo, diagnosed with a terminal illness, is taken on a trip around the world to learn about religion. A spiritual version of *Sophie's World*.

# THEMIDDLEEAST

## GENERAL MIDDLE EAST

*Under the Naked Sky: Short Stories from the Arab World*, Ed. Denys Johnson-Davies
Thirty writers from ten countries carefully selected and translated by the editor, offering a varied and colourful picture of life in the Arab world.

*Mirage*, Bandula Chandraratna
This beautifully written, highly acclaimed debut novel is about a Muslim man who unexpectedly finds love, but treacherous undercurrents conspire to snatch it away. The first of an intended trilogy.

*The Book of Saladin: A Novel*, Tariq Ali
A brilliant and lusty fictional memoir of the Muslim leader who re-conquered Jerusalem in 1187. One of a series of historical novels about Islam.

# EAST MIDDLE EAST

KEYTITLES

*The Prince*, Hushang Golshiri **(Iran)**
*The Kite Runner*, Khaled Hosseini **(Afghanistan)**

## THE PRINCE (1969)
Hushang Golshiri

In 1920s' Iran, the deposed Prince Ehtejab is dying of tuberculosis. On the last day of his life, he is visited by the ghosts of dead relatives. They emerge from picture frames and old paintings to taunt him about his weaknesses and castigate him for the current state of the family's affairs. Scenes from their violent history, including brutal murders and extortion, are gleefully regurgitated.

Ehtejab is the last in line of a now-deposed dynasty, and while his ancestors raped and pillaged at will, he lives in seclusion in a provincial Persian town, Isfahan, with his wife and servant. He is the last of the Qajars, a family notorious for their tyrannical rule, exceptional cruelty and incompetence, whose reign spanned the period from 1785 to their overthrow by what became the Pahlavi monarchy, in 1921. They in turn were overthrown by the Ayatollah in 1979.

The Prince's long-suffering late wife, Fakhronissa, also torments him, with reminders of how sexually vigorous his forebears were compared to him. His grandfather had a different virgin every night of his life, while Ehtejab, a petty tyrant, is reduced to forcing himself on their ignorant maid, Fakhri, whom he obliges to dress up like her mistress before he lays his old impotent body against her chest.

The narrative voice moves from ghost to ghost, and from Prince to maid, producing a hallucinatory effect. Award-winning novelist, James Buchan has done a commendable job in translating what was said to be an untranslatable novella.

An internationally acclaimed film, *Shazdeh Ehtejab*, was made in 1974. It offended the authorities to such an extent that they imprisoned Hushang Golshiri for six months.

*Golshiri was tireless in his political efforts to secure freedom from repression and these efforts doubtless contributed to his early death in 2000. His novel,* The Shepherd and the Lost Sheep *(1978), anticipates the growth of Islamic fundamentalism.*

# THE KITE RUNNER (2003)
## Khaled Hosseini

A rather effusive tale of love and redemption, told through the eyes of one man, Amir, as he relates his journey from his Afghan childhood in the 1970s to his position as a writer in California at the turn of the new century. When he receives an unexpected phone call from an old family friend, Amir knows he must return to his homeland, where he will have the opportunity for redemption. First, he must prove himself worthy.

Amir has spent his whole life trying to win the love and approval of his father, whilst also dealing with the jealousy he feels at his father's affections for his own best friend and low-caste servant, Hassan. Amir recounts how a cowardly act on his part separated the two boys forever. He knows he cannot move forward with his life until he has come to terms with all that his boyhood betrayal meant to those nearest to him.

The sights and smells of the Afghanistan of Amir's childhood are delightfully conveyed and Hosseini brings the tale to life with vibrant descriptions of Afghan life and culture. This book highlights all the major upheavals Afghanistan has undergone in recent times, taking in the conclusion of King Zahir Shah's forty-year reign, the Russian invasion and turbulent times under Taliban control. Amir's life in America is touchingly related, although perhaps the American Dream scenario is somewhat overplayed. Amir's journey to rescue Hassan's orphaned child, through a Taliban-controlled Afghanistan, is quite chilling.

Whilst some of the contrivances of the plot might be said to be a little far-fetched, and the themes somewhat signposted, this huge bestseller is undeniably a magical evocation of a life once lived in a land still fraught with troubles. This was the first Afghan novel to be written in English. *A Thousand Splendid Suns* (2007) is also set in Afghanistan.

# 🐢Read ons

### AFGHANISTAN

*Pashtun Tales: From the Pakistan-Afghan Frontier*, Aisha Ahmad and Roger Boase
A fascinating compendium of oral tales collected in a region that was once the main caravan route from Persia, India and China.

*Earth and Ashes*, Atiq Rahimi
A grandfather and his grandson are the only two survivors from a village bombed by the Russians. They go in search of the boy's father, to tell him the dreadful news. A spare, haunting tale that encompasses years of Afghan history.

*Swallows of Kabul*, Yasmina Khadra
A powerful novel dealing with four people living under the Taliban's oppressive regime. The author, a male Algerian army officer, wrote under a feminine pseudonym to avoid having to submit his manuscripts for approval by the army.

*The Breadwinner*, Deborah Ellis
An excellent novel for older children about the effects on ordinary lives of the Taliban seizure of Kabul. An eleven-year-old girl is forced to dress up as a boy in order to earn money to feed her starving family.

*The Mulberry Empire*, Philip Hensher
A well-researched and possibly over-ambitious tale of a desire to make Afghanistan part of the British Empire.

### IRAQ

*Saddam City*, Mahmoud Saeed
A harrowing account of the wanton brutality of the Hussein regime. A schoolteacher is arrested and held for eighteen months, a period during which he begins to doubt his own sanity.

*When the Grey Beetles Took Over Baghdad*, Mona Yahia
An award-winning book that deals with a Jewish girl trying to live a normal life as her family prepare to leave the increasingly perilous Baghdad of the 1960s.

*Scheherazade*, Anthony O'Neill
Our eponymous heroine is once again forced to spin yarns to save her life when she is abducted in ninth-century Baghdad. Seven unlikely heroes set out to fulfil an ancient prophecy by rescuing her.

IRAN/PERSIA
*Persian Brides*, Dorit Rabinyan
A few days in the lives of two Jewish girls in turn-of-the century Persia. Flora is fifteen, pregnant and abandoned, while Nazie, her eleven-year-old cousin dreams of her own wedding day.

*The Blind Owl*, Sadegh Hedayat
Written in 1937, *The Blind Owl* records an opium addict's descent into madness. It combines dream-like narration with gruesome symbolism and is a book that, at the time of its publication, mothers warned their daughters not to read. Henry Miller described it as the best book he had ever read.

*A Persian Requiem*, Simin Daneshvar
A woman tries to keep the peace between two brothers during the British occupation of Iran in the Second World War. The heat of an Iranian summer is wonderfully evoked.

*My Father's Notebook*, Kader Abdolah
The whole history of twentieth-century Iran is contained in this epic novel. An exiled Iranian dissident tries to translate his deaf-mute father's notebook.

*Women Without Men*, Shahrnush Parsipur
A frank and defiant portrayal of female sexuality. Five oppressed women find their way to a garden where they can decide their own fate. This novella is still banned in Iran.

*My Uncle Napoleon*, Iraj Pezeshkzad
Published in the 1970s and revered as a classic in Iran, this is a comic, at times slapstick novel about a family dominated by the narrator's patriarchal uncle, Napoleon.

OTHER COUNTRIES

*The Railway*, Hamid Ismailov (Uzbekistan)
The author tells thrilling tales of the inhabitants of a small town on the ancient silk route, near Tashkent, as he brings the region and its history to life with rich and vivid language.

*Ali and Nino*, Kurban Said (Azerbaijan)
A tragic love story about an Azerbaijani Muslim boy in love with a Georgian Christian girl, around the time of the Russian Revolution.

*Jamilia*, Chinghiz Aïtmatov (Kyrgyzstan)
A novella described as 'the most beautiful love story in the world'. The eponymous Jamilia, pretty and spirited, falls for and elopes with a reserved newcomer to the village whilst her husband is away at war.

# WEST MIDDLE EAST

## KEY TITLES

*The Rock of Tanios*, Amin Maalouf (**Lebanon**)
*Eight Months on Ghazzah Street*, Hilary Mantel (**Saudi Arabia**)

## THE ROCK OF TANIOS (1993)
Amin Maalouf

This historical romance, based on a folk tale, tells a story within a story and is set in the village of Kfaryabda in nineteenth-century Lebanon.

*The Rock of Tanios* is a throne-like formation. Local legend has it that, 150 years ago, a young boy, Tanios, sat on the rock and promptly disappeared.

Tanios was purportedly the son of Sheik Francis, a Christian Arab and a notorious womaniser. His major-domo was Tanios's 'father' Gerios, whose beautiful wife the Sheik was supposed to have seduced, setting off a series of events that culminated in the ruination of the town. The rumours surrounding the parentage of Tanios upset the Sheikha and her father, the powerful and colourfully named Lord of the Great Jord. He was especially dismayed when the Sheik sent his own grandson, Raad – along with Tanios – to the English School, fearing his spiritual contamination.

When the local Patriarch arranged a marriage between his own nephew and the girl Tanios loved, Gerios rashly murdered him and fled to Cyprus, taking his son with him. There the pair became embroiled in international schemes involving England, France and Egypt. They were lured back to Lebanon, where Tanios was used to help topple the Emir. Tanios found himself temporarily promoted to sheik, but his lenient attitude was at odds with the vengeful society that surrounded him. When Sheik Francis returned from exile, he intended to make Tanios his successor, but the boy was troubled by all that he had seen. He sat on the rock to consider his future and was never seen again.

This is a story of international intrigue and politics written as folklore. The complex storyline is carefully delineated and the cast of characters wonderfully drawn. Lyrical and poetic, Maalouf's story weaves a fable out of fact. It won France's most prestigious literary prize, the Prix Goncourt, in 1993.

*Amin Maalouf is also the author of* Leo the African *(1986),* Samarkand *(1988) and* The Gardens of Light *(1991).*

# EIGHT MONTHS ON GHAZZAH STREET (1988)
Hilary Mantel

Hilary Mantel spent four years in Saudi Arabia and has drawn from her own experiences to write this scathing exposé of women's lives in this hugely repressive regime. After a spell living in Africa, Frances Shore, a cartographer, and her husband Andrew, an engineer, decide to move to Jeddah, where he has been offered a lucrative job. She anticipates a difficult life in a country where women keep their heads covered and also keep them bowed. Nevertheless, she is shocked on arrival at their new apartment to find the front door bricked up. She learns that this was done to prevent the former tenant's wife from encountering her male neighbours on the stairs.

Frances is not allowed to work, or even to drive. Her trips outside the building are generally accompanied. On the odd occasion when she ventures out alone on foot, she is greeted by obscenities from passing drivers. She eventually befriends two neighbours, Yasmin and Samira, both married Muslim women with curious ideas about the West.

One day Frances hears sobbing from the supposedly empty apartment above and then hears rumours about a powerful man using the flat to conduct an illicit affair. She becomes preoccupied with finding out the truth and in the course of her investigations various unsavoury incidents fuel Frances' fear and sense of isolation. She sees her husband become increasingly insensitive, uncommunicative, and dismissive of her concerns.

Saudi Arabia is portrayed as a dangerous place where the police act as moral enforcers. The details of crimes never emerge, but sentences, such as beheading for an adulterous woman or the chopping off of hands for theft, are reported in great detail. Although many Westerners live in the country, they seem to bypass its repressive culture, making their own alcohol and only mixing with their own kind.

Mantel's depictions of the day-to-day lives of women are revealing and the views of her characters often illuminating. Ultimately, this is a brave and fascinating novel which may make uncomfortable reading for some.

## 🕮 Read ons

### SAUDI ARABIA
*The Belt*, Ahmed Abodehman
A wealth of Arabian folk tales are woven into this powerful autobiographical account, set in rural Saudi Arabia, of a young boy caught between traditional and modern ways.

*The Saddlebag*, Bahiyyih Nakhjavani
Subtitled *A Fable for Doubters and Seekers*, this story concerns a mysterious saddlebag that affects all who handle it, as it is passed between pilgrims on the way to Mecca, one day in 1844.

*Adama*, Turki Al-Hamad
It is the 1960s and an eighteen-year-old boy is coming alive to the world of ideas and the need for change. The first in a trilogy, it became a bestseller in the Middle East, despite being banned in several countries.

### LEBANON
*Hikayat: Short Stories by Lebanese Women*, Ed. Roseanne Saad Khalaf
A fascinating and varied collection from this consistently excellent series of short story collections by women from around the world.

*Gate of the Sun*, Elias Khoury
A genuine masterpiece about a peasant doctor who nightly tells stories to a man in a coma to keep him from dying. The reader is told the history of the Palestinians of Galilee since the creation of the state of Israel, in 1948.

*Beirut Blues*, Hanan al-Shaykh
An elegiac novel. A woman writes a series of letters about her love for the city of Beirut before and during the Civil War.

*Unreal City*, Tony Hanania
In war-torn Beirut, a man searches for friends, family and the woman who once betrayed him.

*Somewhere, Home*, Nada Awar Jarrar
Three Lebanese women return to their homes near Mount Lebanon, in a moving debut novel that seeks to discover what is meant by 'home'.

### PALESTINE
*Qissat: Short Stories by Palestinian Women*, Ed. Jo Glanville
An excellent collection that places established names alongside up-and-coming writers, revealing varied and exciting voices.

*A Lake Beyond the Wind*, Yahya Yakhlif
In 1948, the clashes between Zionist forces and the volunteers of the Arab Liberation Army decimate the small town of Samakh, north of Jerusalem, and drive its inhabitants into exile.

*Wild Thorns*, Sahar Khalifeh
Written in 1976, this book tells of the effects on some Palestinian families of the Israeli occupation of the West Bank. Some conform, some rebel, but all suffer.

### OTHER COUNTRIES
*Grandfather's Tale*, Ulfat Idilbi (Syria)
A Syrian woman tells the story of how her grandfather travelled from Chechnya to Damascus in the early nineteenth century, and of how he never stopped dreaming of one day returning to his mother.

*Just Like A River*, Muhammad Kamil al-Khatib (Syria)
An enthralling examination of Syrian political and social life during the 1980s. Many differing opinions come to light when the educated daughter of a middle-class liberal family is courted by a university teacher with radical views.

*Like Nowhere Else*, Denyse Woods (Yemen)
There are vibrant depictions of Yemen in this novel about a woman who falls for an anthropologist with connections to her own past.

*Pillars of Salt*, Fadia Faqir (Jordan)
Two women in an insane asylum in Jordan in 1921 tell the tales of how they came to be there. A remarkable novel about female oppression.

# ISRAEL

KEYTITLES

*The Lover*, A B Yehoshua
*See Under: Love*, David Grossman

## THE LOVER (1977)
A B Yehoshua

Just after the Yom Kippur War, a Jewish garage-owner, Adam, sets out to find his wife's lover, Gabriel, who has gone missing. While Adam scours army recruitment offices and the back streets of Haifa, his schoolteacher wife, Asya, sleeps and dreams. However, their only daughter, Dafi, suffers from insomnia. She walks the streets, or stares out at fellow insomniacs through her window.

Gabriel had initially returned from Paris to Israel for the first time in a decade, believing his grandmother, Veducha, to be dead. In fact, she is in a coma. Gabriel is a gentle soul who seems now to have an uncertain grip on reality. When he comes to Adam for help with his car, claiming all it needs is a screw, Adam has to rebuild the engine. The bill for Adam's work is so high that Gabriel has to work to pay it off. Adam invites Gabriel into his home, hoping his presence will enliven his soporific and emotionally remote wife.

Dafi catches her mother and Gabriel together one day and thus begins her nightly turmoil of sleeplessness and signals Gabriel's sudden disappearance.

In the search for Gabriel, Adam employs a young Arab boy, Na'im, to break into Veducha's flat. An unexpected development opens the door for love to finally enter this fractured family.

Each character's story is told in the first person, giving the reader multiple perspectives on the events, a device that highlights the potential for misunderstanding: between people in different rooms, between nations on each other's land, and between cultures at war. This is a charming and spirited novel.

*The author still lives in Israel and has become a controversial figure in recent years as a result of his ideas on secular Judaism. Hailed by Saul Bellow as one of Israel's 'world-class' writers, Yehoshua has also written* Mr Mani *(1990),* A Journey to the End of the Millennium *(1997) and* The Liberated Bride *(2001).*

# SEE UNDER: LOVE (1989)
## David Grossman

This complex and demanding novel is divided into four parts. The first is set in Israel in the 1950s and concerns Momik, a nine-year-old boy who is the only son of holocaust survivors who reveal to him only fragments of their terrible experiences 'over there'. Momik's great uncle, Anshel Wasserman, once a writer of children's tales, is now a mute deranged old man. Momik decides to hold him hostage in the basement one day so he can lure the 'Nazi Beast' in and slay it.

Part 2 is set thirty years on and Momik, now a writer, has protected himself from hurt by refusing to enter into emotional attachments of any kind. He is obsessed with the Polish writer, Bruno Schulz, who was shot by the Nazis. (The author claimed that he wrote See Under: LOVE to avenge this murder.)

Momik reconstructs the life of his great uncle in Part 3. In this fantasised version, Anshel is in a concentration camp. Every day, the Nazis try but fail to kill him and he ends up telling the camp commandant stories every night. The last story he tells is about a boy, Kazik, whom some friends find in a zoo in Warsaw. The boy lives his whole life in a day. An encyclopaedia of this creature's amazing existence takes up Part 4.

It is difficult to summarise this novel. Grossman's anti-narrative has several themes: the inadequacy of language; the impossibility of knowing historical truths; the power of art to transcend experience; and, the presence of love amid the horrors of mankind.

The power of Grossman's thought and the sheer vigour and beauty of his words make this book more of an occurrence than a read. Although not entirely set in Israel, it is very much about the Jewish experience, especially that of the generation following the war. A rewarding book for those prepared to take the journey.

*David Grossman's other books include* The Book of Intimate Grammar *(1991) and* Be My Knife *(1998).*

## Read ons

*Past Continuous*, Yaakov Shabtai
This groundbreaking book has became a classic of Jewish literature. It deals with the lives of three middle-aged men during a nine-month period in Tel Aviv in the 1960s.

*Four Meals: a Novel*, Meir Shalev
A magical novel about an illegitimate Jewish man who, in order to know his deceased mother, has meals with three men claiming to be his father.

*The Rock: A Tale of Seventh-Century Jerusalem*, Kanan Makiya
This novel describes how Jews, Muslims and Christians built and maintained the Dome of the Rock, showing that the three religions were once just different paths on the same road.

*My Michael*, Amos Oz
First published in 1968, this novel centres on a young couple in 1950s' Israel. The wife finds she is unable to cope with everyday life and slowly drifts into her own fantasy world.

*Our Weddings*, Dorit Rabinyan
An overbearing mother's love, family life and the fate of Persian immigrants in Israel are woven beautifully into the fabric of this book.

*When I Lived in Modern Times*, Linda Grant
An award-winning novel about a young woman learning to live and love in the newly formed state of Israel in 1948.

*Matches*, Alan Kaufman
This brutal tale of love and war sees an American-born Jew leave New York for a new life in Israel and service in the Israeli Defence Force.

*Operation Shylock*, Philip Roth
A bizarre, intellectual comedy in which the author's namesake tours the country telling Jews to return to their homelands, while he suffers from depression and the attentions of Mossad.

*The Bus Driver who Wanted to be God and Other Stories*, Etgar Keret
Short absurd fables from a popular, hip Israeli author. These emotional and often comic stories cover both reality and the surreal with equal aplomb.

*The Secret Life of Saeed: The Pessoptimist*, Emile Habiby
This contemporary classic, first published in 1974, is a comic satire on the illogicality of Israeli politics. A Palestinian becomes an informer for the Zionist state and eventually an Israeli citizen.

*The Little Drummer Girl*, John Le Carré
A brilliant and beautiful actress is recruited into setting a dangerous trap to lure a Palestinian terrorist.

# READONATHEME

## IN THE BEGINNING – BIBLICAL NOVELS

*Quarantine*, Jim Crace
A fictionalised account of the forty days Jesus spent fasting in the wilderness of the Judean desert, battling for survival against searing heat, temptation and an evil merchant called Musa.

*The Red Tent*, Anita Diamant
A vivid portrayal of the lives of women in Biblical times. It re-creates the life of Dinah, the daughter of Jacob, from her happy childhood in Mesopotamia to her death in Egypt.

*The Gospel According to Jesus Christ*, José Saramago
A re-imagining of the life of Jesus, from birth to crucifixion, portraying him as an ordinary human being who has a difficult relationship with a dictatorial and demanding God.

*Only Human*, Jenny Diski
Subtitled *A Comedy*, this is a fascinating love triangle between Sarah, Abraham and God. A sequel, *After These Things*, follows the psychological trail of Isaac and his son, Jacob.

*Mary, Called Magdalene*, Margaret George
Mary is neither a whore nor the wife of Jesus, but a woman who devotes her life to Christ after he drives away her demons. An engaging version of her life.

*The Last Temptation of Christ*, Nikos Kazantzakis
A wonderfully descriptive novel featuring a Christ with human frailties, which makes his resistance to the Devil's temptation especially poignant.

*The Wild Girl*, Michele Roberts
The lost fifth gospel is discovered, written by Mary Magdalene, which throws new light on her relationship with Jesus, suggesting that Tantric love is the road to spiritual enlightenment.

*Seven Days to the Sea*, Rebecca Kohn

A bold re-telling of the Exodus, told by the two women who loved Moses most: his sister, Miryam, and his lover, Tzipporah. *See also* **The Gilded Chamber: A Novel of Queen Esther**.

*My Name Was Judas*, C K Stead

In this teasingly comic rendering, Judas, neither a traitor nor a suicide, lives to be an old man. He tells his version of the events of forty years ago, when a deranged school friend believed he was the Son of God.

# AFRICA

## GENERAL AFRICA

### Read ons

*African Short Stories*, Ed. Chinua Achebe, C L Innes
Twenty stories from the latter half of the twentieth century that serve to represent the very best of modern African literature.

*Under African Skies: Modern African Stories*, Ed. Charles R Larson
Evidence of the rich vein of traditional African storytelling is on display here, featuring twenty-six writers from seventeen countries, with writing spanning the period from 1952 to 1996. Each selection is preceded by an introduction to the writer and a brief discussion of the context for each story.

*Picador Book of African Stories*, Ed. Stephen Gray
This book is arranged into five regions and includes authors from Djibouti and Cape Verde.

# EAST AFRICA

KEY TITLES

*Season of Migration to the North*, Tayeb Salih (**Sudan**)
*From a Crooked Rib*, Nuruddin Farah (**Somalia**)

## SEASON OF MIGRATION TO THE NORTH (1966)
Tayeb Salih

An unnamed narrator returns to his home village in Sudan, after spending several years in Europe studying for a doctorate. No one can tell him anything about the stranger who has moved in, married a local girl and now runs a farm close by. Nothing except his name, Mustafa Sa'eed. So the narrator gradually draws Mustafa into telling his own remarkable tale.

The novel is a whirlwind of prose that offers glimpses of events and reminiscences. The reader learns that Mustafa was born in Khartoum but was sent to Cairo for schooling, eventually landing in London where he became something of a sexual predator. His relationships with women are based on a litany of cultural misconceptions. Valued for his exotic charm, he finds that women fall at his feet, while he aspires to a Western sensibility. Three women commit suicide over him and he murders his own wife.

The novel cleverly highlights how the ravages of colonisation have translated into the psychological make-up of a people. At his trial for murder, Mustafa exclaims: 'I came as an invader into your very homes: a drop of the poison which you have injected into the veins of history.'

Meanwhile, the narrator becomes part of the new leadership in an independent Sudan but gradually feels increasingly uncomfortable about his role. He sees himself as ineffectual in his dealings with those for whom he has responsibility, both publicly and privately.

When Mustafa disappears, presumed drowned, the narrator is made guardian to his two children. Among the possessions now in his charge is the key to Mustafa's study, where the rest of his life story waits to be told. The fate of Mustafa's widow and the narrator's unexpressed feelings for her make him realise just how far removed he is from his own people and from the patriarchal nature of their lives. He feels in limbo, able neither to live in the village nor to live an independent life.

This is a complex, multi-layered novella that is majestically written, with exceptionally vivid descriptions of desert life. It is a passionate and important work, rightly considered to be one of the finest books in modern Arab literature.


# FROM A CROOKED RIB (1970)
## Nuruddin Farah

This is the story of a country girl's life and unhappy marriage in Mogadishu, a story that celebrates the human spirit and challenges male chauvinism. Ebla, an orphaned eighteen-year-old girl, runs away from her village when her grandfather arranges a marriage to a much older man. Illiterate and poor, and with no experience of the outside world, she goes to the neighbouring town, where she has a cousin. She stays there for a while, looking after her cousin's wife and helping with her new baby. However, when her cousin sells her to a local broker, she elopes with the next-door neighbour's nephew, Awill.

The couple flee to 'Mogadiscio' and there they marry, but the hopelessly unworldly Ebla's troubles are far from over. When Awill disappears to Italy for three months, Ebla is left alone with the landlady, whom her new husband has paid to look after his wife. Unhappy with the arrangement, Ebla takes a series of lovers, but soon finds herself alone again and at the mercy of others. Her innate sense of fairness and an inner wisdom see her through this emotional turmoil and she arrives at a resolution that has at least the beginnings of a stand.

Set just before Somalia's independence, in 1960, Farah exposes the inhumanity of the traditional values many Africans were hearkening back to in the aftermath of colonialism, and unmasks the hypocrisy of a society that claims to respect women while neither educating nor valuing them.

*This was a particularly startling perspective for a male, western-educated writer to articulate. Farah returned to Somalia after twenty-two years in exile and went on to write a trilogy of novels examining cultural identity in post-colonial Africa, under the title* Blood in the Sun. *The three novels are* Maps *(1986),* Gifts *(1993) and* Secrets *(1998).*

## 📖Read ons

*Abyssinian Chronicles*, Moses Isegawa **(Uganda)**
An ambitious, vibrant, energetic and lengthy tale of Uganda's recent history that mixes the personal with the political.

*The Last King of Scotland*, Giles Foden *(Uganda)*
This darkly comic novel tells the tale of a Scottish doctor and the time he spent with the crazed dictator, Idi Amin, in the 1970s.

*A Sunday at the Pool in Kigali*, Gil Courtmanche **(Rwanda)**
An important and powerful novel that blends real-life events with a fictionalised love affair against the backdrop of the Hutu genocide.

*Paradise*, Abdulrazak Gurnah **(Tanzania)**
Set before the First World War, this is a poetic tale of a boy's rite of passage and of the outside influences on the Islam of his upbringing.

*An Ice Cream War*, William Boyd **(Tanzania)**
A semi-comic tale of First World War shenanigans in East Africa, told in Boyd's captivating style.

*The Africa Bar*, Nick Maes **(Zanzibar)**
Two women form a friendship and tell of their love affairs, past and present. The sights and sounds of the spice island of Zanzibar are wonderfully evoked.

*Boy*, Lindsey Collen **(Mauritius)**
Four days of a young man's awakening in the lush landscape of Mauritius are told in fractured, exuberant language. Winner of the 2005 Commonwealth Writers' Prize.

# KENYA

## KEYTITLES

*A Grain of Wheat*, Ngugi wa Thiong'o
*Masai Dreaming*, Justin Cartwright

## A GRAIN OF WHEAT (1967)

Ngugi wa Thiong'o

Set in December 1963, as Kenya prepares for independence, this book investigates the preceding Emergency years of 1952–1960 and Britain's brutal suppression of the violent Mau Mau rebellion. This groundbreaking novel presents differing notions of salvation: some believe they will find it through love, some through religion and others through the political goal of a free Kenya.

Told through flashbacks and multiple narrative voices, a number of individual stories deal with the nature of war and show how it changes people from within, revealing the difficulties people face in adapting to normal life once the armed struggle is over. The novel begins with Mugo, a quiet, isolated man who has served his time for the Movement. When the villagers come to him and request he give a speech to celebrate their freedom on Uhuru Day, he is reluctant. He has a past he cannot escape from, yet his reputation as a hero continues to grow, almost mythically, despite his own lack of resolve.

The story then switches to other members of the town, such as Gikonyo, its richest man, who spent time in a detention camp. He is estranged from his beautiful wife, Mumbi, because he believes she has betrayed him with a childhood friend, Karanja, who has since joined the forces of white oppression. Events come to a head during the Uhuru Day celebrations, when the elders want to reveal Karanja as the man who betrayed Kihika, the hero of the revolution, and handed him over to be killed by the authorities. Revenge must be exacted, they have decided, but fate intervenes.

Always passionate and humane, the novel weaves many threads together to produce a truly moving narrative. *A Grain of Wheat* was listed among Africa's top twelve books by *The African Review of Books*.

*Also by Ngugi wa Thiong'o is* Petals of Blood*, a fascinating multi-layered story about the betrayal of the independence struggle, told through the lives of four people at the forefront of a murder investigation. The author was imprisoned for writing this book.*

# MASAI DREAMING (1993)
## Justin Cartwright

Tim Curtiz, a writer, is researching a film about an ethnographer, Claudia Cohn-Casson, who spent time with Masai warriors in the early 1940s. A beautiful French Jew, Casson lived with the tribe and recorded their rituals and way of life. She appeared to have a tremendous effect on all who encountered her. Curtiz interviews those who knew her, including a white Kenyan ex-lover, Tom Fairfax, and a Masai tribal leader whose brother was executed by the authorities, partly because of his involvement with Claudia. She went back to France in an effort to save her family from the Holocaust, but was brutally arrested and exterminated. The savage barbarity that can exist in Africa is contrasted with the sophisticated evil of modern Europe in the shape of Nazism.

Curtiz is struggling with his producer, the sybaritic S O Letterman, to make a film that portrays the truth of the situation while also conveying a positive universality. He is drawn into Claudia's story to such an extent that his own life comes to seem unimportant.

The book beautifully describes the sights, sounds and smells of Kenya and the arid savannah: the spicy Khaki bush, the dry woodsmoke and the omnipresent dust. A complex book by a clever writer, *Masai Dreaming* shows Cartwright to be as comfortable evoking the vast African landscape as he is exploring the intimacies of human relationships.

The character Tim Curtiz also appears in some of Cartwright's other novels, including *Interior* (1988), in which he returns to Africa to investigate his father's disappearance, and *White Lightning* (2002) – *see* **South Africa Read-Ons**.

## 📖Read ons

*Coming To Birth*, Marjorie Oludhe Macgoye

From one of the country's leading literary figures comes this engrossing novel dealing with the troubled development of modern Kenya, told through the life story of a young woman, Paulina, who moves from her rural village to Nairobi.

*The In-Between World of Vikram Lall*, M G Vassanji

A fascinating novel about 'the most corrupt man in Kenya' looking back on his life as an Indian growing up during the struggle for independence and beyond.

*Away From You*, Melanie Finn

A woman goes back to the Africa of her childhood, determined to prove her abusive, deceased father guilty of murder. An atmospheric novel about Kenya in the 1960s and the modern day.

*The Constant Gardener*, John Le Carré

When a human rights activist is murdered, her British diplomat husband finds himself attempting to track down her killers. An intelligent thriller set in the world of the multinational pharmaceutical industry.

*Rules of the Wild*, Francesca Marciano

An Italian woman in Nairobi is torn not simply between her two lovers but also between the raw beauty of Africa and the often uncomfortable realities of living there.

*Red Strangers*, Elspeth Huxley

The damaging relationship between the European settlers and the indigenous population is told in this epic tale of four generations of a family in the savannah.

*Blood Sisters*, Barbara and Stephanie Keating

Three girls form a childhood bond that will be repeatedly tested during their adult lives in the turmoil of an independent Kenya.

# SOUTHERN AFRICA

## KEYTITLES

*Nervous Conditions*, Tsitsi Dangarembga (**Zimbabwe**)
*The Grass is Singing*, Doris Lessing (**Zimbabwe**)

## NERVOUS CONDITIONS (1988)

Tsitsi Dangarembga

A semi-autobiographical novel set in Rhodesia in the late 1960s and 1970s. When thirteen-year-old Tambudzai is sent to her wealthy uncle's mission school after her elder brother's death, she feels it will be the beginning of her 'unburdening' as a woman. But she embarks on a wider education, at the hands of her Western-influenced cousin, Nyasha, who brings colour and confrontation into Tambu's black- and-white world, making the docile young woman question much of what she has taken for granted in the patriarchal and colonial world around her.

A young woman with a deep-rooted sense of tradition, Tambu still has a lot to learn about the ways of the world.

Her cousin Nyasha, however, has been brought up in England and finds herself unable to adapt to African culture. Her more rebellious attitude signals her eventual downfall. In time, Tambu comes to understand that she must free herself from the struggle between tradition and modernity.

*Nervous Conditions* is a fascinating insight into the plight of African women seeking to find their true selves in the face of cultural imperialism and colonial assimilation. It is an absorbing debut novel that offers a delightful and moving perspective on friendship and a frank portrayal of a young girl's awakening. It has been hailed as the first truly feminist novel to come out of southern Africa.

It was awarded the Commonwealth Writers' Prize in 1989 and is included in Africa's top twelve books by *The African Review of Books*. A long-awaited sequel, *The Book of Not,* was finally published in 2006.

# THE GRASS IS SINGING (1950)

Doris Lessing

This remarkable debut novel explores the truth behind a newspaper report of the death of the wife of a white farmer in a desolate farmhouse in 1950s' Rhodesia. The delicate Mary Turner was unprepared both for marriage and for the life she was expected to endure. Living in the rural wastes of southern Africa, in a brick and tin shack, she hates the weather and the isolated conditions and is constantly at loggerheads with the houseboys. Her husband, Dick, is a poor farmer in both senses of the word: penurious and incompetent. Nevertheless, he stubbornly ploughs on with his mismanagement of the land, forcing them ever closer to the brink of bankruptcy. The couple are completely mismatched and it is clear they have married simply to avoid a life of loneliness. Dick wants to have children, but Mary cannot bear the thought of bringing a baby into such an inhospitable environment. A later relationship that develops between Mary and a farm-worker-turned-houseboy scandalises a community in which relations between land-owning whites and black workers are already extremely tense. The couple's descent into emotional hell is superbly handled and vivid descriptions of the blazing sun and the baked earth add to the sense of isolation and despair.

*Doris Lessing arrived in England clutching this manuscript when she was just twenty-five. It was published to universal praise and remains one of her finest novels. See also* This was Old Chief's Country *(1951), a collection of her African short stories.*

## ⏚Read ons

*A Question of Power*, Bessie Head (**Botswana**)
This powerful novel concerns one woman's mental suffering as she leaves a South Africa under apartheid for the apparent freedom of Botswana and yet feels equally repressed in her adopted country.

*Last Flight of the Flamingo*, Mia Couto (**Mozambique**)
There is more than a hint of magic realism and sly humour in this incisive tale of an Italian UN official sent to investigate attacks on their peacekeepers.

*Smouldering Charcoal*, Tiyambe Zeleza (**Malawi**)
A short first novel contrasting the lives of two families who become victims of the increasingly pervasive repression of a corrupt regime.

*The Purple Violet of Oshaantu*, Neshani Andreas (**Namibia**)
This novel explores the value of female friendship in a rural community in northern Namibia. Several interconnected stories are gently threaded together.

*Cowrie of Hope*, Binwell Sinyangwe (**Zambia**)
A single mother struggles to secure the funds for her daughter's education. After exhausting all possibilities in her rural community, she journeys to the capital city of Lusaka.

*The Return of the Water Spirit*, Mayombe Pepetela (**Angola**)
Set in the 1980s, this novel uses mythology to construct a critique of the corrupt and avaricious government of Angola.

*Harvest of Thorns*, Shimmer Chinodya (**Zimbabwe**)
A prize-winning novel about a young man's coming of age during the transition from white rule to the birth of Zimbabwe.

*Without a Name* and *Under the Tongue*, Yvonne Vera (**Zimbabwe**)
Two exceptional and at times shocking novels that deal with the lives of women, set against the backdrop of the guerrilla warfare of the 1970s.

# SOUTH AFRICA

## KEYTITLES

*The Conservationist*, Nadine Gordimer
*In Corner B*, Es'kia Mphahlele
*Disgrace,* J M Coetzee

## THE CONSERVATIONIST (1974)
### Nadine Gordimer

Mehring is a rich, self-satisfied, white property owner. He has a small farm just outside Johannesburg, in apartheid-era South Africa. He is content to be part of a system that oppresses others while keeping him and his kind rich, allowing him to be a weekend farmer who writes his expenses off against tax.

When a dead body is found on his farm, the local police simply bury it where it has fallen. The corpse becomes a voice, a spokesperson for the landless, taunting Mehring with the reality of his diminishing ownership. He may own things in law but they cannot in essence be rightfully regarded as belonging to him. His family moves away and his mistress deserts him. His workers treat him with diminishing respect and the land itself overwhelms him with problems, first with drought, then with floods. And yet Mehring cannot understand that he has no fundamental right to the land.

The novel is written in a stark, modernist style that distances the reader some-what from the action, yet serves to reveal deeper truths. The story flashes back without warning to Mehring's earlier life and often uses a stream-of-consciousness style. The cruel splendour of the veldt and the relationship that others have with the land are used to highlight Merhring's plight. It is through the lives of these others – Mehring's black overseer, Josephus, and a local Indian shopkeeper, for example – that the reader is given a portrait of a society crippled by race laws that arbitrarily determine social status whilst strangling culture and heritage.

The Conservationist *won the Booker Prize in 1974 and Nadine Gordimer was awarded the Nobel Prize for Literature in 1991. All her novels are set in South Africa.*

# IN CORNER B (1967)
## Es'kia Mphahlele

Known as the greatest fiction chronicler of South African life in the apartheid era, Mphahlele writes with humanity and warmth about the everyday lives of the people who inhabit the townships. This collection of short stories includes *Mrs Plum*, his most famous work and regarded by the author as his best. It centres on a young black cook, Karabo, from the township of Phokeng, and her relationship with her liberal white mistress, in the suburbs of Johannesburg. Mrs Plum's hypocritical claim to be working for the equality of blacks and whites from within the apartheid system is expertly conveyed.

In *Man Must Live*, an overly proud orphan's fragile façade is shattered when he leaves his job at the railway station to marry a rich widow who does not respect him. *Women and their Men* shows social uproar and chaos mirrored in the emotional turmoil of male-female relationships. The title story, *In Corner B*, shows Mphahlele is not afraid to reveal his tender side, dealing as it does with a woman mourning the death of an unfaithful husband.

*In Corner B* was originally published in Nairobi in 1967, but was not available in the author's home country until 1979. The 2006 Penguin Modern Classics edition has been revised to include more recent stories.

Ezekiel Mphahlele published his first set of short stories, *Man Must Live*, in 1946. Later he worked as fiction editor on Johannesburg's *Drum* magazine, which showcased the best of black South African writers. He spent twenty years in self-imposed exile, finally returning to South Africa in 1977, at which point he decided to Africanise his name to Es'kia.

*His novels include* The Wanderers *(1969) and* Chirundu *(1979), the latter set in a fictitious African country and dealing with a man torn between African tradition and English law.*

# DISGRACE (1999)

J M Coetzee

A middle-aged professor of Romantic poetry, David Lurie, has an imprudent affair with one of his students. The fallout leads to public censure and dismissal. He leaves Cape Town and takes refuge with his lesbian daughter, Lucy, on her remote farm, attempting to embrace her bucolic lifestyle while planning to write a light opera about Byron's time in Italy. The pair have difficulty forming a relationship but slowly find a way to live together.

Their peace is shattered when the farm is attacked. Lurie fails to understand his daughter's attitude towards the black assailants and to the man next door, Petrus, her occasional help, who seems to know more about the attack than he admits to. Slowly it dawns on Lurie that there are more complicated issues at stake than simple justice or retribution.

Generations of discrimination lie at the heart of the South African psyche and the shifting of power leaves people like the Luries voiceless and abandoned. Just as David Lurie cannot understand his daughter's commitment to the land and her willingness to sacrifice so much to hold on to her way of life, so he fails to grasp the brutal realities of that life. His personal detachment makes him ill fitted for empathy. It is only when helping out at an animal welfare clinic, tending the dead bodies of animals about to be incinerated, that Lurie is made aware of his own mortality and of the ephemeral nature of everything. In spare succinct prose, Coetzee has created an honest howl of anguish.

Disgrace *won the Booker Prize in 1999 and was also voted the best book by a British or Commonwealth writer in the last twenty-five years. Coetzee was awarded the Nobel Prize for Literature in 2003. He has also written* The Life and Times of Michael K *(1983), which won the Booker Prize, and* Age of Iron *(1990), both set in South Africa.*

## 📖 Read ons

*Dinaane: Short Stories by South African Women*, Ed. Maggie Davey
An excellent selection of tales from the rich tradition of South African writing.

*A Dry White Season*, Andre Brink
His sense of justice outraged by the death of a black friend, a white teacher searches for the truth and challenges the assumptions on which his racist society is founded.

*Bitter Fruit*, Achmat Dangor
A vivid and compelling novel about the tragedies suffered by one family, experiences that expose the fragile nature of the the Truth and Reconciliation policy in post-apartheid South Africa.

*The Good Doctor*, Damon Galgut
In a ghost hospital in a former Bantu homeland, a disillusioned doctor is unsettled by the arrival of an enthusiastic new medic. A subtle and desperate parable about a nation ill at ease with itself.

*Frieda and Min*, Pamela Jooste
In mid-1960s' South Africa, a poor Jewish girl and a 'white kaffir' form a lifelong friendship.

*White Lightning*, Justin Cartwright
A richly detailed novel about a failed film director who returns to South Africa to buy a farm. There he reflects on his life back in England, while contemplating the beauty of his surroundings.

*Cry, the Beloved Country*, Alan Paton
In the 1940s, a father searches for his delinquent son through the troubled streets of Johannesburg. His search takes him through a labyrinth of murder, prostitution, racial hatred and, ultimately, reconciliation. A classic of extraordinary power.

*The Long Silence of Mario Salviati*, Etienne Van Heerden
The tumultuous history of South Africa is told in this tale of an art curator sent to a small town in the Karoo to buy a sculpture.

*Triomf*, Marlene Van Niekerk
This seminal Afrikaans novel is a scabrous tale of the everyday life of a poor white-trash family living in the period before the first multiracial elections in 1993.

*Islands*, Dan Sleigh
A beautifully rendered epic tale of the first fifty years of white settlement in the Cape of Good Hope as it affects an indigenous woman. Translated by Andre Brink.

*Red Dust*, Gillian Slovo
A Truth Commission amnesty hearing in a backwater town reunites victim and torturer. This tense courtroom thriller is a moving exposition of the difficulties of reconciliation.

*Tsotsi*, Athol Fugard
A young gang leader finds redemption in learning how to love again in this raw, humane and compelling novel. It was made into an Oscar-winning film in 2005.

*The Whale Caller*, Zakes Mda
In this eccentric, whimsical tale set in Hermanus on the western coast, a man's love affair with a whale is compromised when he falls in love with a woman.

## ONCE UPON A TIME – MYTHS, LEGENDS, FOLKTALES

*The Girl Who Married a Lion*, Alexander McCall Smith
A collection of simple, traditional fables from Zimbabwe and Botswana, retold in McCall Smith's engaging prose.

*Gods, Demons and Others*, R K Narayan
This renowned author skilfully adapts myths and legends from classic Indian texts, including the Ramayana, into a selection of simple, approachable and always fascinating stories.

*Ka: Stories of the Mind and Gods of India*, Roberto Calasso
An impressive interweaving of the best-known Indian myths, presented in a novelistic format. Some chapters revolve around a central character – Shiva, Krishna or Buddha – while others include parts from epics such as the Mahabharata.

*Italian Folktales*, Italo Calvino
Chosen by Calvino and rewritten in his inimitable style, this is a wonderful collection of strange, fascinating and touching tales from all over Italy, in tones reminiscent of the Brothers Grimm.

*Arabian Nights and Days*, Naguib Mahfouz
The Nobel-Prize-winning author continues from where Scheherezade's 1001 Nights left off, with a further collection of stories of genies and moral dilemmas with a more contemporary feel.

*The King Must Die*, Mary Renault
An evocative re-creation of the myth of Theseus and his journey to Knossos to defeat the Minotaur. *The Bull from the Sea* continues the story.

*The Marriage of Cadmus and Harmony*, Roberto Calasso
A master at re-telling myths, Calasso focuses here on ancient Greek tales, presenting a selection of mythical escapades and a discourse on the nature of myths and their effects on Western culture.

*The Penelopiad*, Margaret Atwood
The period surrounding the Trojan War is brought to life in the words of Penelope, wife of Odysseus, who ran the kingdom and kept suitors at arm's length while her husband was away for twenty years.

*The War at Troy*, Lindsay Clarke
The events at Troy and the exploits of Odysseus and Achilles, Paris and Helen et al are masterfully described in this acclaimed retelling of Homer's *Iliad*. Clarke continues Odysseus's story in *The Return from Troy*.

*The Once and Future King*, T H White
A classic retelling of the Arthurian legend. White's enchanting version tells the king's story in five volumes, all included here. It begins with *The Sword in the Stone*.

*Angela Carter's Book of Fairy Tales*, Angela Carter
Originally published in two separate volumes, as *The Virago Book of Fairy Tales*, this recent single-volume edition includes a wealth of humorous, bloody and beastly stories from around the globe.

*The Virago Book of Erotic Myths and Legends*, Shahrukh Husain
An anthology of titillating and tempting ancient myths from various parts of the world. Each is rewritten but faithfully conveyed by the author.

*The Book of Imaginary Beings*, Jorge Luis Borges
A compendium of mythical and fantastical beasts, humorously and cleverly described by the master wordsmith.

# CENTRAL AFRICA

KEYTITLE

*The Poisonwood Bible*, Barbara Kingsolver (**Congo**)

## THE POISONWOOD BIBLE (1998)

Barbara Kingsolver

It is 1959 and the Belgian Congo is on the verge of independence. A committed Baptist preacher, Nathan Price, uproots his wife and four daughters from Bethlehem, Georgia with the aim of bringing salvation to the African people, pitifully unaware of the desire of the Congolese people to be delivered from their white rulers.

The story is narrated by the womenfolk. The docile and repentant mother, Orleanna, looks back on the family's two years in the village of Kilanga. The eldest daughter, Rachel, vain and sarcastic, tells a tale fuelled by fury and laced with biting wit. Her story is followed by that of the highly intelligent twins, Leah and Adah. Leah's initial idolisation of her father slowly evaporates as her experiences and fresh insights lead her to become his fiercest critic. Adah, disabled by hemiplegia, opts not to talk to her family but gives the reader her palindromic story. Ruth May, the youngest at five, is something of a determined spirit.

A series of, at times, hilarious mishaps and setbacks beset the family in a cruel and unforgiving landscape that seems to unsettle their domestic and spiritual certainties. Nathan's aim of creating an Edenic garden is thwarted when it emerges that the seeds he brought from the US are tainted. The result of his horticultural efforts is the lethal Poisonwood. His arrogant imposition of Western values and religious practices antagonises the local people. When they accept democracy, they exercise it by promptly voting against having Jesus as the head of the church.

When tragedy inevitably strikes, the family is separated. The book chronicles the next thirty years in the lives of the children, detailing how their experience in the Congo has affected them. The novel does lose some of its intimacy and drive in this section, as Kingsolver seems determined to make clear the case for the Western world's culpability. Nevertheless, this is an extraordinary novel of scope and power. The author's sensual evocation of place is palpable, while her ability to speak coherently and plainly through the different characters makes this a compelling and formidable achievement.

## Read ons

*Mema*, Daniel M Mengara (Gabon)
When an apparently barren wife has children, her in-laws suspect witchcraft and the woman begins a long struggle to prove her innocence, hindered by the sudden death of her husband.

*The Story of the Madman*, Mongo Beti (Cameroon)
A comic satire in which a chief struggles to maintain his country's traditional way of life in the face of the threat of social change.

*A Bend in the River*, V S Naipaul (Congo)
A young Indian merchant opens a store in a small, sleepy town and watches chaos unfold before him as the newly decolonised nation attempts to forge its own identity.

*The Catastrophist*, Ronan Bennett (Congo)
This lyrical thriller sees a disaffected Irish historian attempting to rekindle a relationship with an Italian journalist committed to a cause he does not believe in.

*The Book of the Heathen*, Robert Edric (Congo)
It is 1897 and an Englishman is on trial for killing a native child. A slow-paced, dark thriller that obliquely unravels colonial misdeeds.

*A Burnt-Out Case*, Graham Greene (Congo)
An excellent psychological study of a world-famous architect who, tired of the high-life, attempts to retire from the world by spending time in a leper colony.

*Heart of Darkness*, Joseph Conrad (Congo)
Classic tale of a man's voyage deep into the 'Dark Continent' in search of maverick ivory trader, Kurtz.

# WEST AFRICA

## KEYTITLES

*Scarlet Song*, Mariama Bâ **(Senegal)**
*A Good Man in Africa*, William Boyd

## SCARLET SONG (1981)

Mariama Bâ

This excellent novel begins as a tender and triumphant interracial love story and develops into a dark and complex tale.

Ousmane Gueye is the eldest son in a poor Muslim family. At university, he falls in love with Mireille De La Valle, the white daughter of a French diplomat. She is sent back to Paris when her father discovers their relationship. The lovers bide their time and eventually elope, to the consternation of both families. Ousmane insists on Mireille converting to Islam before they marry, also stating his desire to live in Dakar, among his people. Mireille agrees, believing her religious conversion to be no great sacrifice, and remaining determined to retain her own identity within their marriage.

Ousmane adopts the manner and customs of traditional Senegalese men and Mireille finds it increasingly difficult to adjust to a life in which her social status is so drastically reduced. Ousmane is too weak to fight the chauvinistic culture of his upbringing and rifts appear between the couple, leading to a shocking conclusion.

The author presents both perspectives with skill and style, at the same time putting the case for the need for Africa's cultural traditions to embrace Western notions of gender equality. This is a poignant tale, beautifully written.

*Mariama Bä died soon after completing this book. Her only other novel is* So Long a Letter *(1980), which won the Noma Award. It deals with a widow having to share the mourning of her husband with his second, much younger wife, once again highlighting women's position in modern Africa.*

# A GOOD MAN IN AFRICA (1981)

## William Boyd

A comic romp through the fictitious West African state of Kinjanja. Morgan Leafy is the drunken, oafish Deputy High Commissioner who falls for his boss's daughter, Priscilla, but is then forced to reject her when he is diagnosed with a venereal disease. She never forgives the rejection and becomes engaged to his subordinate, Dickie Dalmire. Morgan subsequently beds the wife of a local potentate and political candidate, Adekunle, who blackmails Morgan into bribing the university doctor, Murray, to handle a proposed land deal in Adekunle's favour. When the High Commissioner's servant is struck by lightning and killed, no one is prepared to move the body for fear of upsetting Shango, the local god. The servant's corpse lies rotting as the Duchess of Ripon prepares to make a state visit to the area.

When British collusion with Adekunle's corrupt pre-election manoeuvrings comes to light, Morgan is called upon to deal with a host of problems he is ill equipped to tackle. Falling deeper into a dissolute lifestyle, he makes a string of unfortunate decisions that ultimately lead to rioting.

Although essentially a good-natured farce, *A Good Man in Africa* reveals Boyd, who was brought up in Ghana, to be sensitive to the concerns of modern Africa. He handles his material well and it is a remarkably assured debut novel that won the Whitbread Prize for best first novel, as well as a Somerset Maugham Award.

*His other African novels are slightly less knockabout but thoroughly engaging.* Brazzaville Beach *(1990) is an absorbing book in which a woman reflects on her time working on a field study of chimpanzees.* See East Africa listing for An Ice-Cream War *(1982).*

## ☙Read ons

*Beasts of No Nation*, Uzodinma Iweala
Written in conversational patois, this savage novel concerns the brutalisation of a young boy who becomes a child soldier.

*The Healers*, Ayi Kwei Armah (Ghana)
This classic of African literature is set in late-nineteenth-century Ghana and deals with the Healers' attempts to bring harmony and unity to the country as European settlers arrive.

*Changes*, Ama Ata Aidoo **(Ghana)**
Set in modern-day Accra, this novel exposes how the freedom of an educated, financially independent woman is limited by her gender.

*Waiting for the Wild Beasts to Vote*, Ahmadou Kourouma (Togo)
A prize-winning look at post-independence West Africa through the life of a dictator. It veers between fantasy and reality, yet always remains fascinating and funny.

*God's Bits of Wood*, Sembene Ousmane **(Senegal)**
A beautifully written series of interconnected stories about the rail workers' strike of 1947, an event in which women's rights and the class struggle took precedence over racial issues.

*The Viceroy of Ouidah*, Bruce Chatwin **(Benin)**
This novella artfully tells the rags-to-riches tale of a real-life slave trader, Brazilian-born Francisco da Silva. It is set in the early 1800s and in modern-day Benin.

*The Heart of the Matter*, Graham Greene **(Sierra Leone)**
Set during the Second World War, an incorruptible and devout Catholic police officer battles with his beliefs when he falls for another woman.

*Moses, Citizen and Me*, Delia Jarrett-Macauley **(Sierra Leone)**
Moving between scenes of harsh reality and dream-like sequences, this heartfelt and moving story deals with child soldiers in the aftermath of a war.

*The Radiance of the King*, Camara Laye **(Guinea)**
An arrogant white Frenchman is stranded off the coast of an unnamed African country. With the help of local people, he journeys to see the king, an encounter that strips him of all his pretensions.

# NIGERIA

**KEY**TITLES

*Things Fall Apart*, Chinua Achebe
*The Famished Road*, Ben Okri

## THINGS FALL APART (1958)
Chinua Achebe

Set at the end of the nineteenth century, this is a classic novel of one man's fall from grace, written just two years after Nigeria gained independence. Okonkwo is a proud and powerful tribal leader, fearful of weakness and failure. After he accidentally kills a clansman, he is forced into exile for seven years. When he returns, he sees that his culture is disintegrating as a result of the arrival of white settlers. Because Okonkwo loses his place in the world and his identity as a man, he is unable either to accept the changes he sees or to find a place for himself in the new society.

Achebe's powerful and moving tale is a searing indictment of colonial rule, written as a riposte to Joyce Cary's *Mister Johnson*, in which Africans are portrayed as dim-witted clowns. This novel is calm and intelligent in tone and was among the first to give Western readers a glimpse of an authentic African way of life.

*Achebe is generally regarded as the founding father of modern African literature and this novel was included in Africa's top twelve books by* The African Review of Books. *The two further volumes of The African Trilogy are* Arrow of God *(1964) and* No Longer at Ease *(1967).*

*After a long absence, Achebe produced* Anthills of the Savannah *in 1988. Set in the fictional nation of Kangan, it concerns three old school friends with conflicting roles in a postcolonial government. Liberally sprinkled with pidgin English, this is a demanding but ultimately rewarding read.*

# THE FAMISHED ROAD (1991)

Ben Okri

*The Famished Road* is a story told by Azaro, a spirit-child whose destiny is to be repeatedly reborn but who decides to break with fate in order to experience real life. The love of his family enables Azaro to survive, offering hope for the survival of a Nigeria struggling to realise itself as an independent nation.

The spirit world makes constant attempts to claim Azaro back, and these attempts are contrasted with the daily struggles of his poverty-stricken parents: his father's efforts to box his way to wealth and enlightenment are particularly poignant.

The book is replete with fantastical characters and scenes: a forest that walks away after losing its battle with men; a man who becomes hungrier the more he eats; numerous ghosts and spirits that haunt the mighty Madame Koko's bar; an election between the Party of the Poor and the Party of the Rich. Okri's world presents a view of humans as gods hidden from themselves, more afraid of love than death and, consequently, finding it easier to die than to love.

Drawing on Yoruba story-telling traditions and a belief in several layers of existence, the book sees Azaro flit between the real and spirit worlds. The author weaves a multi-layered, fanciful tale full of grotesque and bizarre characters, depicted in rich, hallucinatory language.

The Famished Road *was awarded the Booker Prize in 1991. The dreamscape is continued in* Songs of Enchantment *(1993) and* Infinite Riches *(1998). Both are beautifully written books and are quite astonishing in their language and imagery.*

## Read ons

*Purple Hibiscus*, Chimamanda Ngozi Adichie
A graphic tale of a fourteen-year-old girl's coming to terms with her father's abuse, set against the backdrop of a military coup in Nigeria. Adichie's second novel is *Half of a Yellow Sun*.

*The Joys of Motherhood*, Buchi Emecheta
A highly descriptive narrative about the desperate plight of people in the slums of Laos, focusing on the treatment of women by their men.

*Waiting for an Angel*, Helon Habila
A political prisoner writes poetry in jail in an attempt to hold on to his sanity during the political unrest of the 1990s.

*Efuru*, Flora Nwapa
A landmark book that explores village life through the tale of one woman's struggle to be herself in a land where the spirits still influence people's everyday lives. Nwapa was the first Nigerian woman to be published in Nigeria and the first black African woman to be published in the UK.

*The Icarus Girl,* Helen Oyeyemi
The author was eighteen when she wrote this lyrical story about a little girl of mixed race who finds a soulmate when she visits her mother's family in Nigeria.

*Sozaboy*, Ken Saro-Wiwa
A politically important novel about a naïve recruit facing up to the harsh realities of war. A short novel told in 'rotten English'.

*The Palm-Wine Drinkard*, Amos Tutuola
A series of hallucinatory stories in which a young man embarks on a journey full of magic, humour and horror.

*The Interpreters*, Wole Soyinka
A group of young Nigerian intellectuals return to their homeland and attempt to understand their society and the all-pervasive influence of native traditions.

*God's Medicine Men and Other Stories,* Tanure Ojaide
Ten reflective stories from a winner of the Commonwealth Poetry Prize. They feature Nigerians attempting to cope in a country undergoing major social change.

# NORTH AFRICA

KEY TITLES

*This Blinding Absence of Light*, Tahar Ben Jelloun (Morocco)
*The Sheltering Sky*, Paul Bowles (Sahara)

## THIS BLINDING ABSENCE OF LIGHT (2004)
Tahar Ben Jelloun

In 1991, a handful of survivors were released from the claustrophobic underground cells in which King Hassan II of Morocco confined his political prisoners, cells so cramped that many of the prisoners found on their release that they had shrunk in size by a foot. This is the fictionalised story of one of them.

Salim was a soldier, merely following orders, yet was imprisoned for over eighteen years for his part in an attack on the King's palace. His family had no notion of what had happened to him and presumed him dead. Salim's father, a court jester who was close to the King, disowned and denounced his son.

With no exercise and barely enough food, Salim works to erase his memory while remaining alive intellectually. He tries not to recall his past life, his childhood or his relationship with his fiancée, but memories return to him in his dreams.

Although unable to see each other, the inmates can hold conversations and they invent ways of keeping themselves occupied and sane. They spend their days reciting the Koran and literally counting time. Salim becomes the prison storyteller and relates tales remembered from Balzac and the *Arabian Nights*, and from films such as *A Streetcar Named Desire*, to divert his fellow inmates' minds from the smell of faeces, the palpable presence of disease, and the sounds of scorpions scuttling across the floor.

The inmates find pleasure where they can, adopting a dog ludicrously imprisoned for biting a general and caring for a dove that has taken to visiting them. One by one they die in these cramped and terrible conditions.

Ben Jelloun's genius is to keep the narrative flowing remarkably well in spite of the limited and unvarying location of the story. This is a remarkable book, written in language the spareness of which matches the austerity of the prisoners' condition whilst providing a moving testimony to human dignity.

# THE SHELTERING SKY (1949)
Paul Bowles

Three Americans wander round North Africa in search of new experiences in the period following the Second World War. Port and Kit Moresby have been married for ten years and Port sees this trip as a way of reinvigorating their rather lifeless marriage, an aim in which his wife seems less interested. They bring a friend, George Tunner, along with them, although neither Port nor Kit is particularly fond of George. The group has the means and the time to travel endlessly, changing location on a whim. Emotionally constipated and rather bored by the instant gratification of their desires, they find comfort in the perfunctory.

Frustrated by the claustrophobia of the narrow streets and clamouring Arabs, they travel south, where they encounter the cruel, untamed beauty of the desert. Unable to cope with intimacy, they seek a superficial exoticism which, once found, proves too difficult to accept. Tragedy strikes and death and madness ensue.

Bowles's pellucid, understated style superbly conveys the superficiality of his characters and the self-destructive nature of their flawed ambitions, while the merciless heat and majesty of the desert landscape are rendered with an artist's eye.

The novel is a stunning metaphor for the emptiness of twentieth-century living and the pitiful condition of the human search for meaning and purpose in a loveless and hostile environment.

A visually stunning film was made by Bernardo Bertolucci in 1990.

## 📖Read ons

*Leo the African*, Amin Maalouf **(North Africa)**
This fictional memoir of real-life sixteenth-century Arab traveller, Hassan Al Wazzan, takes the reader on a tour of medieval North Africa and explores the worlds of Islam and Christendom.

*The English Patient*, Michael Ondaatje **(North Africa)**
As the Second World War comes to an end, a nurse looks after a patient burnt beyond recognition. He recalls his time in Africa and the love he left behind.

*Abductor*, Leila Marouane **(Algeria)**
Suppressed family secrets eventually come to light in this often comic tale of a Muslim father of six daughters who attempts to woo his ex-wife after a rash divorce.

*The Outsider,* Albert Camus **(Algeria)**
A classic existential novel set in Algeria. A man's life seems to have no meaning, until he shoots a stranger on the beach.

*The God Who Begat a Jackal*, Nega Mezlekia **(Ethiopia)**
Set in eighteenth-century Abyssinia, this is a magical and lyrical tale, steeped in African mythology, about the forbidden love between a slave and his mistress.

*M'hashish*, Mohammed Mrabet **(Morocco)**
Translated by Paul Bowles, this collection of exotic stories conveys much of the hallucinatory quality of hashish-inspired dreams. Mrabet is also the author of *Love with a Few Hairs* and *Harmless Poisons, Blameless Sins*.

*Hideous Kinky*, Esther Freud **(Morocco)**
This quirky adolescent yarn, set in the 1960s, deals with a mother taking her young family abroad to find enlightenment, told through the eyes of one of the children.

*The Almond*, Nedjma **(Morocco)**
Controversial and erotic, this is a purportedly autobiographical tale of the sexual awakening of a young Muslim woman in Tangiers.

*In the Country of Men*, Hisham Matar **(Libya)**
Family loves and loyalties come under strain in this poignant tale of a young boy growing up in Libya under Gadaffi's brutal regime.

*The Tremor of Forgery*, Patricia Highsmith **(Tunisia)**
In the late 1960s, an American writer sits down to write under the Tunisian sun. We watch as he eats, drinks and sinks into moral decay. Highsmith at her best.

# EGYPT

**KEY**TITLES

*Woman at Point Zero*, Nawal El Saadawi
*The Cairo Trilogy*, Naguib Mahfouz

## WOMAN AT POINT ZERO (1975)

Nawal El Saadawi

This story, based on a true-life case, is told by a journalist visiting a woman on death row. Firdaus has been condemned to death for killing a pimp but has refused to ask the King for clemency. Intrigued as to why Firdaus wants to die, the journalist interviews her and then tells her story.

Firdaus is an intelligent, sensuous woman whose spirit has been crushed by a repressive society. Brought up as a peasant, her early life is one of innocence and harmony, but from the day she is ritually circumcised, life becomes different. Aware of her own needs, yet unable to voice them, she finds herself in Cairo with her abusive uncle, who sends her away to school. Although she performs outstandingly well and is clearly exceptionally intelligent, on leaving she is married off to a repulsive elderly man. When her husband beats her and she complains, she is told by her aunt that she should be submissive, like a good woman.

Unwilling to submit, Firdaus finds she can use her sexuality as a way of gaining power over men and control of her own life, and she carves out a position for herself as a high-class prostitute. Eventually bullied into taking the protection of a pimp, she finds his unfair treatment unbearable and she kills him.

*A highly regarded and important novel about the treatment of women in patriarchal societies,* Woman at Point Zero *earned Nawal El Saadawi a term of imprisonment, years of persecution and the withdrawal of her right to practise medicine. Her other books include* God Dies by the Nile *(1985).*

# THE CAIRO TRILOGY (1956–57)
## Naguib Mahfouz

This remarkable trilogy is a vibrant and engaging study of a turbulent period in Egypt's history. It follows al-Sayyid Ahmad Abd al-Jawad and his family through three generations, beginning during Britain's occupation of Egypt in 1917 and drawing to a close at the end of the Second World War.

Ahmad has a devoted wife, Amina, three sons, and two daughters. A middle-class shopkeeper and professed devout Muslim, Ahmad rules his family with an iron fist whilst indulging his own secret vices. This hypocrisy is emblematic of the Egypt Mahfouz describes, a country hidebound by traditional beliefs, struggling to assimilate into the modern world.

The trilogy begins at a leisurely pace with absorbing descriptions of daily routines, picking up pace when Ahmad's sons venture out into the world. One son involves himself in a demonstration against the British, another falls in love with an unsuitable girl. As Ahmad ages, he sees his grandchildren become emancipated in ways he could not have imagined as a younger man, ways that involve extremism at both ends of the spectrum. He becomes a more introspective man and grows to acknowledge the dwindling power of a patriarchal system that has served him so well.

The trilogy is exceptional in its rendering of detail and its evocation of place. Cairo is brought to life in Mahfouz's florid descriptions of streets, mosques, people and food. Whilst the politics of the period are dissected at some length, it is the human dramas that remain central to the story and provide the focus for the reader's emotional investment. It is an outstanding accomplishment.

*Mahfouz remains the only Arab to win the Nobel Prize for Literature, which he received in 1988. The individual novels are* Palace Walk *(1956),* Palace of Desire *(1957), and* Sugar Street *(1957).*

## 📖Read ons

*Distant View of a Minaret and Other Stories*, Alifa Rifaat
A collection of inventive and intimate stories detailing the everyday lives of people, mainly women, in Cairo, where Allah is never more than a whisper away.

*The Map of Love*, Ahdaf Soueif
An epic saga that tells the story of the life and loves of an English noblewoman settling in fin-de-siècle Egypt.

*The Yacoubian Building*, Alaa Al Aswany
A controversial and best-selling novel that follows the lives of residents of a block of flats in central Cairo.

*The Alexandria Quartet*, Lawrence Durrell
Opinions are divided on this major work, dismissed by some as laughably pretentious and revered by others as an unparalleled metaphysical tour-de-force, this quartet offers four perspectives on a single sequence of events, with modern notions of love at their core. Set in Alexandria in the period before and during the Second World War.

*Moon Tiger*, Penelope Lively
As a woman lies dying in hospital, she recalls her relationship with a soldier whom she loved and lost in Egypt during the Second World War.

*The Levant Trilogy*, Olivia Manning
A wartime saga following a British couple caught up in emotional and political turmoil, told with wit and perception. It is the sequel to *The Balkan Trilogy*.

*The Alexandria Semaphore*, Robert Sole
A panoramic view of Egyptian society, set in the late 1800s against the backdrop of the construction of the Suez Canal, with sensitively drawn characters from all walks of life. This is the third instalment; the preceding volumes are *The Photographer's Wife* and *Birds of Passage*.

*The Pyramid*, Ismail Kadare
A harrowing parable about the construction of a pyramid built simply to enslave the populace and keep rebellion at bay.

*Beer in the Snooker Club*, Waguih Ghali
A lively account of 1950s' Cairo, full of love, politics and alienation. The author gained posthumous fame as the subject of Diana Athill's memoir, *After a Funeral*.

*The Fascination of Evil*, Florian Zeller
Two authors stir up trouble in modern-day Cairo. One searches for sexual encounters but finds murder. A novel about declining morals.

## READ ON A THEME

### ANCIENT EVENINGS – ANCIENT EGYPT

*Warlock*, Wilbur Smith
The hero becomes a warlock in order to save the dynasty of a dead queen. *See also* **River God** and **Seventh Scroll**.

*The Ramses Series*, Christian Jacq
A lively, though historically inaccurate account of Ramses' rise to power, in five volumes. *See also* the **Mysteries of Osiris** series, the **Judge of Egypt** series and the **Queen of Freedom** trilogy.

*Ancient Evenings*, Norman Mailer
An impressive tome dealing with the lives of the pharoahs around 1200 BC.

*The Memoirs of Cleopatra*, Margaret George
A first-person account of the life of the Egyptian queen, replete with exotic and fascinatingly detailed stories.

*The Ptolemies. Book 1: The House of the Eagle*, Duncan Sprott
A gritty, realistic and colourful book which chronicles the rise of the Ptolemies through the generations. Part one of a planned quartet.'

*The Mask of Ra*, Paul Doherty
A Pharaoh's wife sets out to discover who murdered her husband and finds herself becoming ever more powerful. There are six titles in the series so far.

# EUROPE

## GREECE

KEYTITLES

*Zorba the Greek*, Nikos Kazantzakis
*The Magus*, John Fowles

## ZORBA THE GREEK (1946)

Nikos Kazantzakis

Alexis Zorba, a wild and free spirit, is hired by the narrator of the novel, an unnamed Greek man, to look after his lignite mine on the island of Crete. The narrator is a self-confessed bookworm who engages in a study of Buddhist philosophy in order to free himself from material, fleshly concerns. However, Zorba's down-to-earth, lusty good humour and vibrant spirit teach him to enjoy the beauty in everyday life. 'The Boss', as Zorba calls him, tired of the intellectual life, entreats Zorba to tell tales of his travels and his meetings with remarkable people, to brighten up his day. Zorba likes to eat, sing, dance and plays the santuri, a metallic-sounding stringed instrument that he cherishes. He also enjoys the company of women and, if his approach to the opposite sex is a little primitive, his enjoyment of their company is profound. The inhabitants of the island are initially friendly to this odd pair but incidents involving them and the village widow, Madame Hortense, eventually bring outrage and censure.

The details of Greek peasant life are splendidly described, as are the marvels of nature. Grand metaphysical questions are also explored in the text. At one point Zorba asks The Boss, 'One man lives as though he will never die and another as though each day were his last. Who is right?'

*Zorba the Greek* is passionate, vital and bursting with exuberance and raucous good humour. A reader who approaches it with a good heart will be enchanted.

*Nikos Kazantzakis is the most famous modern Greek author. A luscious film was made of this, his most celebrated book, in 1964, with Anthony Quinn as Zorba and Alan Bates as the narrator.*

# THE MAGUS (1965)

## John Fowles

In this spellbinding novel of psychological gameplay, Nicholas Urfe, a disillusioned Oxford graduate bored with life in London, decides to take a position as an English schoolteacher on the island of Phraxos (a fictional location based on the island of Spetses). His flight to Greece is also an escape from a relationship with girlfriend Alison, whom he leaves to pursue his notions of personal freedom but whom he finds himself unable to forget. His new job soon becomes tedious and, unable to concentrate on his own personal projects, and struck by the beauty of his surroundings, he takes to exploring the island. In rather mysterious circumstances, he meets the beguiling Maurice Conchis, who lives in a villa nearby. Conchis subjects Urfe to a series of testing 'games' that bring him close to breaking-point. He finds himself falling in love with Julie, who also lives in the villa, along with, it emerges, a twin sister, June. Various conflicting reasons are given for the twins' presence on the island, and for their involvement in Conchis's life, leaving Nicholas uneasy but nonetheless smitten. So much so that when Alison invites him to Athens for the weekend, he goes along but rejects her offer of a reconciliation, later learning that she commits suicide. Nicholas is hauled before a panel of twelve judges, who proceed to pass judgement on his life.

Fowles himself describes the book as a literary Rorschach test, its meaning decided by whatever reaction this emotional and intellectual maelstrom produces in the individual reader.

Originally subtitled *The Godgame*, it was first published in 1965 and was reissued in a revised version twelve years later.

# 📖Read ons

*Little Infamies*, Panos Karnezis
A collection of interweaving short stories set in a nameless, isolated Greek village and full of curious characters and strange goings-on.

*The Few Things I Know About Glafkos Thrassakis*, Vassilis Vassilikos
Metafiction about a biographer investigating the life and works of a famous, but very mysterious, deceased Greek writer who bears a close resemblance to Vassilikos himself.

*Captain Corelli's Mandolin*, Louis de Bernières
Set on the island of Cephalonia during World War Two, this is an amusing and moving novel about a love affair between an Italian soldier and the daughter of the local doctor.

*The Dark Labyrinth*, Lawrence Durrell
A typically evocative and complex novel from the pen of one of Britain's finest writers, about a group of English tourists lost in Cretan caves in the late 1940s.

*The Late-Night News*, Petros Markaris
The deaths of two Albanians are closely followed by those of two investigating journalists. Athens at its hustle-bustle best is illustrated in this, the first novel in the Costas Haritas detective series.

*Four Walls*, Vangelis Hatziyannidis
An acclaimed, fable-like first novel, set on a Greek island, that explores the themes of solitude, confinement and incest.

*The Jasmine Isle*, Ioanna Karystiani
A modern-day Greek tragedy, set in the Cyclades islands, that tells of a woman forced to marry someone she does not love, whilst the man she does love marries her sister.

*The Island*, Victoria Hislop
Crete and Cretan culture are vividly evoked in this gripping story of four generations of a family beset by tragedy, war, passion and secrets.

*Fugitive Pieces*, Ann Michaels – *see* **Canada**.

## READONATHEME

### HELLENICA – ANCIENT GREECE

*Fire from Heaven*, Mary Renault
The first novel of Renault's 'Alexandriad', a trilogy tracing the life and legacy of the great Alexander, told from the point of view of various characters, including his lover, Bagoas. *The Persian Boy* and *Funeral Games* complete the trilogy.

*Alexander: Child of a Dream*, Valerio Massimo Manfredi
Archaeologist and academic, Manfredi delivers this rip-roaring tale of Alexander the Great's quest to rule the civilised world. *The Sands of Ammon* and *The Ends of the Earth* are the companion volumes.

*The Ten Thousand*, Michael Curtis Ford
A blockbuster retelling of Xenophon's *Anabasis*, the epic account of how he led ten thousand Greek soldiers to safety from deep within enemy Persian territory, across deserts and snow-capped mountains, in 401 BC.

*Gates of Fire*, Steven Pressfield
The last survivor of the Battle of Thermopylae in 480 BC relates the story of the battle to the Persian king, Xerxes, recounting how a mere three hundred Spartan warriors kept the entire Persian army at bay for six days.

*The Double Tongue*, William Golding
Arieka the Pythia, the oracle of Apollo at Delphi, looks back over sixty years as a priestess in the first century BC.

*Olympiad*, Tom Holt
A farcical satire by the renowned historical and fantasy novelist about a cast of inept characters and their attempts to organise the first Olympic Games in 776 BC.

*The Athenian Murders*, José Carlos Spinoza
Heracles Pontor, the Dicipherer of Enigmas, investigates the unaccountable death of one of Plato's pupils. Meanwhile, in modern times, the translator of a rare Ancient Greek whodunnit finds that his own life is in danger.

*The Eye of Cybele*, Daniel Chavarría
This complex whodunnit, set in ancient Athens, revolves around two rival generals, a scheming and seductive courtesan, and the disappearance of a sacred jewel.

*Aristotle Detective*, Margaret Doody
Aristotle and Stephanos, the Morse and Lewis of ancient Athens, set out to find the perpetrator of a puzzling murder. The first in a series of well-researched and entertaining mysteries.

*The Last of the Wine*, Mary Renault
An expert on Ancient Greece, Renault tells the story of Alexias, a young well-to-do Athenian and pupil of Socrates, at the time of the Peloponnesian War in fifth-century BC Athens.

*See also* READ ON A THEME: ONCE UPON A TIME – MYTHS, LEGENDS, FOLKTALES

# TURKEY

KEYTITLE

*My Name is Red*, Orhan Pamuk

## MY NAME IS RED (1998)
Orhan Pamuk

In sixteenth-century Istanbul, the Sultan commissions an illustrated book to commemorate the glories of his realm. However, he wishes the illustrations to be produced in Venetian single-point perspective, rather than in traditional Islamic style. As such a work of representational art is an affront to Islam, it has to be carried out in secret, without the artists knowing for whom they are working. When one of the artists disappears, believed murdered, questions are asked. Was the motive religious fanaticism, professional jealousy or something more sinister?

The book is written from the point of view of several characters, beginning with the dead man himself, and from the 'point of view' of several inanimate objects, including a tree, a gold coin, and some red ink. Although this literary ventriloquism may sound off-putting, it gives each chapter an endearing freshness and Pamuk delivers it in such an assured manner that most readers will allow him these conceits.

Fascinating and richly detailed, this novel, part detective story and part meditation on love and art, completely immerses the reader in time and place. Pamuk highlights the mutual cultural influences of East and West and the book contains scintillating debates on artistic style. To help orientate the reader, it also contains a map and a thousand-year chronology detailing the history leading up to the events of the story.

*Orhan Pamuk was awarded the Nobel Prize for Literature in 2006. His novels, all of which are set in Turkey, include* The New Life *(1995), the fastest-selling book in Turkish history, and* Snow *(2002).*

## 📖Read ons

*Memed, My Hawk*, Yashar Kemal
An exceptional novel about a peasant boy who becomes a Robin Hood figure as a result of his brutal treatment at the hands of a feudal lord.

*Young Turk*, Moris Farhi
Thirteen different narrations are interwoven to produce a portrait of a multi-racial Turkey between 1930–1955.

*The Flea Palace*, Elif Shafak
An acclaimed story about the residents of a block of flats in Istanbul, and the rather bad smell emanating from the building. The author was tried for 'insulting Turkishness' in her novel, *The Bastard of Istanbul*.

*Birds Without Wings*, Louis de Bernières
Stories of the people of a village in southwest Turkey during the last years of the Ottoman Empire run parallel with the history of Kemal Atatürk, the father of modern Turkey.

*Belshazzar's Daughter*, Barbara Nadel
The first in a series of Inspector Ikmen crime novels set in a vividly depicted Istanbul, about an old Jewish man who is tortured to death.

*The Janissary Tree*, Jason Goodwin
A succession of barbaric murders seem to indicate that a banned group of elite soldiers are still operational, in the first of a mystery series set in late nineteenth-century Istanbul and featuring Yashim, the Ottoman detective.

*The Towers of Trebizond*, Rose Macaulay
This witty novel features the problems faced by a group of eccentric travelling companions on their way from Istanbul to Trebizond.

*The Maze*, Panos Karnezis
A retreating brigade of Greek soldiers, on the run from the Turkish army in Anatolia in the 1920s, seek refuge in a town untouched by the war.

# RUSSIA/SOVIET UNION

## KEYTITLES

*Dr. Zhivago*, Boris Pasternak
*Soul*, Andrey Platonov
*And Quiet Flows the Don*, Mikhail Sholokhov

## DOCTOR ZHIVAGO (1957)
Boris Pasternak

Against the backdrop of the Russian Revolution of 1917, this grand narrative ostensibly tells the story of the life of Yuri Zhivago and his love for Larisa Feodorovna. Tolstoyan in its epic sweep, this is also one of the great love stories of modern literature.

Yuri and Lara are both married when they first meet. In the course of marathon adventures across Russia, their love flourishes and then founders time and again. Zhivago is a poetry-writing physician who is concerned as much with spirituality as he is with physicality. While he believes in the ideals of the Revolution, he deplores its brutal methods and its equivocal outcomes.

Boris Pasternak brings his poet's lyrical sensibility to the prose, filling the pages with vivid descriptions of the magnificently vast Russian landscape he so obviously adores, together with quite graphic descriptions of war and bloodshed that brought not only political change but a fundamental alteration in the character of the Russian people.

Doctor Zhivago *was smuggled out of Russia after it was written and was first published in Italy. It was not available in Russia until 1987. Pasternak was awarded the Nobel Prize for Literature in 1958, a prize which the Soviet government forced him to renounce. He died two years later.*

The book is overdue for re-translation: the 1958 rendering loses much of the rhythm of the original language. It was made into a highly successful film by David Lean in 1965.

# SOUL (1935)

## Andrey Platonov

Andrey Platonov has been hailed as the best writer to come out of the Soviet Union, although he also seems to be among the least well known.

The opening chapters of *Soul* announce that this is a somewhat unusual read. In them the recently graduated Nazar Chagataev hugs 'dead objects' (so they won't forget him), marries a pregnant woman he has only just met, and falls in love with her fourteen-year-old daughter. He is then sent from Moscow back to his homeland in the desert heart of Turkmenistan, to bring socialism to the Dzhan tribe. This arduous trek involves boat and train journeys and endless days of walking, with a sick camel that Chagataev eventually eats 'without appetite'. When he arrives, he finds that only a few members of the tribe are still alive and he quickly trades his elderly mother in for a ten-year-old girl, Aidym.

Chagataev attempts to integrate the tribe into the modern world in the belief that 'the future is in our minds and the past in our hearts', but these people have nothing, materially, and so are bound to be guided by their hearts.

Platonov has revealed that it was his original intention to write a novel demonstrating how the Soviet system had brought barefoot beggars into a modern technological paradise. However, his own experiences in the desert taught him that this was not the reality for many people. 'Dzhan' means 'a soul in search of happiness' and the soul-searching struggle of the Dzhan is movingly and compellingly handled in the book. Chagataev comes to realise that, in order to live happily, people must be free to choose how to live their lives, a view not knowingly encouraged by the Soviet authorities.

Andrey Platonov's writing is highly individual in style and content, with every page bringing a linguistic gem of some sort. His descriptions of harsh desert life give *Soul* a remarkable sense of place, which is conveyed intelligently and effortlessly.

*Soul* remained unpublished for thirty years, only then being available in a bowdlerised version. This splendid Harvill translation, published in 2003, required the attentions of six (!) translators, owing to the author's eccentric use of Russian. All of Platonov's novels are recommended, especially *The Foundation Pit* (1930).

# AND QUIET FLOWS THE DON (1928)

Mikhail Sholokhov

This book is the first of a two-part novel set among the Cossacks living in the Don valley in southwestern Russia. The Melekhov family is descended from an eminent soldier who took a Turkish wife. His progeny were therefore forever known as 'The Turks'. The novel concerns one of his grandchildren, Gregor Melekhov, and his love for a neighbour's wife, Aksinia Astakhov. They cause a scandal by openly conducting an affair while Aksinia's soldier husband, Stepan, is away fighting. Their eventual elopement leads to a feud between the Astakhovs and the Melekhovs.

The story opens under the shadow of the approaching First World War and it continues into the 1917 Revolution and the subsequent Civil War. Through this period the author charts the demise of the Cossacks and the birth of a new society in the shape of the Soviet Union. The tension between tradition and modernity is played out as much on the battlefields, in clashes between guns and sabres, as it is in the minds of the protagonists.

Notwithstanding modern accusations that Sholokov was a Stalinist lackey, the author explores in detail the Don Cossacks' desire for independence and their hostility toward the Bolsheviks, whose bloodthirstiness is not circumvented. The novel portrays with depth and feeling the brutish existence of Cossacks on the bleak Steppes, and is peopled with a wealth of wonderfully drawn characters.

*Mikhail Sholokhov was awarded the Nobel Prize for Literature in 1965. The story continues with the sequel,* The Don Flows Home to the Sea *(1940).*

## ⮾Read ons

*Russian Short Stories from Pushkin to Buida*, Ed. Robert Chandler
Covering the last two hundred years, and including many previously censored stories, this excellent collection includes such giants as Tolstoy, Chekhov and Gogol, as well as more recent writers such as Platonov and Bulgakov.

*Mother*, Maxim Gorky
A woman becomes politicised by the activities of her socialist son, whom she in turn humanises, in this brilliant novel set in pre-revolutionary Russia.

*One Day in the Life of Ivan Denisovich*, Aleksander Solzhenitsyn
This short novel recounts in shocking detail one soul-destroying day of convict Shukhov's 3,500-day sentence in the sub-zero living hell of a Gulag.

*A Life's Music*, Andreï Makine
An old man tells his life story to a fellow passenger on a train journey to Moscow. It is the story of a life decimated by the horrors of Stalinist Russia, war and unrequited love.

*The Life of Insects*, Victor Pelevin
From one of modern Russia's most prominent authors comes this satire on post-Soviet-Russian life, concerning a trio of businessmen, who are also insects, in a Crimean seaside resort.

*Red Cavalry and Other Stories*, Isaac Babel
This collection combines Babel's masterpiece on the Soviet-Polish war, first published in 1926, with many of his stories focusing on Jewish life and the city of Odessa.

*Life and Fate*, Vassily Grossman
A masterpiece of the twentieth century that centres on the everyday life of the Russian people during the battle for Stalingrad.

*Life With an Idiot*, Victor Erofeyev
A superb collection of short stories from this controversial writer, ranging from the surreal to the fiercely humorous.

*The Case of Comrade Tulayev*, Victor Serge
This masterpiece deals with the Stalinist purges of the 1930s and is a shocking account of a totalitarian state flexing its mighty muscles in an effort to track down the killer of a government official.

*Love of Worker Bees*, Alexandra Kollontai
Kollontai, who was a radical feminist, produces a collection of stories that portray ordinary Russian people at work and at play. Originally published in 1923, it was denounced as pornographic.

*The Gift*, Vladimir Nabokov
Although set in Berlin, this novel about an impoverished poet dreaming of writing a successful book is the last to be written in Nabokov's native tongue and is a hymn to Russian literature, evoking the works of Pushkin and Gogol.

*The Ice Road*, Gillian Slovo
The compelling story features a handful of people living in St. Petersburg during the first wave of genocide in Stalinist Russia between the wars.

*The People's Act of Love,* James Meek
A highly regarded epic of civil war in Siberia in 1919, this novel follows an escaped convict, Samarin, as he stumbles across a remote community of religious fanatics. He has an amazing tale to tell about his journey, and a self-prophesying destiny to fulfill.

# MOSCOW/ST PETERSBURG

KEYTITLE

*The Master and Margarita*, Mikhail Bulgakov

## THE MASTER AND MARGARITA (1966)
Mikhail Bulgakov

Once hailed as Stalin's favourite playwright, Bulgakov has enjoyed widespread acclaim in modern times owing to the posthumous publication of novels such as this, a scathing satire on Russian communism. Two separate stories run simultaneously: the first is set in Moscow in the 1930s, when the Devil and his entourage turn up in Red Square; the second is set in Jerusalem at the time of Christ.

The Devil is disguised as Professor Woland and he is in the capital city looking for The Master, a writer who, following criticism of his novel and extended state persecution, has retreated to a psychiatric hospital. The Master's mistress, Margarita, sells her soul to the Devil and agrees to host his spring ball in return for her lover's release. The novel that The Master has written centres on the repressive regime of Pontius Pilate and its condemnation of Jesus (Yeshua) in Jerusalem. It appears in many forms – for example, as a dream experienced by one of the inmates, and as a tale told by Satan – throughout the book.

Professor Woland is accompanied by various bizarre characters, including a talking black cat, a naked witch and an expert assassin. They wreak havoc in the bureaucratic and literary circles of Moscow and the story features decapitations, arson and abductions.

The Devil symbolises the need for evil as a necessary juxtaposition to good. Atheism is presented as the predominant Soviet 'religion', and the book features comic scenes in which people deny the existence of the Devil when faced with his very person. A highly original book dripping with cynicism and amusing theological debate, *The Master and Margarita* is generally hailed as a masterpiece of twentieth-century literature. It was written in the 1930s but was not published for over thirty years, when it was serialised in expurgated form. Only in 1973 did the full work appear for the first time. There are currently several different translations available, each with its individual merits.

## 📖Read ons

*Novel With Cocaine*, M Ageyev (Moscow)
A fascinating, if grim, account of a young man's philosophical ideas and the rampant self-loathing that eventually leads to drug addiction and tragedy. Set in Revolution-era Moscow, it was first published in the 1930s.

*Angels on the Head of a Pin*, Yuri Druzhnikov (Moscow)
A host of colourful characters inhabit this epic tale set in Moscow in the late 1960s. Sinister political machinations surround the collapse of an editor of a communist newspaper.

*The Dream of Sukhanov*, Olga Grushin (Moscow)
A stylish debut novel about a former artist looking back on a life of mediocrity through a series of dreams.

*The Beginning of Spring*, Penelope Fitzgerald (Moscow)
It is spring, 1913, and Englishman Frank Reid is running his printing business in Moscow when his wife, Nellie, suddenly leaves him. How he copes is the subject of this gloriously crafted comic oddity.

*The Russian Interpreter*, Michael Frayn (Moscow)
An English businessman uses an interpreter to help him conduct an affair with a Russian woman. Complications ensue when the interpreter also falls in love with her.

*Darkness at Noon*, Arthur Koestler (Moscow)
A philosophical novel set in 1930s' Soviet Union. A hero of the Revolution is accused of crimes against the state and is tortured in order to make him publicly confess.

*The Winter Queen*, Boris Akunin (Moscow)
May 1876. When a wealthy young student shoots himself, the police's newest recruit, a charming ex-government clerk, is sent to investigate. The first in the thrilling Detective Erast Fandorin series.

*Petersburg*, Andrei Bely **(St Petersburg)**
This complex masterpiece of twentieth-century literature is a dense and highly imaginative book concerned with the political and social ferment around the time of the 1905 revolution.

*The Master of Petersburg*, J M Coetzee **(St Petersburg)**
This novel features an imagined event in Dostoyevsky's life, as the exiled writer returns to St Petersburg in order to investigate the sudden death of his stepson.

*The Siege*, Helen Dunmore **(Leningrad)**
A story of love and survival set in Leningrad in 1941, as Hitler prepares his troops for the siege of the city and winter prepares to set in.

*To The Hermitage*, Malcolm Bradbury **(St Petersburg)**
A dual narrative follows an academic journeying to St. Petersburg to discuss a project on Diderot, and follows the French philosopher himself, two hundred years earlier, visiting the court of Catherine the Great in the same city.

## TO THE ENDS OF THE EARTH – EXPLORERS, DISCOVERERS, ADVENTURERS

*Voss*, Patrick White
Based on a true story, White evocatively charts the doomed expedition of Johann Ulrich Voss, who tried to cross the Australian continent in the mid nineteenth-century.

*The Discovery of Slowness*, Sten Nadolny
A novelisation of the life of Sir John Franklin, a nineteenth-century explorer who overcomes his early difficulties to find the Northwest Passage across the Arctic Circle.

*The Voyage of the Narwhal*, Andrea Barrett
A historical adventure imbued with the cold of the Arctic Circle. It tells of the ill-fated mission, in 1855, of the *Narwhal* and its crew to chart Siberian waters.

*This Thing of Darkness*, Harry Thompson
An epic retelling of the journey to South America undertaken by Charles Darwin aboard the *HMS Beagle* in 1828, and of Darwin's friendship with the captain, Robert Fitzroy. A thought-provoking and intelligent novel.

*Wegener's Jigsaw*, Clare Dudman
This vivid, fictionalised account documents the extraordinary life of Alfred Wegener, a German meteorologist and Arctic explorer, and his arduous expeditions to Greenland.

*The Syme Papers*, Benjamin Markovits
Samuel Highgate Syme, an eighteenth-century inventor, was never given proper credit for his theory of continental drift. Douglas Pitt, a modern man obsessed with Syme, sets out to reveal Syme's genius.

*Bering*, Edward John Crockett
An adventure story detailing the disastrous exploratory mission to the Siberian seas undertaken by Vitus Jonassen Bering, the eighteenth-century navigator after whom the Bering Strait is named.

*Water Music*, T C Boyle
A fictional and comic account of the insane quest of Mungo Park and Ned Rise in 1795 for the source of the river Niger, via the gutters of London and the Scottish Highlands.

*Rifling Paradise*, Jem Poster
A gripping historical novel, set in the Victorian era, which vividly describes the native flora and fauna of Australia. An Englishman sets off for Australia hoping to escape past misdeeds and with ambitions to become a naturalist.

*Explorers of the New Century*, Magnus Mills
Mills constructs a parallel universe in which things are not quite as they seem. Two teams of explorers race to reach the 'agreed furthest point' from civilisation. Loosely based on the Scott/Amundsen battle to the South Pole in the early twentieth century.

*See also* **READ ON A THEME: POLE TO POLE – ARCTIC/ANTARCTIC**

# EASTERN EUROPE

## GENERAL EASTERN EUROPE

---

**KEY**TITLES

*Spring Flowers, Spring Frost*, Ismail Kadare **(Albania)**
*The Good Soldier Svejk*, Jaroslav Hašek

---

## SPRING FLOWERS, SPRING FROST (2000)
Ismail Kadare

Ismail Kadare is Albania's finest literary export and this novel is set in his home country after the collapse of Enver Hohxa's forty-year totalitarian regime. The novel alternates between chapters and counter-chapters. The chapters limn the normal life of Mark Gurabardhi, a painter working in the local art centre in a mountain town, simply called B -. Strange events occur, beginning with a bank robbery, an activity unheard of in previous times and a sure sign of slackening government control and of western trends infiltrating the country. Yet the secret police are still seemingly in operation.

The counter-chapters set out Mark's dreams and musings on various matters, including old legends such as the woman who married a snake, the myth of Tantalus and the iceberg that sank the *Titanic*. When Mark's boss is murdered, Brezhnev and a resurrected Hohxa make appearances. Mark paints his girlfriend in the nude and wonders whether she would love him less if he gave up painting. He worries about whether he should have joined the police force, like his father and grandfather, and also wonders why his friend Zef has disappeared.

Mark's worries are comically handled in free-flowing prose, although the light tone belies the serious issues addressed, issues including the question as to whether there is a copy of *The Book of Blood* in circulation, signifying that the country will return to the ways of the Kanun (the ancient system of blood feud and vendetta): an important concern for every citizen. The seemingly impossible reconciliation of these apparently disparate elements occurs in a final search for the disused tunnel in the mountain where the secret State Archives are hidden. This novel portrays in an elegant fashion a country uncertain about how to use its new-found freedom.

*Curiously, the only edition available in the UK has been rendered from a French translation. Ismail Kadare was the first winner of the Man Booker International Prize in 2005. His other books include* Broken April *(1980) and* The Successor *(2006).*

# THE GOOD SOLDIER SVEJK (1921–22)

Jaroslav Hašek

A compatriot and contemporary of Kafka, Jaroslav Hašek was ahead of his time as a writer. His treatment of the absurdities of bureaucracy predates Kafka, his anti-war message anticipates Remarque, and his modernism steals a march on Hemingway and Faulkner. Joseph Heller has stated that he would not have attempted *Catch-22* if he had not first read *The Good Soldier Svejk.*

This hilarious satire follows the fortunes of the hapless Svejk during the First World War. Dismissed from the army as feeble-minded, he is arrested after making some careless remarks about the shooting of Franz Ferdinand. This bungling, naïve fool is then drafted back into the army and embarks on a string of farcical adventures with, amongst others, a drunken chaplain and an amorous lieutenant. The reader is never sure whether Svejk is a genuine nincompoop or whether his idiocy masks a shrewdness that he deploys to fool everyone.

Although this is a war novel, it features no descriptions of battles, fighting or injuries. However, there is a continual biting satire on the pompous nature of army organisation and a jeering attitude towards the recently lost Austro-Hungarian Empire. Lampooned when it was first published, and written in the language of the people (i.e. Czech), *The Good Soldier Svejk* soon became the ordinary man's favourite and critics were quick to revise their opinions.

*The book was superbly illustrated by Jose Lada, after Hašek's death. Lada depicts Svejk as a bald, fat, unshaven, middle-aged man. Hašek originally intended to write six volumes, but only managed to complete four before his death in 1923.*

# CZECH REPUBLIC/SLOVAKIA/ CZECHOSLOVAKIA

*This Side of Reality: Modern Czech Writing*, Ed. Alexandra Büchler
An eclectic selection of the best new Czech authors, including Klima, Skvorecky and Jachym Topol.

*I Served the King of England*, Bohumil Hrabal
Hrabal is considered one of the greatest Czech writers of the twentieth century. This comic novel, which opens in the 1930s, concerns a lascivious and diminutive waiter who marries a Nazi gym teacher and pursues his greedy ambitions.

*The Engineer of Human Souls*, Josef Skvorecky
In this eloquent and compassionate novel, a writer examines the three stages of his life: his youth in wartime Czechoslovakia, the communist takeover, and his exile in Canada.

*Waiting For Leah*, Arnost Lustig
A novel of love, war and the Jewish experience during the Holocaust, as circumstances force three young people to share an attic room. This is a prequel to *Lovely Green Eyes*, another excellent novel.

# PRAGUE

## THE UNBEARABLE LIGHTNESS OF BEING (1984)
Milan Kundera

Kundera's most famous novel is set in the Prague Spring of 1968. Tomas lives with Tereza, a former waitress who has followed him to Prague, seemingly happy to dedicate her life to him. She becomes a politically committed photographer, while he is a surgeon and a serial seducer. Tomas loves Tereza but because he separates sex from love, he sees no contradiction in his pursuit of other women. Tereza knows of his infidelities and does not condemn him outright, although she does find it increasingly difficult to love him wholeheartedly. For her, love is a serious duty. Sabina, Tomas's favourite lover, is a rebellious and rash woman who has affairs with other men, all equally at the mercy of her cavalier approach to relationships.

The central message of the novel is that human life is futile and the decisions we make have little bearing on what actually happens to us. This is the reality for Tomas, when the Russian tanks arrive in Prague and he loses his job for criticising the Communist Party. Tomas and Tereza leave the city and join Sabina in Switzerland, but when Tereza decides to return to Prague, Tomas must decide whether to return with her or not.

*The novel is written in Kundera's trademark ironic and cynical style. A rather rueful film was made in 1987, in which Kundera was so disappointed that he has refused to allow any of his other novels to be filmed.*

*His earlier novels are also set in the Czech Republic or have the communist regime at their centre, including* The Joke *(1967),* Life is Elsewhere *(1969) and* The Book of Laughter and Forgetting *(1979).*

# LOVE AND GARBAGE (1986)

Ivan Klíma

A banned writer takes a job as a street sweeper in Prague before the Velvet Revolution. His job gives him the time to contemplate his life and there are musings on his lover, his time in America, his relationship with his father, and his childhood experience in a concentration camp.

While sweeping the streets he observes the lives of his fellow sweepers – a one-eyed foreman who is a failed inventor, a sickly teenager called 'the kid', a former pilot known as 'The Captain', and the only woman in the crew, Mrs Venus, a fading beauty who comes to work with bruised eyes.

Apparently written as a riposte to the unconcealed misogyny in Kundera's work, *Love and Garbage* is a warm and gentle story. The narrator meditates on the nature of love, while his lover, a fiery sculptress, and his wife, for whom he has great tenderness, wait for him to choose between them. The agony of his indecision is heartfelt and the character is redeemed by the sincerity of his feelings, while his relationship with his dying father is both poignant and powerful.

This novel is more of a wandering through the mind than through the actual streets of Prague, but the spirit of the great city is present in the heart of all Klíma has to convey, and his conversational style is very endearing.

*Love and Garbage* was initially banned by the Czech authorities and was first published in Sweden. Also set in Prague is *A Summer Affair* (1987), about a dedicated biologist who risks everything for the love of a girl he meets at a funeral.

## 📖 Read ons

*The Castle*, Franz Kafka
A land surveyor attempts to gain access to the mysterious castle and gain acceptance in the town. Written when Kafka lived in the shadow of the Hrad itself.

*Life With a Star*, Jiri Weil
An arresting and moving novella about a sickly Jewish bank clerk striving to survive as the Nazi purge of the city gathers momentum.

*The Prague Trilogy*, Sylvie Germain
In *The Weeping Woman on the Streets of Prague*, Germain tours the city using each locale as a poetic representation of a different suffering. The trilogy continues with *Infinite Possibilities* and *Invitation to a Journey*.

*Utz*, Bruce Chatwin
An art historian travels to Prague to carry out research but becomes enthralled by Utz, a man who has lost the privileged life he once led but has managed to hold on to his amazing collection of Meissen porcelain.

*The Golem*, Gustav Meyrink
Every thirty-three years a ghostly figure appears and haunts the people of the city. An unnatural creation in a wonderfully depicted Prague at the turn of the twentieth century.

*The Prague Orgy*, Philip Roth
An American novelist, on the hunt for an unpublished manuscript, embarks on a series of bizarre adventures in the mid 1970s. This novel completes the *Zuckerman Unbound Trilogy*.

# FORMER YUGOSLAVIA

*Made in Yugoslavia*, Vladimir Jokanovic
Three young men are forced to grow up quickly and face the reality of war. They must also choose which side to fight on. A fascinating look at the realities of the recent conflict in Yugoslavia.

*The Ministry of Pain*, Dubravka Ugresic
A young Croatian professor in Amsterdam encounters considerable resistance when she attempts to teach Yugoslavian literature to a disparate group of exiled students.

*The Question of Bruno*, Aleksandar Hemon **(Bosnia)**
Eight moving and well-observed stories about exile and the trauma of war are brought together in this debut collection by a half-Ukrainian, half-Serbian, writing in English.

*Lie in the Dark*, Dan Fesperman **(Bosnia)**
In shell-shocked Sarajevo, a detective is asked to investigate the death of a high-ranking police official. A plaintive paean to a suffering city.

*The Bridge on the Drina*, Ivo Andric **(Bosnia)**
In the sixteenth century, an Ottoman pasha built a bridge over the river Drina that was destroyed in 1914. This classic novel spans the period of the bridge's existence. It deservedly won the author the Nobel Prize for Literature in 1961.

*Croatian Nights*, Ed. Various **(Croatia)**
This fascinating anthology is the product of the annual Festival of Alternative Culture in Croatia and brings together nine British authors whose stories are set in Croatia, and nine authors native to Croatia, many appearing in translation for the first time.

# POLAND

KEYTITLE

*Satan in Goray*, Isaac Bashevis Singer

## SATAN IN GORAY (1935)

Isaac Bashevis Singer

Set in the seventeenth century, *Satan in Goray* centres on an isolated Polish village that becomes prey to a bout of messianic fever during the period following the Chmelnicki massacres of the 1640s. The Jews of Goray are attempting to recover from the worst period of persecution since the Crusades and believe that the end of the world is coming. When Shabbati Shevi arrives, claiming to be the Messiah, they are ready to have faith in him. The Chief Rabbi of Goray, Rabbi Benish Ashkenazi, resists him, but many others are taken in.

First published in serial form, this episodic story is told in a fractured, piecemeal way. It begins with descriptions of the brutal massacre of thousands of Jews by Ukrainian national leader, Bogdan Chmelnicki, and then recounts the return to Goray of its deeply scarred former inhabitants fifteen years after its destruction. The chief rabbi is determined to restore order and meaning to the community but when rumours of the Messiah's imminent arrival break out, a fanatical leader, Reb Gedaliya, encourages people to live for the present and religious fervour, sexual promiscuity and moral mayhem ensue.

Written in Yiddish and first published in 1935, when Singer was twenty-six and still living in Poland, *Satan in Goray* was Singer's first book and was viewed as prophetic in the light of the world events that followed shortly after. It is also a controversial book, partly because of certain historical inaccuracies, but also because of the negative light in which Jews are depicted. Nevertheless, it remains an incredibly powerful study of religious mania.

## 📖 Read ons

*The Eagle and the Crow*, Ed. Teresa Halikowska and George Hyde.
There is no better introduction to post-war Polish writing than this collection of short stories. Allegorical, comical and topical, it includes Pawel Huelle, Natasza Goerke and the playwright Slawomir Mrozek.

*Mercedes-Benz*, Pawel Huelle
A whimsical novel about a man learning to drive in post-communist Gdansk. He tells his pretty driving instructor stories from his own and Poland's history, through tales about cars.

*Pornografia: A Novel*, Witold Gombrowicz
In a country house, two middle-aged men derive vicarious sexual pleasure from the liaisons of others.

*House of Day, House of Night*, Olga Tokarczuk
An award-winning collection of interlinked short pieces that illustrate life in a small village, Nowa Ruda. Now located in Poland, the village has at various times been German, Czech and Austro-Hungarian.

*Death in Danzig*, Stefan Chwin
A beautifully realised Danzig (Gdansk) is at the heart of this impressionistic novel, set in 1945. As the Germans flee and the Russians arrive, people's lives are in chaos.

*The Fictions of Bruno Schulz*, Bruno Schulz
An epistolary novel about an eccentric family in a small 1930s' town in eastern Poland. Surreal and imaginative.

# HUNGARY

## EMBERS (1942)

Sándor Márai

Henrik, an aged reclusive general, waits in a castle beneath the Carpathian Mountains for Konrad, an old friend whom he has not seen for over forty years. The last time they met, there took place an act of betrayal so profound that it shattered both their lives and that of the general's wife, Krisztina. While he is waiting, Henrik reminisces about his life and his friendship with Konrad, whom he has known since childhood. Henrik describes their different backgrounds, lifestyles and attitudes towards life.

Henrik is rooted in the material world, its order and its traditions, while Konrad is a more passionate and artistic soul. Despite these differences, and until that fateful day, Henrik always looked upon Konrad as a brother. The question that hangs over the novel is, of course, what happened to drive the two friends apart?

When Konrad arrives, the friends partake of the same meal they ate all those years ago and Henrik proceeds to tell Konrad what has been troubling him for the past forty years. He is seeking not merely the facts but the meaning attached to them. What results is an unexpected denouement that is richly satisfying in spite of its ambiguity.

*In* Embers*, Marai poses serious questions about the nature of friendship and the role of passion in our lives, in lean, tense and atmospheric prose. This is a quiet classic which, although written in 1942, has only recently been translated into English.*

## 📖Read ons

*Leopard V – An Island of Sound*, Ed. George Szirtes
This is Hungarian poetry and fiction from before, during, and after the existence of the Iron Curtain. Labelled the 'literature of anxiety', this wonderful collection shows Hungarian writing at its most varied, exciting and inquiring.

*Transylvania Trilogy*, Miklós Bánffy
Three huge romantic and historical novels recording the decline of the aristocracy. First published in the 1930s, the books are *They Were Counted*, *They Were Found Wanting* and *They Were Divided*.

*Celestial Harmonies*, Peter Esterhazy
Over three centuries of turbulent eastern European history are covered in this extraordinary tale of an aristocratic family and its eventual decline.

*Under the Frog*, Tibor Fischer
Set in post-war communist Hungary, this amusing novel follows two young men in their adventures on the road with a travelling basketball team.

*The End of a Family Story*, Peter Nadas
In 1950s communist Hungary, an old man invents a fantastical family history for his grandson.

*The Door*, Magda Szabó
The story of a female writer and the relationship she has with her elderly house-keeper as secrets are unveiled.

*Fatelessness*, Imre Kertesz
A Jewish teenage boy relates his life as he is taken from his family home in Budapest to various concentration camps. A powerful and important book from this Nobel-Prize-winning author.

*The Book of Fathers*, Miklós Vámos
Beginning in 1705, each first-born son of the Csillag family writes down his experiences before passing the book and a genetic psychic gift on to the next generation.

*Century in Scarlet*, Lajos Zilahy
Two aristocratic brothers fight on opposing sides in revolutionary Europe in 1848. A passionate, epic novel with vivid portraits of Budapest and Vienna, from the leading Hungarian novelist of the twentieth century.

# OTHER EASTERN EUROPEAN COUNTRIES

*The Land of Green Plums*, Herta Muller **(Romania)**
This novel portrays the reality of day-to-day existence under an oppressive regime, as a group of ex-students attempt to live a normal life.

*The Balkan Trilogy*, Olivia Manning **(Romania)**
Three autobiographical novels, written in the 1960s, tell of a British couple living in Bucharest during the Second World War. Forced to flee to Greece, they eventually arrive in Egypt, where their story is continued in *The Levant Trilogy*.

*Treading Air*, Jaan Kross **(Estonia)**
This admirable novel from a highly regarded Estonian author covers most of the last century through the eyes of one man. He has to deal with both the German invasion during the war and the Soviet occupation that existed both before and after it.

*Headcrusher*, Garros-Evdokimov **(Latvia)**
A fast-paced cult novel written by two Latvian authors. A man obsessed with computer games loses touch with reality and sets out on a killing spree.

*Death and the Penguin*, Andrey Kurkov **(Ukraine)**
This is the strange tale, set in Kiev, of an obituary writer and his pet penguin and their dealings with the local mafia.

*Everything is Illuminated*, Jonathan Safran Foer **(Ukraine)**
A humorous yet deeply moving novel in which a young American journeys to the Ukraine to try to find the woman who saved his grandfather from the Nazis in the Second World War.

## CLOCKWORK ORANGES – TIME-TRAVEL

*Timeline*, Michael Crichton
Whilst viewing new technology that allows travel to another time, a professor goes missing somewhere in France in 1357. A group of historians are sent to track him down.

*My Dirty Little Book of Stolen Time*, Liz Jensen
In Copenhagen at the turn of the twentieth century, a cleaner discovers something in the basement of the strange mansion where she works and finds herself transported to twenty-first-century London.

*Orlando*, Virginia Woolf
A mock-biographical fantasy that examines notions of love and gender, this novel features a character who begins as a sixteenth-century nobleman and ends as a female writer in the 1920s.

*Slaughterhouse 5*, Kurt Vonnegut
This fantastical novel and cult classic combines the bombing of Dresden, alien abductions and time travel to highlight the atrocities and absurdities of war.

*The House on the Strand*, Daphne du Maurier
Dick Young takes a drug that sends him back to fourteenth-century Cornwall. Captivated by the period, and by a local beauty, he returns time and again until he begins to meddle with the course of history.

*The Time Traveler's Wife*, Audrey Niffenegger
A love story centring on a man who suffers from an illness that interferes with his genetic clock and pulls him unexpectedly into the past or the future. He and his long-suffering partner, Clare, struggle to lead a normal life.

*The Discovery of Chocolate*, James Runcie
This comic and quixotic tale sees a time-travelling Lothario and his dog seeking the perfect chocolate and the meaning of life.

*Live From Golgotha*, Gore Vidal
A camera crew, using newly designed technology, goes back in time to film the crucifixion live to boost their station's ratings in this clever, surreal satire on religion and the media.

*Time's Arrow*, Martin Amis
An immigrant doctor in America finds his life suddenly moving in reverse, taking him back to a dark secret from his past. A stunning and imaginative novel of the Holocaust.

*Cross Stitch*, Diana Gabaldon
In the period after the Second World War, a woman on a second honeymoon steps into a stone circle in the Scottish Highlands and finds herself whisked back in time to war-torn Scotland in the eighteenth century. Danger, and a surprising love affair, ensue.

*A Scientific Romance*, Ronald Wright
In this moving and compelling novel, set in London in 1999, David Lambert comes across H G Wells' time machine. He uses it to travel five hundred years into the future, where he finds Britain a very different place.

# SCANDINAVIA

## FINLAND

*The Summer Book*, Tove Jansson

## THE SUMMER BOOK (1972)
Tove Jansson

A grandmother and her six-year-old granddaughter spend the summer together on an island in the Gulf of Finland. Sophia's mother has died and her father has work to do, so the two of them have plenty of time on their hands. They build animal sculptures and boats from bark, pick berries, swim, and clear up in the Magic Forest. They also chat, argue and have tantrums, displaying behaviour that is subtly interchangeable. The unvoiced love in their relationship imbues the novel with tremendous warmth.

This humorous, charming and poignant book is based on a relationship between Tove Jansson's own grandmother and her niece, and is set on the very island that the Jansson family discovered and cultivated. The author uses her intimate knowledge of the place to craft wonderfully detailed descriptions of this tiny island.

*Tove Jansson is famous for the* Moomin *stories for children but she also wrote ten adult novels,* The Summer Book *being her own favourite. It was reissued in 2003, with photographs of the island and of the real Sophia and Signe, to huge acclaim.*

*The* Winter Book *(2006) was published as a companion volume and is a collection of her short stories. It includes thirteen stories from her first book for adults,* The Sculptor's Daughter *(1968), plus seven of her later stories, translated into English for the first time.*

## 📖Read ons

*Wonderful Women by the Water*, Monika Fagerholm
A melancholic account of Finnish-Swedish middle-class family life in the 1960s as two women compare lives on their annual seaside holiday.

*House of Orphans*, Helen Dunmore
An exquisitely written story of the Finnish uprising against their Russian rulers in 1901, as seen through the eyes of an orphan desperate to return to her old life in Helsinki.

*The Year of the Hare*, Arto Paasilinna
A disillusioned journalist travels around Finland with a hare for company in this wonderfully offbeat tour of the Finnish landscape and psyche. Something of a cult classic in Europe.

*Lang*, Kjell Westo
A famous chat-show host becomes involved with a mysterious woman and an increasingly dangerous love triangle develops. A tale of love and murder in a neatly visualised Finland.

*Not Before Sundown*, Johanna Sinisalo
A charming novel about a photographer who finds a troll and brings it home only to discover it has magical powers.

# SWEDEN

## DOCTOR GLAS (1905)

Hjalmar Söderberg

Set in Stockholm during the closing years of the nineteenth century, Doctor Glas is a darkly comic psychological study of a troubled and complex man. It is the journal of a misanthropic and romantic physician whose love for one of his female patients drives him to contemplate killing her husband, a local clergyman, a monstrous act rationalised by the fact that the Reverend Gregorius is elderly, odious and thoroughly undeserving of his pretty wife. The doctor advises the reverend to refrain from sexual relations with his wife, owing to her delicate medical condition, and subsequently hatches a plan to poison the pastor.

His sensitive nature makes Doctor Glas ill-suited for a profession that provides constant reminders of the sordidness and wretchedness of human existence, qualities inherent in the fact that he finds himself able to love only women who are in love with other men.

*Doctor Glas* caused a scandal when it was first published, with its views on abortion and euthanasia and its attack on the hypocritical nature of Swedish society. This modernist masterpiece continues to be well served by its 1963 translation by Paul Britten Austin.

A companion novel, *Gregorius*, by Bengt Ohlsson, considered the same circumstances from the clergyman's point of view. It won the prestigious August Prize in 2004.

## Read ons

*Hanna's Daughters*, Marianne Fredriksson
A poignant and fascinating novel that interweaves the lives of three generations of women and brings the country and its history alive. It won Book of the Year in Sweden.

*Frozen Music*, Marika Cobbold
A witty and keenly observed novel about two would-be lovers, one in Stockholm and the other in London, who are destined to be together.

*Popular Music*, Mikael Niemi
In a small isolated town in northern Sweden in the 1960s, adolescent boys grow up and do the things boys do. Crude and more than a little surreal.

*Faceless Killers*, Henning Mankel
In southern Sweden, an old couple are viciously slain. What might have been an ordinary police procedural novel is cleverly turned into an examination of a nation's racial prejudice. It is the first in the Inspector Kurt Wallander series.

*Blackwater*, Kerstin Ekman
A complex novel about a woman who believes that her daughter's new boyfriend was responsible for a murder nearly twenty years earlier.

*Roseanna*, Maj Sjowall and Per Wahloo
When a dead woman is dragged from the canal her identity remains a mystery until detective Martin Beck is put on the case. Originally published in 1967 and recently re-released, it is the first in a series.

*Missing*, Karin Alvtegen
A homeless woman with a fascinating past goes into hiding when she is suspected of murder. She decides to investigate the crime herself.

# NORWAY

| KEY TITLE |
|---|
| *The Half Brother*, Lars Saabye Christensen |

## THE HALF BROTHER (2001)
### Lars Saabye Christensen

This lengthy and dense novel centres on the relationship between two half-brothers. Barnum, the novel's narrator, is a screenwriter. Constantly in the shadows of his life lurks his half-brother, Fred, the product of the rape of their mother and a boxing sociopath whom Barnum loves and fears in equal measure. Barnum's father, Arnold, is a mysterious diminutive man who once left his family to join a circus and regularly indulges in unexplained absences. Barnum, who has inherited his father's diminutive stature, displays a dependent personality that has clearly been formed by these absences, although it is the absence of Fred that affects him most keenly, leaving him feeling incomplete.

Christensen's novel is slow-paced but the relationship between the brothers is well drawn and moving and the author moves effortlessly from comedy to pathos. Barnum's filmic exploits and his attempts to turn his family life into art illustrate the uncertainty of truth that is one of the novel's central themes.

The Half Brother *won the Nordic Prize for Literature. Christensen's other novels include* Beatles *(1984), about growing up in Norway in the late 1960s and early 1970s, and its sequel* Bly *(1990).*

## 📖Read ons

*Leopard VI – The Norwegian Feeling for Real*, Ed. Harald Bach-Wiig, Birgit Bjerck and Jan Kjaerstads
Over four decades of writing are included in this enthralling anthology of short stories, which includes pieces by Saabye Christensen, Karin Fossum and Jostein Gaarder.

*Dreamers*, Knut Hamsun
A humorous and eccentric tale set in a small Norwegian fishing village in the 1920s about the romantic escapades of a telegraph operator seeking his fortune through the manufacture of fish-glue.

*Kristin Lavransdatter*, Sigrid Undset
Fourteenth-century Norway is the setting for this magnificent trilogy of novels that centre on a woman's life and embrace politics, religion and romance. Undset won the Nobel Prize for Literature in 1928.

*Beyond Sleep*, W F Hermans
A deadpan 1960s comedy set in the Finnmark area. A Dutch geologist attempts to make a momentous discovery but is hampered by the harsh environment, his dead father and his own failings.

*The Ice Palace*, Tarjei Vesaas
This is a haunting tale from a major Norwegian author. Two eleven-year-old girls in a Norwegian village find their friendship cut drastically short.

*Out Stealing Horses*, Per Petterson
An old man looks back over his teenage years and recalls an occasion when he and a friend stole some horses, an incident that had a profound effect on both their lives.

*Beyond the Great Indoors*, Ingvar Ambjornsen
A highly original and humorous novel concerning two misfits who live together. One of a series of four novels featuring the character, Elling.

### *Don't Look Back*, Karin Fossum

When a young girl's naked body is found by a lake at the top of the Kollen Mountain, a sleepy village's innocence is lost forever. The first book in the Inspector Sejer Series.

### *The Butterfly Effect*, Pernille Rygg

A research student in a chilly Oslo finds herself applying psychology and chaos theory to the supposedly accidental death of her private detective father, whose last case she has taken over.

### *The Seducer*, Jan Kjærstad

An award-winning novel about a TV producer who returns home one day to find his wife dead. He embarks on a quest to find her killer and to assess his complicated life.

### *Shyness and Dignity*, Dag Solstad

A carefully drawn portrait of a middle-aged teacher who feels out of step with society. His life changes one fateful day.

# ICELAND

## INDEPENDENT PEOPLE (1934–35)
### Halldór Laxness

After eighteen years as a farmworker, Bjartur of Summerhouse finally has his own sheep farm, in a remote spot in the frozen wastes of Iceland. Although a modest establishment, and reputed to be haunted, it is a possession of which he is proud. A stubborn, unpleasant man who is suspicious of others and of modern ways, Bjartur takes a wife, Rosa, who quickly becomes lonely and miserable and desperate to return to the comfort of the life she knew before marriage. She dies giving birth to the daughter of the bailiff's son, a child whom Bjartur adopts as his own. The unfortunate farmer later takes another wife, who also dies.

Bjartur finds himself constantly in the face of a battle: with the elements, with strangers, with the vagaries of the economy, with the supernatural, and with death itself. Fiercely opposed to modernity, and to what he regards as creeping socialism, he finds himself abandoned by those of his sons who survive into adulthood. The only child to remain is his favourite first daughter, Asta Solilja, although, when she falls pregnant, he banishes her from his life.

This is a long book full of black humour and humanity, a moving story of love and survival. Beautifully written, it has a cast of marvellous characters: especially enchanting are the poet wife of the bailiff and their politically ambitious son, Ingolfur. The novel gives an interesting insight into Iceland's economic and political development through the early part of the twentieth century as it affects a remote farming community.

*Halldór Laxness won the Nobel Prize for Literature in 1955 for 'renewing the great narrative art of Iceland'.*

## 🐚Read ons

*The Journey Home*, Olaf Olafsson

In the mid 1960s, a hotel manager discovers she is terminally ill and decides to travel from England to the Iceland of her childhood. Rich and painful memories of her troubled life come flooding back.

*101 Reykjavik*, Hallgrimur Helgason

A tour of Reykjavik's seedier side. A thirty-something slacker, living at home with his mother, has to take action when her lesbian lover moves in and his girlfriend announces she is pregnant.

*Tainted Blood*, Arnaldur Indridason

When an old man's murder reveals many hidden secrets, Detective Erlendur discovers a purely Icelandic solution. An award-winning novel set in a bleak and rainy Reykjavik, this is the first of a series.

*The Killer's Guide to Iceland*, Zane Radcliffe

A Scotsman moves in with his Icelandic girlfriend's family in Reykjavik, but when his past catches up with him, they are all at risk.

# DENMARK

KEYTITLE

*Miss Smilla's Feeling for Snow*, Peter Høeg

## MISS SMILLA'S FEELING FOR SNOW (1992)
Peter Høeg

When a neighbour's six-year-old boy, Isaiah, falls to his death from the roof of a block of flats in Copenhagen, Smilla Jaspersen seems to be the only one who doubts the police's assessment that the death was an accident. Smilla is an intelligent and determined woman with an instinctual knowledge of snow that she uses to read the tracks at the crime scene, an examination that leads her to the conclusion that the boy's death was murder. The boy, a Greenlander like herself, was her only real friend and her investigation into his death places her own life at risk and leads her all the way to the Arctic Circle.

Høeg's descriptions of place are vibrant and the pace of this psychological novel is suitably slow. The character of Smilla is cleverly drawn and the most is made of her Inuit roots and outsider status, allowing her to see what the Danes cannot. Through her, Høeg reveals the problems caused by Denmark's colonisation of Greenland and the harsh treatment that Inuit Greenlanders receive in Danish society. Smilla's relationships with her father and prospective lover are portrayed with sly humour and intelligence.

What begins as an unconventional detective story becomes a global spy thriller when a connection emerges between the boy's death and operations run by a mining company in Greenland. At this point, the mystery surrounding the death begins to melt away.

*Miss Smilla's Feeling For Snow* gives the reader an invigorating sense of place that perfectly articulates the tension between between nature and the modern world. It was made into a film by Bille August in 1997.

## ⮛Read ons

*Anecdotes of Destiny*, Isak Dinesen (Karen Blixen)
These tales show Denmark's most famous author at her gothic and florid best, weaving magic out of myth.

*The Visit of the Royal Physician*, Per Olov Enquist
Based on a true story, this novel tells of a German doctor summoned to help the mentally unstable King of Denmark, Christian VII, in the eighteenth century.

*Lucca*, Jens Christian Grondahl
A young actress is blinded in a car accident and spends her recovery with an emotionally damaged doctor. A reflective and beautifully written novel.

*Imago*, Eva-Marie Liffner
An unidentified body found in a peat bog provokes an amateur historian to turn detective in this entertaining and unusual thriller.

*Prince*, Ib Michael
An enchanting novel about a twelve-year-old boy who spends the summer of 1912 in a small Danish coastal village.

*Music and Silence*, Rose Tremain
Set in the seventeenth century, this novel sees an English lute player discover a world of intrigue and temptation at the Danish Royal Court, to which he has been summoned to play for the King.

## READONATHEME

### NORSE ODES – VIKINGS

*Meadowland*, Thomas Holt
A fascinating story from a renowned historical novelist about the Vikings' discovery, settlement and abandonment of a place they called Meadowland, which Columbus would famously discover 450 years later.

*Thunder God*, Paul Watkins
An action-packed and thought-provoking drama about a humble Viking who, after being kidnapped, embarks on an odyssey that takes him to Constantinople, Wales and across the Atlantic to the New World.

*The Last Kingdom*, Bernard Cornwell
The first in a series, this novel is set during the reign of King Alfred, when England was under siege by Viking hordes. The events are recounted through the eyes of Uhtred, a man with conflicting loyalties.

*Viking: Odinn's Child*, Tim Severin
The first part of a trilogy that follows the adventures of Viking Thorgils Leifsson, from his childhood in Greenland to the battlefields of England in 1066.

*Saga: A Novel of Medieval Iceland*, Jeff Janoda
A skilful retelling of an ancient Norse saga that brings to life tenth-century Iceland. Two rival chieftains fight for control of the land.

*The Greenlanders*, Jane Smiley
Smiley recreates the Norse sagas in this epic tale of the Gunnarsson family struggling to deal with family feuds and the hostile elements as a mini ice age approaches in fourteenth-century Greenland.

*The Sea Road*, Margaret Elphinstone
The Vikings' first attempts to settle in Newfoundland in the eleventh century are recounted through the eyes of the remarkable Gudrid, a strong and adventurous woman in a male-dominated world.

## POLE TO POLE – ARCTIC/ANTARCTIC

*North*, Roger Hubank
Based on a true story, this novel describes the tragic consequences of America's attempts to join the Arctic exploration race in the late nineteenth century.

*Afterlands*, Steven Heighton
A fictionalised version of the 1871 Polaris expedition to reach the North Pole, in which half the expedition's crew became stranded on an ice floe for several months. The novel describes the effects of the expedition on the survivors as they return to their various native countries.

*White*, Marie Darrieussecq
An intriguing and poetic novella, set in 2015 AD, about two runaways who join an assorted group of scientists attempting to build a permanent European base in Antarctica.

*The Birthday Boys*, Beryl Bainbridge
An enthralling account of the ill-fated Antarctic expedition led by Captain Scott in 1912, re-told by key members of the team in absorbing first-person narratives.

*Antarctic Navigation*, Elizabeth Arthur
This gargantuan book chronicles a woman's obsessive recreation of Scott's expedition and describes her fascinating experiences at the South Pole.

*Mrs. Chippy's Last Expedition: The Remarkable Journal of Shackleton's Polar-Bound Cat*, Caroline Alexander
This novel offers a different perspective on Shackleton's 1914 expedition to reach the South Pole aboard the *Endurance*. It includes photographs and drawings from the original members.

*Victim of the Aurora*, Thomas Kenneally
In this murder mystery, set in 1909, a captain has to investigate his own crew when, during an Antarctic expedition, one of its members is found dead on the ice.

*Cold Skin*, Albert Sánchez Piñol
A surreal psychological thriller about a weather observer on a tiny island at the edge of the Antarctic Circle, visited nightly by sea creatures.

*See also* **READ ON A THEME: TO THE ENDS OF THE EARTH – EXPLORERS, DISCOVERERS, ADVENTURERS**

# GERMANY

**KEY**TITLES

*The Reader*, Bernard Schlink
*The Dark Room*, Rachel Seiffert
*The Tin Drum*, Günter Grass

## THE READER (1995)
### Bernhard Schlink

In 1954, a teenage boy, Michael Berg, falls ill on the way home from school and is rescued by a tram conductor, Hanna Schmitz, a woman in her thirties. They embark on a sexual relationship. Each time he visits, she gets him to read to her before their lovemaking. When she suddenly disappears after a misunderstanding, he is devastated and blames himself for her departure.

Their paths cross again, years later, when he is a law student. Hanna has been convicted of war crimes. He feels guilty for having loved such a person and yet is keen to understand her motives, which seem to spring more from pragmatism than anything more sinister and he believes he can help her, but has a philosophical dilemma about whether anyone has the right to help another, if they are not prepared to help themselves. Hanna, seemingly, has no comprehension of her guilt until she reads up on the subject and it is as though there are set reactions one must have if one is to be human.

Years pass and Michael marries and is later divorced. He seems to exist in an emotional void, as though the guilty secret of his adolescent relationship has stripped him of feeling. Eight years into Hanna's incarceration, he decides to read some of his favourite novels onto tape and he sends them to her, with no accompanying letters or notes. This one-way correspondence continues for a decade, until Hanna's imminent parole and the prospect of a meeting.

*Bernhard Schlink, a judge and a writer of detective fiction, produces in this work a narrative that is both insightful and heartfelt.*

# THE DARK ROOM (2001)
Rachel Seiffert

This book consists of three novellas linked by similar themes. The central character of the first novella is Helmut, born in Berlin in 1921, with a disability that makes him unable to use his right arm properly – significant in the fact he cannot give the Nazi salute. His isolated upbringing makes him an outsider who cannot function in the real world. Obsessed by trains and photography, he spends hours every day in the station, making a photographic record of deportations with a dispassionate eye. His disability notwithstanding, he is a loyal supporter of the Nazi party.

The second novella tells the story of twelve-year-old Lore and her flight across postwar Germany with her three younger siblings, escaping the condemnation and imprisonment that would be visited on these children of a high-ranking Nazi. Their mother, facing imprisonment herself, urges the children to flee to Hamburg to be with their grandmother. It is a harrowing journey undertaken at a time when Germany was divided into zones through which passage was extremely difficult without the relevant papers.

Thirdly, in modern-day Berlin, a young teacher, Micha, begins to question his devotion to his grandfather, Askan, when his grandmother inadvertently reveals that he was a member of the Waffen SS. He begins to explore his family's history and official records, an obsessive search that takes him to the heart of the problem of redemption.

Written in sparse, cool prose, this thought-provoking and intelligent book asks serious questions not just about the legacy of the Nazi period but about human nature itself.

*Seiffert's* Field Study *(2004) is a collection of short stories, most of which are set in post-Communist East Germany and Poland.*

# THE TIN DRUM (1959)
Günter Grass

Oskar Matzerath is telling his life story from an asylum where he has been incarcerated after being falsely accused of murder. He is a drum-playing midget who intentionally stopped growing from the age of three, when he received his first tin drum. Oskar begins his story at the turn of the twentieth century with the tale of his grandparents. They were Kashubes from a northern region of Poland, who moved to Danzig, where Oskar's mother, Agnes, was born. She marries a member of the Nazi party, Alfred Matzerath, but maintains a life-long affair with her cousin, Jan Bronski, with the result that Oskar does not know which of the men is his real father. His mother dies before the outbreak of war and Jan is executed for his part in resisting the German invasion. His putative father, Alfred, then marries an employee of his, Maria, believing he has made her pregnant, when in fact the father of the baby is Oskar. Their son, Kurt, rejects Oskar, who eventually becomes rich as the drummer in a jazz band.

This highly symbolic novel presents the reader with a cavalcade of grotesquery in which the surreal mixes with the very real. Oskar is symbolic of a German people refusing to mature and take responsibility for past actions. When Oskar arranges his own arrest for a murder he did not commit, it is an action expressive of the collective guilt felt by the German people in the postwar years.

*Günter Grass received the Nobel Prize for Literature in 1999, notwithstanding revelations that he had been a member of the SS in his youth.*

*The Tin Drum* is the first part of *The Danzig Trilogy*, of which the companion volumes are *Cat and Mouse* (1961) and *Dog Years* (1963). An Oscar-winning film was made of *The Tin Drum* in 1978.

## 🐦Read ons

*The Hothouse*, Walter Koeppen
In postwar Germany, a once-idealistic politician wrestles with his conscience before a vote in parliament over disarmament. The first of a loose trilogy of which the companion volumes are *Pigeons on the Grass* and *Death in Rome*.

*Buddenbrooks*, Thomas Mann
An excellent new translation has recently reinvigorated this 1901 classic, which Mann wrote when he was just twenty-five, about the decline of four generations of an aristocratic family.

*The Lost Honour of Katharina Blum*, Heinrich Böll
A woman is driven to extremes when she is hounded by the press over her innocent involvement with a member of the Red Army Faction, in a terrorist-obsessed Germany in the 1970s

*Narziss and Goldmund*, Herman Hesse
A serious exploration of Dionysian and Apollonian philosophies. In a medieval monastery, a monk, Narziss, sends his friend and novice, Goldmund, away to experience the world, while he stays behind in spiritual contemplation.

*All Quiet on the Western Front*, Erich Maria Remarque
A classic anti-war novel about a generation destroyed by the Great War. A nineteen-year-old student is encouraged to enlist by his schoolmaster and is unable to cope with the horrors he witnesses.

*The Blue Flower*, Penelope Fitzgerald
A short lyrical novel, based on a true story, about the poet Novalis and his engagement to a twelve-year-old girl, Sophie, in eighteenth-century Saxony.

*A Legacy*, Sybille Bedford
A story set in the Kaiser's Germany. Two families connected by marriage – one Jewish and residing in Berlin, the other aristocratic in rural Baden – live in ignorant bliss of the military conflict to come.

*How German Is It?*, Walter Abish
A writer returns to Germany to a town built on a former concentration camp and is forced to confront a country struggling to cope with its present difficulties and past actions.

*Elizabeth and Her German Garden*, Elizabeth von Arnim
A witty account of life in Pomerania, written by a young Englishwoman who marries a German count and has little aptitude for running a family in a large country house.

*In a German Pension*, Katherine Mansfield
Published in 1911, this is a wonderfully observant series of satirical sketches of German characteristics.

*Heart's Journey in Winter*, James Buchan
A compelling and complex thriller set in 1983 as the Cold War enters its final phase. British Agent Richard Fisher, working on an assignment, falls for an American undercover spy.

*The Quest for Christa T*, Christa Wolf
One of the first significant books to come out of the former East Germany, it tells the story of a woman growing up under Communist rule.

*The Emigrants*, W G Sebald
A moving account of exile and loss that combines elements of fiction, biography and autobiography. It traces the personal histories of four Jewish émigrés.

*Reunion*, Fred Uhlman
A slim but profound novel that describes an intense friendship between two teenagers, one Jewish, the other an aristocratic German, which is soon dissolved after Hitler's rise to power.

# BERLIN

**KEY**TITLES

*The Wall Jumper*, Peter Schneider
*Goodbye to Berlin*, Christopher Isherwood

## THE WALL JUMPER (1982)
Peter Schneider

*The Wall Jumper* begins more like an essay than a novel in the conventional sense, and gradually builds into a series of observations and stories about people living on both sides of the city. Schneider makes good use of his journalistic skills to paint a picture of Berlin before the Wall came down. Most readers will find their assumptions about the lives of Berliners challenged by this most rare of books.

The Berlin Wall is a potent symbol of divided ideologies but it is its concrete presence that inspires the tales of many of the book's characters, such as three young moviegoers who disappear over the Wall every Friday afternoon to watch westerns in a cinema in West Berlin; and Kabe, the Wall Jumper, who tackles the Wall from the Western side with all the dedication of a mountaineer.

*Schneider's approach is humanistic, enquiring, and laced with sly humour.* The Wall Jumper *was reissued as a modern classic in 2005, with an introduction by Ian McEwan.*

# GOODBYE TO BERLIN (1939)

Christopher Isherwood

The famous opening sentence – 'I am a camera with its shutter open, quite passive, recording, not thinking' – sets the tone of the book. The character Christopher Isherwood, who, the reader is assured, is not Christopher Isherwood the author, moves through the novel like a ghost upon the water, observing and noting without judging.

The setting is Berlin in the early 1930s, and Nazism is on the rise but has not yet taken hold. The book presents a vivid picture of the demi-monde of Weimar Berlin. 'Isherwood' lives with Fraulein Schroeder and a host of interesting characters: prostitutes, bartenders and former stars of the stage, the most famous of whom is Sally Bowles, a vivacious and sexually reckless English girl who is one of the greatest creations of modern English literature.

The author lived in Berlin during this period and his experience feeds into this vivid portrait of a society on the brink of extinction, dancing itself into a frenzy before the music stops.

Originally written as parts of a planned episodic novel provisionally entitled *The Lost*, these fragments nonetheless constitute a powerful piece of work, one that formed the basis of a play, *I Am a Camera* (1951), and, of course, the renowned musical *Cabaret* (1972), featuring Liza Minnelli's tour-de-force performance as Sally Bowles.

*Mr Norris Changes Trains* (1935), also known as *The Last of Mr Norris*, is a prequel of sorts. *The Berlin Stories* brings the books together in a single volume.

## 📖 Read ons

*Berlin Alexanderplatz*, Alfred Döblin
A prisoner is released from jail and attempts to make a better life for himself, but circumstances and society bring him down, in this stream-of-consciousness novel set in 1929.

*Right and Left*, Joseph Roth
1920s' Berlin is brilliantly evoked in this story of two contrasting brothers reacting differently to the economic and political upheavals around them.

*The Innocent*, Ian McEwan
A naïve English postal worker is caught up in Cold War shenanigans in the 1950s, when he becomes involved in a plot to dig a tunnel to gain access to a Soviet communications system.

*Pleasured*, Philip Hensher
On the eve of the year the Wall came down, the lives of two aimless drifters change irrevocably when they accept a lift from a shadowy Englishman with a plan to flood East Berlin with Ecstasy pills.

*The Spy Who Came in From the Cold*, John Le Carré
Graham Greene called this book 'the best spy novel ever written'. It concerns a British operative who defects in order to save a double agent already operating in East Germany.

*Funeral in Berlin*, Len Deighton
Bluffs and double-bluffs abound in this tale of a Russian scientist offered to British intelligence for a price. MI5 send their best man to negotiate terms.

*The Berlin Noir Trilogy*, Philip Kerr
These three novels follow the criminal investigations of smart-talking private investigator, Bernie Gunther, during and after the Second World War. The individual books are *March Violets*, *The Pale Criminal* and *A German Requiem*.

### *All Souls' Day*, Cees Nooteboom
A widowed Dutch filmmaker walks the streets of Berlin reflecting on life and his latest film project – the world through his eyes. Then he begins an affair with an impulsive student.

### *King, Queen, Knave*, Vladimir Nabokov
In 1920s' Berlin the young wife of the owner of a clothes shop seduces his myopic and naïve nephew and together they plan her husband's murder.

# THE NETHERLANDS

*The Assault*, Harry Mulisch

## THE ASSAULT (1982)
Harry Mulisch

This fascinating novel, based on a true incident, is told in five episodes over forty years. The saga begins with twelve-year-old Anton Steenwijk, living with his parents and older brother, Peter, in Haarlem, at the end of the Second World War. The Chief Inspector of police and Nazi collaborator, Fake Ploeg, is shot outside a neighbour's house, but someone moves the body to the doorstep of the Steenwijk house. Anton's family is shot in reprisal and their house is burnt down. Anton is taken away to a police station where he shares a cell with a woman who is, unbeknown to him, a Resistance fighter.

Anton is later sent to live with his uncle and aunt in Amsterdam, where he attempts to carve out a normal existence. He grows up learning to suppress his feelings (and chooses a career as an anaesthetist) but finds himself constantly tormented by his past. He meets Fake Ploeg's son, an old schoolfriend who has now fallen on hard times. He claims that his own father was as innocent as Anton's. Anton also meets the man who actually did shoot Fake Ploeg and, here again, the question of guilt and responsibility is blurred. Eventually he discovers which neighbour moved Ploeg's body and why they chose his family's house as the place in which to lay it.

The novel has a restrained approach to its subject matter, with something of the quality of a detective story, albeit one with a passive, reluctant investigator.

With references to Dutch politics and world events, including the Hungary uprising, Vietnam, and the release from prison of the Dutch head of the Gestapo, this enthralling book attempts to shed light on questions of culpability and the actions of ordinary people forced to live in extraordinary times.

*The Assault* was made into an Oscar-winning film in 1986.

## Read ons

*The Darkroom of Damocles*, W F Hermans
An excellent novel about a psychologically damaged man given a series of missions by a dubious doppelgänger. A morally ambiguous tale set during the Second World War.

*The Vanishing*, Tim Krabbé
Eight years after his girlfriend vanished at a petrol station whilst travelling in France, writer Rex Hoffman is still obsessed with her disappearance. A stranger contacts him, claiming to know her whereabouts.

*The Following Story*, Cees Nooteboom
A slim, surreal tale from one of Holland's most acclaimed writers. Herman Mussert goes to bed one night in Amsterdam and awakes the following day in a hotel in Portugal.

*The Twins*, Tessa De Loo
Two elderly and estranged twins meet by accident at a health resort and relate their wartime experiences on opposing sides of the conflict.

*A Heart of Stone*, Renate Dorrestein
A pregnant single woman moves into her old family home and recalls an unhappy incident that marred her otherwise blissful childhood.

*On the Water*, H M van den Brink
Two young men find friendship and freedom through rowing, in the shadow of the impending war, as they prepare for the 1940 Olympics that never happened.

*The Apothecary's House*, Adrian Mathews
When an art archivist investigates the claims of two very different people on a painting in Amsterdam's Rijksmuseum, she uncovers Nazi connections and starts receiving sinister threats.

*In Babylon*, Marcel Möring
While holed up in a snow-bound country house, an elderly writer of fairy tales entertains his niece with the story of their eccentric clock-making East European ancestors. Winner of two major European prizes.

*The Two Hearts of Kwasi Boachi*, Arthur Japin
This novel is based on the astonishing true story of two Ghanaian princes sent to a Dutch boarding school in 1837. Kwasi, now in Indonesia, recalls his life and the fate of his cousin, Kwame.

# BELGIUM

*Bruges-la-Morte*, Georges Rodenbach
This is ostensibly the account of a doomed love affair, but the real purpose of this bizarre novel is to celebrate the 'dead city' of Bruges.

*Cheese*, Willem Elsschot
A delightfully comic novella, set in the 1930s, about an inept office clerk who leaves his day job to set up a business selling Edam cheese.

*The Sorrow of Belgium*, Hugo Claus
This classic novel is a wickedly funny autobiographical portrait of one boy's coming-of-age in wartime Belgium.

*Antwerp*, Nicholas Royle
An American film director turns detective when the film he is making about a surrealist artist is halted owing to the deaths of two prostitutes employed as extras.

*The Folding Star*, Alan Hollinghurst
The nature of desire is explored in detail as a gay English tutor falls for his seventeen-year-old student. In a different era, a painter obsessively paints his dead lover's portrait.

# AUSTRIA

**KEY**TITLES

*The Man Without Qualities*, Robert Musil
*The Radetzky March*, Joseph Roth

## THE MAN WITHOUT QUALITIES (1930–1942)
Robert Musil

This three-volume unfinished novel of ideas is set during the decline of the Austro-Hungarian Empire, opening in Vienna in 1913. Ulrich, the hero of the title, is involved in planning the jubilee celebration of Emperor Franz Josef's seventieth year. They are looking for a unifying idea that will stir the patriotic soul of the Austro-Hungarian people.

Ulrich finds himself unable to engage in the world in a way that makes sense to him. Lacking in what society terms 'qualities', he seeks to find some meaning in life and to discover what to believe in if there is no God. He is seeking to marry together a scientific view of the world with the mystical, what he calls 'the hovering life' that is all round us. Meanwhile the whole of society is fascinated by the trial of a murderer, Moorbrugger. Ulrich is especially intrigued, seeing the killer as the physical representation of the 'monster in the mind' which is the human capacity for monstrous acts, which lays dormant in most individuals, but is accessible to artists – and obviously violent criminals. Only by the third volume do the true themes begin to express themselves, as we find Ulrich drifting into 'the last love story of all', a relationship with his 'forgotten' sister, Agathe, seeing their bond as a mystical union with the 'other'.

Musil's style is precise to the point of being essayistic, but it is also witty and urbane. He claims that his novels are written for people who do not exist. That fact notwithstanding, Milan Kundera, among others, has declared *The Man Without Qualities* to be one of the best literary works of the twentieth century.

The first two volumes were published in 1930 and 1932. Musil was still working on the third volume at the time of his death in 1942, having regretted publishing the first two volumes early. The third volume was published posthumously, but the whole work remained unfinished in the eyes of the author.

A new and rather Americanised translation by Sophie Wilkins and Burton Pike was published in 1995. The earlier Eithne Wilkins and Ernst Kaiser translations are recommended.


# THE RADETSKY MARCH (1932)
## Joseph Roth

A modern masterpiece about the Habsburg dynasty and three generations of the Trotta family in particular. The book begins with the 'hero of Solferine', an army lieutenant ennobled after saving the life of the Kaiser in 1859. It ends with the end of the First World War and the demise of the Austro-Hungarian Empire.

The original baron, Joseph von Trotta, drifts into obscurity, while his son, Franz, becomes a government functionary depressed at his own nondescript existence. Franz's son, Carl Joseph, joins the army and sets about developing a roistering identity for himself, which he does scandalously well through extra-marital affairs, the non-payment of gambling debts, the fighting of duels, and general excess. He is redeemed by the good name of his family, earned through the bravery of his grandfather. Carl Joseph's dissolute lifestyle is emblematic of the unravelling of the empire.

Roth's writing has a lucid quality and the story features impressive set pieces and haunting descriptions of landscape and place. The epic and the intimate are dealt with equally well and the relationship of increasing irrelevance between the fading generations is poignantly handled.

*The Radetsky March*, perhaps Roth's best-known and most successful book, was banned by the Nazis. A new edition was published by Granta in 2002, expertly translated by the poet Michael Hoffman.

*The Emperor's Tomb* (1938) continues something of the story of *The Radetsky March*. Roth also wrote *The String of Pearls* (1939), which is wonderfully evocative of old Vienna.

## 📖Read ons

*The Piano Teacher*, Elfriede Jelinek
A forty-year-old, virginal piano teacher who secretly trawls the red light district begins a bizarre sexual affair with one of her students.

*Homestead*, Rosina Lippi
Twelve poignant interconnected stories link three generations of women in a remote Alpine village, spanning eighty years and centring on pivotal moments in their lives.

*Badenheim 1939*, Aron Appelfeld
A group of middle-class Jews arrive at an Austrian holiday resort in spring 1939, hoping for a relaxing time. They are unprepared for the horror that is to come.

*Dream Story*, Arthur Schnitzler
Set in turn-of-the-century Vienna, this is a dream-like novella that follows two days in the life of a doctor as he roams from one erotic encounter to the next.

*Beware of Pity*, Stefan Zweig
Zweig's elegant and assured prose is at its finest in his only full-length novel. An army officer's life is turned upside down when he takes pity on a disabled rich girl who has fallen in love with him.

*The Third Man*, Graham Greene
When writer Rollo Martins arrives in postwar Vienna in search of Harry Lime, his old friend who has offered him work, he arrives just in time for Lime's funeral. But who is it that has died?

*The Fig Eater*, Jody Shields
An inspector finds his psychic wife intruding upon his investigation into the death of Sigmund Freud's famous patient, Dora, in 1910 Vienna.

# SWITZERLAND

*Her Lover (Belle de Seigneur)*, Albert Cohen
Hailed as 'the most beautiful love story ever told', this story sees a Jewish official at the League of Nations risk his reputation by starting an affair with the beautiful wife of a colleague.

*The Cow*, Beat Sterchi
A Spanish guestworker experiences racism and hardship when he goes to work as a farm labourer and ends up in a slaughterhouse.

*Thumbprint*, Friedrich Glauser
From the pen of a troubled author known as the Swiss Georges Simenon, this is the first of five novels about Sergeant Studer, a police detective who discovers sinister goings-on behind cool Swiss exteriors.

*Hotel du Lac*, Anita Brookner
An idealistic single woman is sent to Switzerland by friends exasperated by her rejection of a suitable but dull fiancé. Her stay makes her realise what it is she wants from life.

READONATHEME

## TRAVELS WITH OR WITHOUT AUNTS – FICTIONAL ODYSSEYS

*Travels With My Aunt*, Graham Greene
After a dull suburban life, a retired bank manager meets his seventy-year-old aunt at a funeral. She shows him what life has to offer as they travel the world together.

*Balthasar's Odyssey*, Amin Maalouf
As 1666 approaches, Balthasar sets out from his Levantine shop on a journey across Europe in search of a rare book that may contain the secrets of how to survive the 'Year of the Beast'.

*You Shall Know Our Velocity*, Dave Eggers
Two Americans, shocked by the death of a close friend, embark on a week-long trip around the world to assuage their western materialist guilt by giving away money to people in need.

*The Bastard Boy*, James Wilson
A man on the trail of his missing nephew goes from Georgian England, across the Atlantic, to Revolutionary America. He find himself in a prison cell with no idea how he came to be there.

*Summer in Baden-Baden*, Leonid Tsypkin
A double-narrative novel that follows Tsypkin journeying to Leningrad to see the place where Dostoevsky died, and also recounts a journey made by Dostoevsky himself in 1867 across Europe to Baden-Baden.

*Ingenious Pain*, Andrew Miller
A superbly written atmospheric novel that tells the story of a man insensitive to pain who travels to Russia to inoculate the Empress Catherine against smallpox.

*Hallucinating Foucault*, Patricia Duncker
A young Cambridge student sets out for the South of France to track down a highly revered but mad writer. A stylish literary thriller that poses questions on gender and madness.

*The Riders*, Tim Winton
A panic-stricken Fred Scully trails around Europe with his daughter to track down his wife when she fails to get off a flight from Australia.

*To the Wedding*, John Berger
A poetic and moving novel about a woman who, shortly before her wedding, discovers she is HIV positive. Meanwhile, her estranged parents are making separate journeys, from Slovakia and France, to be at the wedding.

*To the Last City*, Colin Thubron
Five Europeans trek through the Peruvian Andes to visit the ancient ruined cities of the Incas. The journey, intended to be mesmerising and enlightening, is a physical and mental challenge to all, leading to soul-searching, dissatisfaction and disaster.

# ITALY

## KEYTITLES

*The Leopard*, Giuseppi Tomasi di Lampedusa
*The Moon and the Bonfires*, Cesare Pavese
*The Garden of the Finzi-Continis*, Giorgio Bassani
*Journey by Moonlight*, Antal Szerb

## THE LEOPARD (1958)

Giuseppe di Lampedusa

Giuseppe di Lampedusa was descended from an old aristocratic Italian family and based this novel on the life of his own great-grandfather. The book is the product of twenty-five years' work and the studied prose speaks of labour and dedication. It is the story of Don Fabrizio, Prince of Salina, at the time of Italy's Risorgimento (circa 1860). He is a proud, sensual man who knows the aristocracy's days are numbered as Italy prepares for unification and democracy.

Don Fabrizio's allegiances are with the old regime but he is wise enough not to become involved in the conflict. His favourite nephew, the charming Tancredi, is a supporter of the leader of the revolution, Garibaldi. He initially has designs on the Prince's daughter, Concetta, but turns his attentions to the wealthy but less aristocratic Angelica. Through a series of wonderfully described set pieces, we see Don Fabrizio's family at play, luxuriating in a world that is already crumbling.

Lampedusa's elegant prose takes us into the heart of the characters: Concetta's unrequited love for Tancredi, the dialogue between Don Fabrizio and Father Pirrone on the Prince's infidelities, even the antics of the dog, Bendicò, are all brought vividly to life with humour and pathos.

*The author died in 1957, soon after receiving the assessment that, owing to political pressures, his novel would never be published. It was, however, rescued by Giorgio Bassani and published posthumously the following year. It became an instant success, although it did attract controversy, not least because of its portrayal of the Catholic Church.*

A lavish film by Luchino Visconti was made in 1963.

# THE MOON AND THE BONFIRES (1950)
## Cesare Pavese

After twenty years in America, Anguilla returns to his home town, the Piedmontese village where he was born. He was a foundling, left on the steps of the local church and raised by a poor farmer who, although paid for his parenting, treated the boy no better than he did his animals. Anguilla returns to Gaminella having made his fortune in America, believing that, despite his uncertain parentage, he belongs to this part of the world. He even contemplates settling down.

He spends time with his old friend, Nuto, and recalls episodes from his unhappy childhood. These episodes, together with revelations from local villagers, enable him to better make sense of the wartime tragedies that still have reverberations for everyone concerned. Many ex-fascists and their victims have lived side by side since the war and the ghosts of the past cannot easily be laid to rest. The emptiness that seems to mark the lives of the locals, set against the beauty of their surroundings, makes Anguilla feel once more that he is outside the society to which he seeks to belong.

Written in cold, dispassionate prose, its lyrical evocations of the countryside around Turin are beautifully, if starkly, rendered. Generally regarded as a master-piece of twentieth-century literature, *The Moon and the Bonfires* is now available in an award-winning translation by R W Flint.

*The Moon and the Bonfires* was published posthumously, as Pavese committed suicide not long after its completion. Notoriously cynical, his published journals were given the suitably sardonic title of *The Business of Living* (1952).

*Cesare Pavese was a major postwar Italian literary figure who wrote nine short novels, including* The Devil in the Hills *(1949) and* Among Women Only *(1953). Together they constitute a rich portrait of modern Italy. A selection of his major works is available in one volume,* Selected Works of Cesare Pavese *(2001).*

# THE GARDEN OF THE FINZI-CONTINIS (1965)
Giorgio Bassani

This autobiographical novel is a poignant tale of unrequited love in the Jewish community in Mussolini's Italy, in the author's hometown of Ferrara. The Finzi-Continis are an aristocratic Jewish family who live in a villa in the middle of a large park – the 'garden' of the title. When their eldest child dies, they retreat into their own world by educating their daughter and younger son themselves, only rarely being seen outside, at the Synagogue or at school exam times. The unnamed narrator catches glimpses of the children as he too is growing up, but they do not speak to each other.

Although the action of the story only occasionally strays from the garden, the reader is given a sense of the world outside the walls. The beautiful descriptions of the flora mirror the countryside beyond, while the dynamics of the family and the relationships between the friends highlight the shifting sands of Italian society as hostilities increase. When Jews are excluded from the town's tennis club, the brother and sister invite some friends, including the narrator, to their own private court. He gradually falls in love with the Finzi-Contini's daughter, Micòl, who does not return his affection. Lives are shattered when the Finzi-Continis are arrested and deported to a concentration camp, where they suffer a brutal and anonymous fate.

*The Garden of the Finzi-Continis* is a haunting book that, in spite of the horrors it contains, recalls a lost period of simple elegance. William Weaver's translation is the more accomplished of those available and captures the tone of the book perfectly.

An excellent award-winning film was made by Vittorio de Sica in 1971.

# JOURNEY BY MOONLIGHT (1937)
Antal Szerb

A Hungarian businessman, Mihály, and his new wife, Erzsi, are on honeymoon in Italy. Already Mihály has discovered that he is unsuited for marriage and he begins to fantasise about his wife leaving him, almost as soon as they arrive in Venice. Having forced himself to marry in an effort to cultivate a maturity that escapes him, he comes to the conclusion that he is not like other men.

A chance meeting with an old friend brings memories of an intense youthful friendship Mihály enjoyed back in Hungary with Tamás and Éva, bohemian school friends of his who committed suicide. These memories reveal Mihály to be something of an old romantic, nostalgic for a more passionate and carefree past.

The couple journey around Italy visiting its art treasures and architectural splendours. When they are accidentally separated at the train station in Terontola, Mihály quite happily spends time on his own, sending Erzsi a telegram instructing her not to try to find him. He promptly takes up with an American art student called Millicent.

Erzsi is also on a journey of her own, hoping to escape her bourgeois life by marrying the unconventional Mihály, but her tendency to get mixed up with manipulative men who treat her badly does not desert her, even when she goes to Paris.

This wonderful novel is a serious comedy, farcical and ironic and yet also heavily symbolic. Len Rix's translation captures the tone of the original very well, although the free translation of the title is something of a mystery.

# ⬚Read ons

*I'm Not Scared*, Niccolò Ammaniti
In southern Italy during a sweltering summer, a young boy makes a horrifying discovery that has repercussions for him and his whole family. A shocking drama from one of Italian literature's brightest stars.

*The Name of the Rose*, Umberto Eco
This richly layered historical novel engages with semiotics, theology and philosophy. It features a medieval monk investigating a series of crimes in a Franciscan monastery.

*The Wine-Dark Sea*, Leonardo Sciascia
Thirteen stories told in the realist style from this excellent Sicilian author who masterfully evokes the people and the attitudes of the island.

*Contempt*, Alberto Moravia
A short modernist masterpiece about an intellectual writer reduced to writing screenplays who becomes convinced that his wife no longer loves him.

*Casa Rossa*, Francesca Marciano
Casa Rossa, a crumbling family estate in Puglia, is up for sale. As she packs up the house, Alina Strada recounts the history of three generations of her extraordinary female ancestors.

*History: A Novel*, Elsa Morante
This long and serious novel looks at war though the eyes of ordinary people. An Italian woman is raped by a German soldier and attempts to ensure the survival of her child.

*Conversations in Sicily*, Elio Vittorini
First published in 1941, this groundbreaking anti-fascist novel, for which the author was imprisoned, deals with a son who returns to his homeland after learning that his father has left his mother.

*The Talented Mr Ripley*, Patricia Highsmith
The first in Highsmith's excellent series of crime novels featuring sinister Tom Ripley. Roaming through various fashionable areas of Italy, he murders a wealthy socialite, assumes his identity and outwits the police.

*A Room With A View*, E M Forster
While touring the Italian countryside with her governess, young Lucy Honeychurch meets the sullen but passionate George Emerson in Florence. He opens her eyes to the world outside Edwardian convention.

*Zeno's Conscience*, Italo Svevo
Written in 1923, this is a humorous and astute novel about a neurotic Italian businessman who tells five interrelated stories about various aspects of his life, at the behest of his psychiatrist.

*Aurelio Zen Series*, Michael Dibdin
Set all over Italy, but mainly in Venice and Rome, there are over ten novels featuring the complex and world-weary Italian police commissioner as he unweaves the intricate texture of Italian life. All are recommended.

*The Shape of Water*, Andrea Camilleri
The first in the series of atmospheric crime novels featuring the irritable and uncompromising Sicilian police inspector, Salvo Montalbano. Here he investigates the death of a local politician.

*The Woman and the Priest*, Grazia Deledda
A tale of love and duty that features a young priest in Sardinia who is having an affair with a village widow, while his devout mother disapprovingly looks on. Also published as *The Mother*.

*Troubling Love*, Elena Ferrante
An intense psychological story about a middle-aged woman who returns to her childhood home of Naples to discover the truth behind her mother's suspicious death.

*Cara Massimina*, Tim Parks
A delicious black comedy about an impoverished English teacher who runs off with
a teenage heiress. They travel the country dispatching ransom notes in an attempt
to blackmail her parents.

# VENICE

**KEY**TITLES

*Invisible Cities*, Italo Calvino
*Death in Venice*, Thomas Mann

## INVISIBLE CITIES (1972)
Italo Calvino

Italo Calvino has based this 'novel' on the thirteenth-century *The Travels of Marco Polo*. It features a young Marco Polo telling an ageing Kublai Khan stories of the cities he has visited in the emperor's vast empire. There are short fantastical accounts of fifty-five cities, each of which is given a feminine name. The descriptions are interspersed with dialogue between the two men, conversations during which they discuss a wide range of metaphysical subjects.

Polo describes each city by focusing either on something physically outstanding, such as the city's architecture or its geographical location, or on a subtler characteristic, such as a trait of its people or the feelings it evokes in the visitor. In Eutropia, for instance, when the inhabitants become tired of their lives, they pack up, change jobs, change partners, and move on to the next city. There are cities built on spiders webs, cities built on people's memories, and cities that induce melancholia: all intricately imagined places beautifully realised.

*Calvino is a wonderfully inventive and thought-provoking writer whose work never ceases to surprise and enthral. This timeless escapade mixes past and present and is as much a discourse on life itself as it is on the notion of place. Marco Polo's cities may be in his mind, but they remain curiously one city, the unmentioned city of his birth, Venice. It is more than a discourse on cities and how we live; it is a poem to the dream of living itself.*

# DEATH IN VENICE (1912)

Thomas Mann

Gustav von Aschenbach is an ageing German writer, an ascetic who believes in discipline and order. When he decides he has been working too hard and uncharacteristically takes a holiday, he goes to Venice, hungry for 'distant scenes'. There he encounters a beautiful fourteen-year-old Polish boy, Tadzio, holidaying with his family at the same hotel. He gradually becomes obsessed with the boy and follows him around the city, watching him swim, eat and frolic in the sun-soaked fading grandeur of Venice. The canalled city is splendidly revealed in all its magnificence.

Von Aschenbach's discipline and reason seem to be failing him. Tadzio represents something Dionysian and wild and the writer has inadequate inner resources with which to respond. He risks death (Venice is in the grip of a cholera epidemic) and loses his dignity (he dyes his hair and rouges his face in order to make himself look more attractive) in his pursuit of the boy who seems to him to embody the ideal of beauty. Eventually his dreams reveal to him the sexual nature of his attraction, with his repressed desires rising to the surface. Mythological motifs litter the story, with the clash of the opposing philosophies of Apollo and Dionysus at its core.

This is a sumptuous novella, echoing with psychological insight, and Mann's elegant and restrained prose throbs with meaning and truth.

Luchino Visconti's famous 1971 film features Dirk Bogarde as Von Aschenbach.

*Thomas Mann remains one of Germany's most influential writers and won the Nobel Prize for Literature in 1929.*

# 📖Read ons

*Miss Garnet's Angel*, Salley Vickers

When her flatmate of thirty years dies, a retired teacher and spinster settles in Venice for six months, to recuperate. Here she learns how to feel for the first time.

*The Wings of the Dove*, Henry James

Set in London and Venice, this novel follows an impecunious journalist wooing a dying American heiress with the aim of inheriting enough money to marry his aristocratic lover.

*The Comfort of Strangers*, Ian McEwan

An unsettling novel about a beautiful young couple on holiday. They encounter a man who leads them into a sexually compromising and potentially violent situation.

*The Stone Virgin*, Barry Unsworth

Three parallel stories in three different ages show how the stone Madonna on a fifteenth-century Venetian church has affected the lives of the people closely associated with it.

*By the Grand Canal*, William Rivière

This enchanting novella, set just after the First World War, concerns a British diplomat and his old friends who must learn to live and love again after the misery of war.

*Across the River and Into the Trees*, Ernest Hemingway

A touching and introspective love story between an embittered American colonel and a young Italian countess, in the days following the end of the Second World War.

*Death at La Fenice*, Donna Leon

When an eminent German conductor is found dead in his dressing room at Venice's famed opera house, vice-commissario Guido Brunetti is called in to investigate. The first in a series of Venetian detective novels.

*The Floating Book*, Michelle Lovric

Using different typefaces for different characters, this story centres on a love triangle in the early days of the printing press, in a highly evocative fifteenth-century Venice.

*The Palace*, Lisa St. Aubin De Teran

In order to win the love of a nineteenth-century noblewoman, a peasant turns successful gambler and begins to build a palace suitable for his love.

## FRIENDS, ROMANS, COUNTRYMEN – ANCIENT ROME

*I, Claudius*, Robert Graves
Claudius tells of his development from young, stammering family embarrass-ment, through various imperial upheavals, to the position of emperor. A grip-ping depiction of debauchery in Ancient Rome, continued in *Claudius the God*.

*Memoirs of Hadrian*, Marguerite Yourcenar
Written in the form of a valedictory letter, this moving and graphically depicted novel brings the Emperor Hadrian and second-century Rome vividly to life.

*Julian*, Gore Vidal
This engrossing and well-researched novel elegantly recreates the Roman Empire in the fourth century BC, as the last pagan emperor, Julian the Apostate, attempts to halt the rise of Christianity.

*Augustus*, Allan Massie
The first Roman emperor relates his rapid rise to the top and his subsequent authoritative rule. Part of a series of imagined biographies of Roman rulers which includes *Tiberius*, *Caesar*, *Antony*, *Nero's Heirs* and *Caligula*.

*Emperor: The Gates of Rome*, Conn Iggulden
This book begins a lavish and thrilling four-book adventure series following the struggles and successes of Julius Caesar, from ambitious youngster to all-conquering, military genius and 'Dictator for Life' of the Roman Empire.

*The First Man in Rome*, Colleen McCullough
The opening book of a 'Masters of Rome' series that chronicles the lives of various characters during the period in which the Roman Empire was con-verted from republic to imperial monarchy.

*Pompeii*, Robert Harris
A gripping recreation of the Roman world set in Pompeii and Herculaneum in August 79AD, just as Vesuvius is about to erupt.

*A Song For Nero*, Thomas Holt
History is re-imagined in this witty and ironic Roman romp. Emperor Nero lives, thanks to a double who is sacrificed, and embarks on a journey with his double's outspoken brother.

*Spartacus*, Lewis Grassic Gibbon
The story of the inspirational gladiator, Spartacus, who led the slave uprising against the Romans in 73BC. *See also* Arthur Koestler's *The Gladiators*.

*See also* **READ ON A THEME: PORTRAIT OF THE ARTIST – ART AND ARTISTS**

# FRANCE

## KEYTITLES

*In Search of Lost Time*, Marcel Proust
*Bonjour Tristesse*, Françoise Sagan
*Perfume*, Patrick Süskind
*The Water of the Hills*, Marcel Pagnol

## IN SEARCH OF LOST TIME (1913–1927)
Marcel Proust

The decline of the bourgeoisie, between 1870 and 1920, is recalled by a writer, also named Marcel, in a novel that is widely regarded as the greatest of the twentieth century. Proust recounts the period through the lives of a group of French socialites who attend soirées, discuss the various events of the day (the Great War, women's emancipation), give critiques on art and music, and fall in love. A host of characters are subtly and finely drawn with superb irony and wit.

Proust's key technique is to take an experience and unfold it before the reader. Pages are devoted to detailed descriptions of sunlight through a window and the pattern on an embroidered blanket. These moments of enlightenment are triggered by sudden lightning flashes of connection to the past through smell, taste and feeling.

The author excels at describing emotions and the various love affairs throughout the book, especially Marcel's with Albertine, are expertly rendered. After years of failed attempts to become a writer, distracted by love and the superficiality of society life, there is a sublime moment when Marcel's mind fixes onto the past through an involuntary memory. This is the famous 'madeleine moment', when he dips the cake into his tea and takes the first bite, the taste setting off the spontaneous recollections that are the material of the book.

An exceptional achievement that stands at over three thousand pages and seven volumes, it took fourteen years to write, during which Proust rarely left his now-famous cork-lined room. The collection, formerly known under the title *Remembrance of Things Past*, has had a tortuous publishing history, especially in translation. The 2002 edition is the work of several translators.

# BONJOUR TRISTESSE (1954)
Françoise Sagan

Written when the author was just eighteen, this slim and assured novel caused quite a stir in its day. It concerns seventeen-year-old Cécile and her forty-year-old father, Raymond. Fresh from convent school, Cécile lives with her libertine father, moving between Paris and the South of France, mixing with the jet set and enjoying a sexually and morally liberated life.

A mature and contrite Cécile recounts the events of one particular summer on the Riviera, spent with Raymond's live-in girlfriend, Elsa Mackenbourg, and Cyril, a man with whom Cécile enjoys an innocent relationship. Also invited is Anne Larsen, an intelligent and bourgeois woman much closer in age to Raymond and whose presence drives away both Elsa and Cyril. When Raymond announces his intention to marry Anne on their return to Paris, Cécile decides to prevent the match at whatever cost.

This is a delightful novel, full of wit and insight, that perfectly captures the awkward condition of a teenager determined to be treated as an adult while still essentially being a child.

Jean Seberg and David Niven starred in a 1958 film version.

# PERFUME (1985)

## Patrick Süskind

This highly individual novel is dark and seductive, portraying with wicked glee the decadence of eighteenth-century bourgeois French society. It concerns the remarkable Jean-Baptiste Grenouille, the unwanted son of a fishwife who was born on a rubbish tip in Paris. He has no personal odour yet is endowed with a sense of smell so acute that he can smell such qualities as trust, adoration and innocent hope. He becomes an apprentice to a perfumier in an effort to create the world's most beautiful scent, something he smelt once in his youth and now seeks to recreate: the aroma of young virgins. Wishing to capture the scent for himself, to compensate for his lack of personal aroma, he sets about murdering ripe young women in order to steal their smells. Grenouille is a sociopath who becomes a psychopath, believing that his olfactory abilities place him above the common herd and allow the most heinous of crimes to be excused.

Originally written in German, it is available in an excellent translation. Once deemed unfilmable, it was brought to the screen in 2006.

# THE WATER OF THE HILLS (1962)

## Marcel Pagnol

Two novels are collected here: *Jean de Florette* and **Manon des Sources**. This powerful tale of greed and dishonour, set in the early twentieth century in the tiny southern French village of Les Bastides Blanches. It features a tax collector, a hunchback called Jean Cadoret, who inherits a house and land from his mother and moves to Provence with his wife and daughter, intent on making a success of growing pumpkins and raising rabbits. They are befriended by the wily and covetous César Soubeyrand and his simple-minded nephew Ugolin, who block up the spring that feeds Cadoret's land, thwarting his agricultural ambitions and bringing his family into a ruinous state that forces them to accept the derisory price César subsequently offers for the farm. Ugolin pursues his dream of growing carnations, while César wants to make the Soubeyrand family the most powerful in the area. He also harbours a grudge against Jean Cadoret's mother, with whom he was once in love. She left him to move to Crespin and marry another man.

This is a beautifully written study of provincial prejudice and devastating tragedy. The sequel, **Manon des Sources**, restores natural justice. It is set three years later and follows the fortunes of Cadoret's beautiful daughter, Manon, in her attempts to seek retribution for her family's treatment.

*Marcel Pagnol was a filmmaker who wrote and directed* Manon des Sources *in 1953, later developing the screenplay into* L'Eau des Collines*, which brace of novels in turn inspired two beautiful awarded-winning films,* Jean de Florette *and* Manon des Sources *(1986), directed by Claude Berri and featuring a galaxy of French stars.*

## 📖Read ons

*Le Grand Meaulnes*, Alain-Fournier
This is unfortunately the author's only novel. Set in the Loire Valley in the late nineteenth century, it touchingly chronicles an affecting friendship between a charismatic schoolboy and his enchanted friend.

*A Very Long Engagement*, Sebastien Japrisot
When her fiancé is condemned to death in the First World War for refusing to fight, Mathilde attempts to discover the true story.

*Thérèse*, François Mauriac
A collection of four moving and powerful stories that follow the tormented and passionate life of Thérèse Desqueyroux, a woman imprisoned for poisoning her husband. Set in Bordeaux and Paris.

*Strait is the Gate*, André Gide
A haunting novel set in Normandy. Alissa fears her relationship with her cousin, Jérome, is damaging his soul. She sacrifices all and ends the affair.

*The Murdered House*, Pierre Magnan
In an effort to find out the truth about his parents' murder when he was a child, a man returns to Provence to the house where they were massacred.

*Suite Française*, Irène Némirovsky
The first two parts of an intended quintet, this novel relates the experiences of various characters in occupied France during the Second World War. First published in 2006, over 60 years after the author died in Auschwitz, it was instantly hailed as a masterpiece.

*A Brief Stay with the Living*, Marie Darrieussecq
A day in the lives of a mother and her three grown-up daughters as they try to come to terms with the death of her son and their brother, Pierre.

*Querelle of Brest*, Jean Genet
In a fogbound seaport, Querelle, a homosexual murderer and thief struts among the sailors, dockers and petty thieves, playing sexual games of surreal and oblique fantasy. A highly original book.

*Atomised*, Michel Houellebecq
A bleak existential novel, by France's new bad boy of literature, about two half-brothers with very different ideas on life and fulfilment. Full of ideas, graphic sex and philosophical angst.

*The Girl at the Lion D'Or*, Sebastian Faulks
Almost cinematic in its vividness and detail, this is a sumptuous story of a brief and intense love affair between an enigmatic waitress and a restless married man, set in small-town France in the 1930s.

*Daughters of the House*, Michèle Roberts
Dark secrets permeate this absorbing tale of two adolescent girls growing up in 1950s' France.

*Tender is the Night*, F Scott Fitzgerald
Set mainly on the French Riviera in the 1920s, this is an elegant and emotional autobiographical novel about the marriage of an alcoholic psychologist and his mentally unstable wife.

*A Sport and a Pastime*, James Salter
Two Americans are staying in a small French town in the 1960s. When one of them begins an affair with a local girl, the other imagines the romance in every erotic detail.

*A Place of Greater Safety*, Hilary Mantel
This fictionalised account of the French Revolution details the lives of the main protagonists: Danton, Desmoulins and Robespierre.

# PARIS

*The Mandarins*, Simone de Beauvoir
*The Age of Reason*, Jean-Paul Sartre

## THE MANDARINS (1954)

Simone de Beauvoir

This semi-autobiographical novel follows the fortunes of a group of Left Bank intellectuals just after the close of the Second World War. De Beauvoir famously based many of the characters on high-profile figures within her social circle, including her long-term partner, Jean-Paul Sartre, Albert Camus, Arthur Koestler and her one-time lover, Nelson Algren, to whom the book is dedicated, although he was less than enamoured with her portrayal of him.

It concerns itself with the social responsibilities of intellectuals and the notions of personal freedom and loyalty. The opposing themes of death and life surround the question of what, now the war is over, one should dedicate one's life to: the cynicism of fatalism or the optimism of action. Ultimately, the Mandarins must decide whether it is right to abandon their educated elite status and resort to political activism.

The central character of the novel is Anne Dubreuilh, a psychoanalyst, married to Robert. Older than Anne, he is a renowned intellectual who fought with the Resistance during the war. They have a daughter, Nadine, an unlikeable character who, mourning of the death of her Jewish lover, descends into a maelstrom of self-destructive behaviour. Anne begins an affair with Lewis Bogan, an American writer who is a little rough round the edges.

The beauty and charm of Paris are faithfully rendered, as are the uncertainty and confusion of the newly liberated country and the bitter aftertaste of the German occupation and Nazi collaboration. This is a sharp, stimulating novel that drives home the importance of personal and political commitment.

# THE AGE OF REASON (1945)
## Jean-Paul Sartre

Jean-Paul Sartre's existential trilogy, *Roads to Freedom*, begins with this book. The novel takes place over a few days in the heat of September 1938. Mathieu, a professor of philosophy, is wrestling with the notion of liberty. His disabled girlfriend, Marcelle, is pregnant. Fearing a loss of personal freedom, he believes an abortion is the only solution. Mathieu's brother offers to pay for the operation if Mathieu agrees to marry Marcelle, but, although Mathieu's conscience tells him this is the right thing to do, his philosophy leads him in a different direction. Meanwhile, outside Paris the forces of war are gathering.

While Mathieu wanders around Montparnasse in search of the four thousand francs he needs for the operation, he is unable to shake off an obsession with the sister of one his students: Boris, a Russian émigré.

Mathieu believes he is free because he does not have any illusions. Yet he will not commit himself to any of the possible courses of action he considers: fighting in Spain, marrying Marcelle, or going to Russia to work as a labourer. The impending war will force him and his friends to realise that true autonomy comes in fact from making choices, not from avoiding them. It is a testament to Sartre's genius that this dilemma always remains fascinating.

Replete with philosophical debates in smoke-filled cafés and drunken episodes in fashionable nightclubs, the book has a wonderful cast of vividly drawn characters whose personalities and notions of free will are revealed through incisively observed dialogue.

*The remaining books of the trilogy are* The Reprieve *(1947) and* Iron in the Soul *(1949). Sartre was awarded the Nobel Prize for Literature in 1964, an honour which he declined to accept.*

## 📖 Read ons

*Zazie in the Metro*, Raymond Queneau

Puckish and unruly, the foul-mouthed prepubescent Zazie goes to stay with her uncle in the capital and embarks on all manner of entertaining adventures in this 1959 French classic.

*Claudine in Paris*, Colette

The second in a semi-autobiographical series, about a young girl growing to maturity at the turn of the last century, sees Claudine being propositioned, molested and sexually awakened among the socialites of Paris.

*The Fairy Gunmother*, Daniel Pennac

A stylish thriller about a plot to get old people hooked on drugs as a way of fleecing them of their apartments. The plot has the police baffled until the wrinklies start to fight back. The second book in the ongoing Benjamin Malaussène series.

*The Devil in the Flesh*, Raymond Radiguet

Shockingly bold for its time, this novel details the affair between a sixteen-year-old schoolboy and a married woman whose husband is away at the front during the First World War.

*Paris Stories*, Mavis Gallant

A near-legendary figure, this Canadian writer has lived in Paris for many years and writes mainly of the lives of exiles. This magnificent collection is edited by Michael Ondaatje.

*The Way I Found Her*, Rose Tremain

A precocious adolescent English boy falls for a forty-something Russian émigrée whose writings his mother is translating, during a hot and eventful summer in the French capital.

*Tropic of Cancer*, Henry Miller

Brash and vulgar poetry oozes from these autobiographical and starkly sexual sketches of a young Henry Miller wandering around Paris in the 1930s.

*The Holy Innocents*, Gilbert Adair
It is 1968 and a young American befriends cinema-loving twins. They play games of increasing sexual danger as the city around them is consumed by political rioting.

*Good Morning, Midnight*, Jean Rhys
An absorbing novel about a disillusioned woman who returns to Paris in the 1930s. She relives her past romances by spending time in bars and cafés, secretly hoping to find love again.

*Giovanni's Room*, James Baldwin
An American in Paris waits for his fiancée to arrive from Spain. While waiting, he falls in love with an Italian barman.

*Just Like Tomorrow*, Faïza Guene
A tough and poignant novel about immigrant life on a Parisian housing estate.

*A Man's Head*, Georges Simenon
One of the scores of Maigret stories written between the 1930s and 1960s. Here, the detective tries to prove the innocence of an escaped convict condemned to death for a brutal murder.

## PORTRAIT OF THE ARTIST –  ART AND ARTISTS

*The Painted Kiss*, Elizabeth Hickey
Emilie Floge tells the story of her long-term relationship with Gustav Klimt. She first meets the artist in Vienna, when she is twelve years old and he is engaged as her art tutor. Later, she becomes his mistress.

*The Painter*, Will Davenport
In 1662, Rembrandt pays for a sea passage by painting portraits of the captain and his wife, Amelia Dahl. In the present day, artist Amy Dale works on the restoration of a manor house once owned by her ancestors. She stumbles upon Amelia's journals.

*Girl with a Pearl Earring*, Tracy Chevalier
A fictionalised account of the painting of one of Vermeer's most famous works of art. Griet, a new maid in the Vermeer household, rises to become his assistant, then his model. Set in seventeenth-century Delft.

*The Passion of Artemesia*, Susan Vreeland
The life story of post-renaissance artist, Artemesia Gentileschi, who rises above the prejudices of a male-dominated world to become one of Italy's greatest female artists.

*The Way to Paradise*, Mario Vargas Llosa
This absorbing novel covers Paul Gauguin's years in Tahiti, and his grandmother's campaign for women's rights in France. Their stories parallel one another in their pursuit of dreams and obsessions.

*Caravaggio: A Novel*, Christopher Peachment
This notorious figure of Italian baroque art recounts his turbulent life, from his early artistic failures in Rome to his time on the run for murder, in this engaging and illuminating novel.

*The Agony and the Ecstasy*, Irving Stone
A gripping fictionalised biography of Renaissance man extraordinaire Michelangelo.

*I Am Madame X*, Gioia Diliberto
This novel tells of Virginie Gautreau, who posed for one of Singer Sargent's most famous portraits, Madame X, and of the huge scandal that ensued in 1880s' Paris when it was first exhibited.

*Keeping the World Away*, Margaret Forster
This fictionalised account of Gwen John's love affair with Rodin also tells of how one of her paintings subsequently touches the lives of the different people who own it throughout the twentieth century.

*The Dark Clue*, James Wilson
A slow-starting novel about a second-rate artist trying to write a biography of the secretive painter J M W Turner. It features some of the characters from Wilkie Collins' classic *The Woman in White*.

*The Voyages of Alfred Wallis*, Peter Everett
This moving novel tells the story of the fisherman from southwest England who took up art late in life in the 1920s.

# SPAIN

**KEY**TITLES

*The Carpenter's Pencil*, Manuel Rivas
*The Seville Communion*, Arturo Perez-Reverte

## THE CARPENTER'S PENCIL (1998)
Manuel Rivas

A tale of love and survival during the Spanish Civil War. Doctor Daniel da Barca, an uncompromising Republican, has returned from exile in Mexico following Franco's death and is being interviewed by a journalist about his experiences during the war. Condemned to death in 1936, the doctor was saved by what seems to him to have been a miracle. The doctor's story is then taken up by Herbal, an unlikely guardian angel who, unbeknown to da Barca, was instrumental in his survival throughout the Civil War and managed to commute the doctor's death sentence to life imprisonment.

Herbal, a perfunctory illiterate Falangist guard, had once executed an unnamed painter who had been sketching prisoners in Santiago de Compostela. He kept the artist's pencil as a keepsake, putting it behind his ear. This becomes his conscience, as though the ghost of the artist is whispering to Herbal to intervene and help the doctor, whenever he can. Herbal may have other motives however, for he is in love with de Barca's lover, the beautiful Marisa, who, despite her own family's attempts to separate them, follows the doctor on his journey through various Spanish prisons. Herbal even helps them engage in their 'secret honeymoon', without either of them suspecting his involvement.

The splintered style of the novel occasionally makes the story difficult to follow, but Rivas's exquisite writing grips the reader, aided by Jonathan Dunne's superb translation. Originally written in Galician, the stunning prose and striking imagery reveal the author's skills as a poet.

*The Carpenter's Pencil* is the most widely translated and best-selling Galician book. It was made into a film in 2003, directed by Antón Reixa. Rivas's other works include *Butterfly's Tongue* (1996), a collection of short stories.

# THE SEVILLE COMMUNION (1995)
## Arturo Pérez-Reverte

The fate of a little church in Seville is brought to the attention of the Pope when a hacker breaks into the Vatican's computer system and sends him a personal message requesting help. The situation is compounded by two 'accidental' deaths that are suspicious in their proximity to each other. Father Lorenzo Quart is dispatched to Spain to discover the identity of the hacker and to report on the situation there. Quart is a fine-looking, well-dressed and disciplined man driven more by pride than by faith. In the Santa Cruz area of the city he finds an old recalcitrant priest, Father Ferro, a beautiful estranged wife of a local gangster, Macarena Bruner, and a dilapidated Baroque church, Our Lady of the Tears.

The rapacious archbishop of Seville, Monsignor Corvo, is about to sign a deal to demolish the church and build a multi-million-dollar development, but Father Ferro's presence thwarts this plans. The pastor has powerful supporters in the shape of a family with long-standing ties to the three-hundred-year-old church and good reason to keep the church out of the hands of the property developers. Father Quart's investigations take him further into the conflict surrounding the church.

This delightful tongue-in-cheek thriller gives a flavour of the historical magnificence of Seville. Arturo Pérez-Reverte is the author of several other literary thrillers, including *The Fencing Master* (1988) and *The Flanders Panel* (1994).

## 📖 Read ons

### The Soldiers of Salamis, Javier Cercas
During the Spanish Civil War, Rafael Sanchez Mazas, a writer, escapes death twice in one day, thanks to an unknown enemy soldier. He becomes a national hero as a result of his exploits. But who is the real hero?

### A Man of Feeling, Javier Marias
While rehearsing Verdi's *Otello* in Madrid, a tenor, known as 'the Lion of Naples', becomes part of an obsessive love triangle in this prize-winning novella.

### The Hive, Camilo Jose Cela
This is a series of interlinked vignettes, centred on a café in Madrid, that show the effects of the Civil War on Spain's lower middle-class in the 1940s.

### The Curriculum Vitae of Aurora Ortiz, Almudena Solana
Thirty-year-old Aurora, recently widowed and never previously employed, looks for work, armed with an unconventional CV and an eccentric attitude to life, in this charming debut novel set in Madrid.

### The Yellow Rain, Julio Llamazares
High in the Spanish Pyrenees a village lies deserted, save for one elderly dying man who is haunted by the ghosts of the past.

### Shadows of the Pomegranate Tree, Tariq Ali
The first in a quartet of novels about the history of Islam. A Moorish family tries to survive the fall of Granada as the Christians seek to re-conquer Spain in the late fourteenth century.

### Misericordia, Benito Pérez Galdós
In nineteenth-century Madrid, a once-wealthy family fallen on hard times receives a sudden windfall that brings unexpected results. A delightfully gloomy novel from one of Spain's greatest novelists.

### Winter in Madrid, C J Sansom
Painful memories are stirred up when a reluctant British spy is dispatched to Madrid during the Second World War, to seek out a former schoolfriend suspected of shady dealings.

### A Thousand Orange Trees, Kathryn Harrison
This spellbinding novel features two women born on the same day in the seventeenth century, one a future Queen of Spain, the other imprisoned for having an illicit affair.

### For Whom the Bell Tolls, Ernest Hemingway
A seminal novel of the Spanish Civil War, about a young American volunteer working with guerrillas planning to blow up a strategic bridge.

### The South, Colm Tóibín
An Irish painter leaves her husband and family behind to travel to Spain in the 1950s, to start a new life. She becomes involved with an artist opposed to the Franco regime.

# BARCELONA

*The Shadow of the Wind*, Carlos Ruiz Zafón

## SHADOW OF THE WIND (2001)
Carlos Ruiz Zafón

In 1940s' Barcelona, ten-year-old Daniel Sempere is taken to the Cemetery of Forgotten Books by his father and is allowed to choose one item. He must treasure this book for the rest of his life, for it houses the soul of the person who wrote it. He chooses *The Shadow of the Wind* by Julián Carax. The book is extremely rare and, over the years, Daniel refuses many generous offers to buy it.

It transpires that a man called Laín Coubert wants to destroy every copy of all of Carax's books, and soon he is on Daniel's trail. This is also part of the plot of *The Shadow of the Wind*, just as Laín Coubert is a character within it. Daniel finds himself also to be replicating the life of the book's author, a hugely successful 1930s writer who had an unhealthy influence on people who came into his life.

In pursuit of answers, Daniel finds time to fall in love with a blind woman, Clara, and come to the aid of a man, Fermín, who provides an eccentric guide to the secret history of the city. The plot becomes increasingly labyrinthine when Daniel's activities attract the interest of the sadistic chief of police, Ignacio Fumero.

Barcelona is lovingly painted as a city of shadows and secrets in which every doorway seems to be a portal to another place and every foggy alleyway houses old, inextinguishable hatreds.

This energetic and romantic novel, from the pen of a children's author and screenwriter, has great fun hopping between genres, from Victorian gothic novel to love story to bildungsroman, which is all done with flair and a knowing wink.

**Read ons**

*Marks of Identity*, Juan Goytisolo
An autobiographical novel about a Spanish exile returning from Paris to his family home in Barcelona following the Civil War. The first of a trilogy that continues with *Count Julian* and *Juan the Landless*.

*Lizard Tails*, Juan Marsé
The suburbs of Barcelona in the late 1940s are the setting for this prize-winning coming-of-age novel, concerning a young boy growing up in a family of Republican sympathisers.

*An Olympic Death*, Manuel Vázquez Montalbán
José 'Pepe' Carvalho, an unorthodox private eye, is hired to find a missing Greek husband on the eve of the 1992 Olympics, in this splendidly realised picture of the city. The first of a long-running series.

*A Light Comedy*, Eduardo Mendoza
Set in the 1940s, just after Franco's victory in the Civil War, a playwright and playboy is suspected of murder when a member of the local underground is killed.

*The Lone Man*, Bernardo Atxaga
The Basque country's best-known novelist sets this literary thriller during the 1982 World Cup. A retired ETA operative is asked to harbour two terrorists.

*The Lonely Hearts Club*, Raul Nunez
A hotel night porter with a resemblance to Frank Sinatra joins a lonely hearts club and encounters a variety of oddballs and lowlifes. Set just off the Ramblas in the 1980s.

*The Colour of a Dog Running Away*, Richard Gwyn
An intriguing thriller in which a musician moves into Barcelona's seedy gothic quarter and finds himself kidnapped by the Cathars.

# PORTUGAL

KEYTITLE

*The Year of the Death of Ricardo Reis*, José Saramago

## THE YEAR OF THE DEATH OF RICARDO REIS (1984)
José Saramago

Ricardo Reis returns to Lisbon in 1936, after practising medicine in Brazil for sixteen years. He begins an affair with a chambermaid, Lydia, at the same time falling in love with an aristocrat, Marcenda. When he meets his old friend, Fernando Pessoa, Portugal's most famous writer, the pair discuss philosophy, poetry, life and love. But all is not as it seems, for Pessoa is a dead man and 'Ricardo Reis' is one of many pseudonyms under which Pessoa wrote poetry.

The rise of Fascism exercises the pair in particular, at a time when neighbouring Spain has succumbed to a civil war, Hitler's rise in Germany is evident, and the Italians are involved in a conflict in Ethiopia. Portugal itself is in the grip of the repressive regime of Salazar.

Although its subject matter is weighty, the novel is written in a conversational, almost intimate style. There are large passages where they stroll through the steep, rain-sodden streets of Lisbon conjuring up that magical city in such a vivid way that the book has been labelled the Portuguese *Ulysses*. The author may not be a fan of punctuation, but his prose is so graceful and elegant, the reader will soon learn to follow where he leads.

*Saramago's other books include* The History of the Siege of Lisbon *(1989). He won the Nobel Prize for Literature in 1998.*

## 📖Read ons

*The Book of Disquiet*, Fernando Pessoa
This is the putative diary of an assistant bookkeeper in Lisbon, detailing the monotonous life that surrounds him in meditative and poetic prose. The only novel by Portugal's leading writer.

*The Tragedy of the Street of Flowers*, Eça de Quieroz
This beautiful novel, set in nineteenth-century Portuguese high society, was written in the 1880s but not published until 1980. It is a tragic love story about a young man and a prostitute.

*Creole*, José Eduardo Agualusa
An epistolary novel about a Portuguese writer and traveller falling in love with a Creole woman who is a former slave, in the late nineteenth-century. Set in Lisbon, Angola and Brazil.

*The Last Kabbalist of Lisbon*, Richard Zimler
A young manuscript illustrator tells the story of the famous Lisbon massacre of 1506, when Jews were forced to convert to Christianity or die.

*Tales and New Tales from the Mountain*, Miguel Torga
Set in the author's birthplace in the remote northeastern region of Portugal, these are poetic tales of the lives of ordinary people in a barren landscape.

*Adam Runaway*, Peter Prince
This boisterous and bawdy tale, set in eighteenth-century Lisbon, sees a young Englishman trying to make good after fleeing impending bankruptcy and his father's suicide in London.

## POSTCARDS FROM THE EDGE – HOLIDAYS IN FICTION

*Leisure*, Kevin Sampson
This novel describes the highs and lows of various English holidaymakers looking to enjoy a week of sun, sea and sex on the Costa del Sol.

*Summer Things*, Joseph Connolly
A farcical romp that follows a group of friends and neighbours as they make merry in an English seaside resort. The characters continue their frolics in Connolly's sequel, *Winter Breaks*.

*August*, Gerard Woodward
The Jones family take their holiday at the same idyllic spot in Wales every year, but behind the façade of contentedness lurk serious problems. The family's story is continued in the Booker-shortlisted *I'll Go To Bed at Noon* and concluded in *A Curious Earth*.

*Rapids*, Tim Parks
A group of English people arrive in the Italian Alps for what they hope will be an exhilarating canoeing holiday. Their journey through the white waters stirs up trouble and violence between them.

*The Enchanted April*, Elizabeth von Arnim
Four women rent a castle in Italy for a month's holiday. The beautiful, atmospheric surroundings inspire each of them to reassess her life and find new happiness.

*Lanzarote*, Michel Houellebecq
On an impulse, a man seeking to escape the usual dreariness of New Year books a week's holiday to Lanzarote. He finds an island with an unnerving landscape, peopled by odd tourists and hedonistic youngsters.

*What We Did on our Holidays*, Geoff Nicholson
A comic caper about a man who coerces his reluctant family into taking a caravan holiday to Skegness. Humiliation and disaster confront him at every turn.

*Mr Golightly's Holiday*, Salley Vickers

Feeling out of tune with the world, 'Mr Golightly' decides to take a holiday. He finds himself in an ancient village on Dartmoor, where he keeps his true identity secret and immerses himself in the community.

# REPUBLIC OF IRELAND

**KEY**TITLES

*That They May Face the Rising Sun*, John McGahern
*The Country Girls Trilogy*, Edna O'Brien
*My Oedipus Complex and Other Stories*, Frank O'Connor
*The Last September*, Elizabeth Bowen

## THAT THEY MAY FACE THE RISING SUN (2002)
John McGahern

This novel concerns a community in a remote corner of County Leitrim, on the border near Enniskillen. Joe Ruttledge was brought up in the area and has now returned with his wife Kate, after years of living in London. A host of colourful characters visit them in their renovated farmhouse on the lake: a gossipy couple who affect a worldy knowledge while claiming never to have moved from the area; cruel, charming and sexually voracious John Quinn; maverick Patrick Ryan, their occasional builder; and the tragic Johnny Murphy, who followed a woman to England once, in search of love.

The reader arrives in this novel much like a stranger in town, piecing together a sense of this community through snippets of the conversations the visitors have with Joe and Kate. McGahern's prose is spare and unaffected and his descriptions of weather, landscape and the routines of country life are presented with the skill of a specialist painter. Witty, poignant and pertinent, this is a lyrical and under-stated book that perfectly captures the rhythms of everyday life.

*All of John McGahern's novels are set in Ireland. Recommended are* Amongst Women *(1990) and his first novel,* The Dark *(1965), banned for alleged pornographic content, which after a ruling by the Archbishop of Dublin led to McGahern losing his job as a teacher.*

# THE COUNTRY GIRLS TRILOGY (1960–1964)

Edna O'Brien

This lively and affecting trilogy follows the fortunes of two Irish girls from their severe Catholic upbringing in the West of Ireland, through their brief burst of freedom in Dublin, to their disillusioned middle age in London.

When the trilogy beings, Caithleen Brady (Kate) is the only child of a drunken father and unhappy mother, living in a rundown farmhouse in County Clare. When her mother dies in a boating accident, while out with another man, Kate is sent to a convent school, from which she and her best friend Baba are expelled for writing an obscene letter about a nun.

The pair move to Dublin, where the sexually aware Baba enjoys letting her hair down. Kate moves in with an older man, Eugene, with whom she has a child. He proves himself to be a bully and a bore and she eventually leaves him and their son behind. Baba, meanwhile, makes a loveless marriage for the sake of financial security.

The final section, narrated mainly by Baba, with vicious humour, sees the women living unhappy lives in London.

Criticised by feminists for its portrayal of women dependent on men, and banned in Ireland because of its graphic sexual content, this is essentially a story of the legitimate dilemmas of real women. There is a perfect balance between humour and pathos, with some genuinely moving scenes.

The individual novels are *The Country Girls* (1960), *The Lonely Girl* (1962), republished as *The Girl with Green Eyes*, and *Girls in Their Married Bliss* (1964). A single volume containing all three novels is available, with an epilogue.

# MY OEDIPUS COMPLEX AND OTHER STORIES
(1963)

Frank O'Connor

WB Yeats said Frank O'Connor did for Ireland what Chekhov did for Russia.

He was a master craftsman and the stories in this unmissable collection recreate worlds that take the reader into the soul of the Irish people. His favourite terrain is the lives of ordinary people, influenced as it is by the bullying, comforting and insidious Catholic Church, as well as by a typically Irish obsession with respectability and how a simple act can become a moral dilemma. He has a sharp ear for dialogue and his characters all display the Gaelic penchant for discourse, revealing truths about their situation through unaffected language, which is a true delight when read aloud.

The story *My Oedipus Complex* is an inspired tale of a boy alone with his mother while his father is away fighting in the First World War. On the occasions his Dad returns the boy looks upon him jealously, regarding him as a rival for his mother's attention and love. Like so many of O'Connor's stories, it is narrated with an adult voice imbued with childish sensibilities. It is also poignant, playful and wise.

Frank O'Connor declared the extent of his own talent in his frankly autobiographical story *The Genius*, whereby he decries the fact that, 'it was a poor, sad, lonesome thing being nothing but a genius'. He wrote over a hundred and fifty short stories and was also a novelist, playwright and poet, translator and biographer. As he said himself, a genius.

# THE LAST SEPTEMBER (1929)

## Elizabeth Bowen

This paper-thin masterpiece is an elegy to a lost time, portraying as it does a side of Ireland very rarely captured: the lives of Anglo-Irish Protestants as independence approaches.

The aristocratic Naylors appear and sound English but consider themselves to be Irish. It is 1921 and Sinn Fein's forces are getting nearer by the day, while the British Army attempts to flush them out with a cruel determination. The Naylors' orphaned niece, Lois, is staying with them on their country estate in Cork. On the cusp of womanhood, she enjoys the attentions of the young British officers who come over to play tennis and have lunch on the lawn. Matters become more serious when her friend becomes engaged and she herself receives a proposal of marriage.

This novel is rich in graceful observations and well-tuned descriptions, and the underlying feeling of dread is communicated effectively. Bowen's wonderfully mordant humour mocks the affectations of the Naylors and their guests and the ridiculous lengths they go to to ignore the terrors that surround them. The tension between the decline of traditional mores and the encroaching of a modern political and spiritual state of independence is rendered in prose that is both psychologically piercing and poetically haunting. A rare feat.

A film was made in 1999, starring Michael Gambon and Maggie Smith.

## Read ons

*The Blackwater Lightship*, Colm Tóibín

When a woman discovers her brother is dying of AIDS, she is forced to face up to her own past and contacts her estranged mother and grandmother. A moving and understated story of a troubled family.

*Inishowen*, Joseph O'Connor

The fates of three troubled characters from different walks of life converge and lead them all to the Donegal peninsula of Inishowen. A novel featuring strong characters, sharp dialogue and black comedy.

*The Whereabouts of Eneas McNulty*, Sebastian Barry

After being branded a British collaborator in the 1920s, Eneas flees Sligo, leaving all his loved ones behind. As he wanders halfway round the world for the next forty years, memories of home remain deeply embedded in his mind.

*The Essential Jennifer Johnston*, Jennifer Johnston

Three early novels from the pen of one of Ireland's finest writers, featuring well-drawn characters experiencing the elusiveness of love. They are *Captains and the Kings*, *The Railway Station Man* and *Fool's Sanctuary*.

*The Third Policeman*, Flann O'Brien

A gloriously dark and multi-layered satire by a comic genius, featuring many bizarre goings-on, including unrequited love between a man and his bicycle.

*A Goat's Song*, Dermot Healy

A powerful novel dealing with Ireland's political history. A Catholic playwright in Mayo re-imagines the life of the Protestant actress with whom he enjoyed a tempestuous love affair.

*The Butcher Boy*, Patrick McCabe

Teenager Francie Brady narrates the story of his descent into insanity, which culminates in an act of savage barbarity. A compelling stream-of-consciousness novel filled with humour.

*The Sea*, John Banville
When his wife dies, art historian Max Morden retreats to the coastal village in which he holidayed as a child and where he previously experienced the death of a loved one. An intimate novel that won the 2005 Booker Prize.

*Collected Stories*, William Trevor
A collection of over eighty stories from a gifted storyteller. Funny, inventive, and with unexpected twists, these stories show the full range of a master craftsman.

*Tarry Flynn*, Patrick Kavanagh
A highly evocative rural novel, set in County Monaghan in the 1930s, that tells the life story of a lustful young farmer and his dreams for the future. Full of gentle humour and sly observations.

*Good Behaviour*, Molly Keane
Aroon St Charles narrates the story of her dysfunctional family in the 1930s, living in the fading glory of their once-majestic mansion and struggling to abide by strict codes of behaviour.

*I Could Read the Sky*, Timothy O'Grady and Steve Pyke
A prose poem of a novel in which an Irish emigrant in England movingly recollects his happy childhood in the West of Ireland. Accompanied by beautiful black-and-white photographs by Steve Pyke.

*Ireland: A Novel*, Frank Delaney
Seduced by the life of a wandering storyteller, Ronan becomes fascinated by myth and legend and travels round Ireland emulating his hero. A fascinating novelisation of Irish history and folklore.

# DUBLIN

## ULYSSES (1914–1922)
James Joyce

This ultimate stream-of-consciousness novel follows two very different men, Leopold Bloom and Stephen Dedalus, going about their business during the course of one day in 1904. With the ostensible aim of creating a complete picture of Dublin, Joyce shows the men defecating, urinating and even masturbating. Indeed, the book ends with an orgasmic yelp, one reason why it was declared obscene and banned in the USA.

Stephen Dedalus, the autobiographical hero of Joyce's earlier *Portrait of The Artist as a Young Man*, is a fledgling writer and intellectual whose mother has recently died. He begins the day by teaching at a local school, later going for a walk along the beach. Leopold Bloom is a likeable, visceral Jewish advertising salesman. He wanders the town to avoid going back to the home where his wife, Molly, is about to take a lover to the marital bed. The two men's paths cross amid a host of unforgettable characters, and the sights, sounds and smells of Dublin are artfully conveyed.

In exploring his theme of interpretation, Joyce uses numerous stylistic devices that make great demands on the reader, but persistent readers are well rewarded for their efforts.

*Ulysses* was written over a seven-year period from 1914 to 1921 and was first published in its entirety in 1922. Universally hailed as a masterpiece, it was ranked first in the list of the hundred best novels in English of the 20th century, compiled by the Modern Library.

A more stylistically conventional portrait of the Irish capital is available in Joyce's book of short stories, *Dubliners* (1914).

# PADDY CLARKE HA HA HA (1993)

Roddy Doyle

This hugely successful book is a series of vignettes about a working-class Barrytown childhood in the late 1960s, as told through the eyes of a ten-year-old boy. The eponymous hero lives with his warring parents and younger brother, whom he bullies mercilessly and ridicules with the nickname 'Sinbad'. There are marvellous episodes of childish mischief and barbarousness in the early part of the book, as the reader follows Paddy larking about with his mates.

When the fighting between his parents intensifies, Paddy makes unrealistic plans to run away. Doyle handles this episode particularly well, illustrating the confusion of a child who loves his parents and cannot understand why they are not happy. When his father eventually leaves, the family breakdown affects the young Paddy in unexpected ways: it has a detrimental effect on his relationships with schoolfriends, but it brings him closer to his younger brother.

The book paints a perfectly convincing picture of the mind of a child, with all its fears and misunderstandings. Hilarious and poignant in turns, this charming and heart-warming coming-of-age book won the Booker Prize in 1993.

Most of Roddy Doyle's books are set in Dublin's northside, and the three novels that comprise *The Barrytown Trilogy* are all recommended. Telling of the exploits of the Rabbitte family, the series begins with *The Commitments* (1987), which spawned the Alan Parker film of 1991, continues with *The Snapper* (1990), and ends with *The Van* (1991).

##  Read ons

*The Ginger Man*, J P Donleavy
Reluctant and irresponsible family man and law student, Sebastian Dangerfield gallivants his way around Dublin and London, drinking and womanising. A hugely funny modernist novel that was once banned.

*The Red and the Green*, Iris Murdoch
Set in Murdoch's Dublin birthplace, this novel deals with complex relationships within an Anglo-Irish family in the tense week leading up to the Easter Rebellion in 1916.

*At Swim, Two Boys*, Jamie O'Neill
In imaginative prose that bears comparisons to Joyce, this novel tells the tender and tragic story of the love between two teenage boys before and during the 1916 Easter Rebellion.

*The Portable Virgin*, Anne Enright
Dublin-born Enright is a highly talented and original novelist. This collection of stories offers an unusual and imaginative look at the Irish capital. It won the Rooney Prize in 1991.

*More Pricks Than Kicks*, Samuel Beckett
A collection of stories from the early career of the Nobel-Prize-winning playwright, novelist and poet. The stories chart the life of anti-hero, Belacqua, a philanderer and a failure. Set in and around Dublin.

*The Visitor*, Maeve Brennan
When her mother dies, a young woman returns from Paris to Dublin to live with her paternal grandmother. A spare and touching novella of heartache and cruelty.

*The Journey Home*, Dermot Bolger
The darker side of contemporary Dublin is portrayed in this powerful and shocking story concerning two friends, Hano and Shay, who become embroiled in a life of drugs, drink, corruption and violence.

*At Swim-Two-Birds*, Flann O'Brien
A novel that combines farce, parody and audacious linguistic skill to tell the story within a story within a story of a drunken student writing a novel.

*Dublin: Foundation*, Edward Rutherfurd
An epic historical novel covering the history of Ireland from pre-Christian times to the sixteenth century, as it affects its greatest city. *Ireland Awakening* continues the story to the modern day.

# UNITED KINGDOM

## NORTHERN IRELAND

**KEY**TITLES

*No Bones*, Anna Burns
*Eureka Street*, Robert McLiam Wilson

## NO BONES (2001)
### Anna Burns

This debut novel takes the reader from the beginning of the Troubles in 1969 to the ceasefire of 1994, through the life of one person. Amelia Lovett is just six years old on that fateful Thursday when a neighbour's child tells her that if they don't get out of Ardoyne, they will be burned in their beds. Amelia grows up amid raids, beatings and murders. Schoolgirls shoot each other in the playground, memorial services are held regularly for dead friends, and cocky children are kneecapped. The violence takes its toll on Amelia, initially driving her into anorexia and when her dysfunctional family disintegrates, she eventually becomes an alcoholic.

If violence is never a solution, it seems at least that humour is always an option, for amidst all the brutality there is a certain amount of knockabout comedy. The novel switches from third to first person seemingly at random, and the intimacy of Amelia's own voice is touching and poignant.

She moves to London temporarily in order to escape the life she has known, but discovers it is no escape at all. When she revisits home, she finds it impossible not to get involved again with friends and family because, in spite of the lunacy that surrounds them, she has the decency to care.

Anna Burns has written about a Belfast that is literally haunted by the past and the novel is really just a series of interlocked snapshots of its inhabitant's fleeing the violence in various, often ill-advised ways. *No Bones* is a book full of trouble and wonder about the darkest days of Northern Ireland's recent history.

# EUREKA STREET (1996)

## Robert McLiam Wilson

Set in Belfast, six months before the 1994 ceasefire, this story follows Jake Jackson, a Catholic ex-bouncer with a soft centre, wondering what to do with his life. Now working as a repo man, he misses the girlfriend who recently left him to move to London. His fat, balding, Protestant friend, Chuckie Lurgan, embarks on a number of vaguely ludicrous but amazingly successful business ventures in which Jake is tangentially involved. When Chuckie follows his American girlfriend to the States, Jake is left behind with her feisty Republican flatmate and a rather spiky relationship develops between them.

This is a richly descriptive novel portraying with delicacy the struggle of living from day to day in a Belfast under the constant threat of bombing. When the bomb does come, Chuckie's mother, Peggy, is deeply scarred by the incident and her anguished response is handled with sensitivity.

McLiam Wilson is keen to highlight the absurdity of sectarian attitudes in this comically inventive and invigorating novel that paints an achingly beautiful picture of a Belfast with a heart.

A mini series was made by the BBC in 1999.

**Read ons**

*Reading in the Dark*, Seamus Deane
Poet Seamus Deane's autobiographical and fittingly poetic novel set in Derry in the 1940s, a dangerous place engulfed in IRA activities.

*The Anatomy School*, Bernard MacLaverty
A vivid and seductive coming-of-age story about an insecure teenager growing up in a strict Catholic family in Belfast during the Troubles in the 1960s.

*Collected Short Stories*, Michael McLaverty
A selection of stories spanning the career of an esteemed short story writer and novelist. The stories vividly and movingly portray the people and landscapes of Northern Ireland.

*The Ultras*, Eoin McNamee
This gripping novel deals with the controversial life of British Army Captain Robert Nairac, accused of stirring up Republican/Loyalist troubles. He disappeared without a trace in the late 1970s.

*Shadows On Our Skin*, Jennifer Johnston
Eleven-year-old Joe Logan lives in Derry in the 1970s. He has ambitions to become a poet until his brother returns from England and the encroaching sectarian violence around him shatters his dreams.

*The Lonely Passion of Judith Hearne*, Brian Moore
Judith is a Catholic spinster in 1950s' Belfast. Desperate for love, she falls for a fellow lodger in her boarding house. A masterful insight into loneliness and disillusionment.

*Number 5*, Glenn Patterson
The story of a house, and a social history of Belfast, told through the eyes of the various families that have lived at number 5 from the 1950s to the 1990s.

*This Human Season*, Louise Dean
Two narratives intertwine in this eloquent novel, set in Belfast in 1979: those of a mother whose son is an inmate at the Maze prison, and of an ex-army prison guard who is his gaoler.

*One by One in the Darkness*, Deirdre Madden
An acclaimed novel that focuses on one week in the lives of a family trying to deal with the brutal death of their father.

*Divorcing Jack*, Colin Bateman
The first in a popular series featuring the hard-drinking and womanising Belfast journalist, Dan Starkey, who, despite his best intentions, finds himself constantly in trouble, both political and amorous.

*Nothing Happens in Carmincross*, Benedict Kiely
After years in America, a man travels home to Carmincross for a family wedding, only for it to be disrupted by an IRA bomb. A black-humoured satire on Irish nationalism and sectarian brutality.

*Death and Nightingales*, Eugene McCabe
A powerful book set in 1883 in Fermanagh, centring on a young Catholic woman's tragic relationship with her bitter and abusive Protestant stepfather.

# SCOTLAND

**KEY**TITLES

*Sunset Song*, Lewis Grassic Gibbon
*The Crow Road*, Iain Banks

## SUNSET SONG (1932)
### Lewis Grassic Gibbon

Set in a rural community in the northwest highlands of Scotland at the beginning of the twentieth century, this novel, the first of a trilogy, follows Chris Guthrie from her birth to the end of the Great War. It begins with a prelude that outlines the history of the village of Kinraddie and its inhabitants, in language that blends Scots and English. An eight-page glossary of Scots terms is included to aid the uninitiated reader.

Chris Guthrie is a farmer's daughter and she has to decide whether to pursue her education, which would take her away from the land and the community she knows, or marry and become a farmer's wife, which she does, maintaining her ambivalent relationship with Scotland, a country she loves and hates in equal measure. Vibrant characters litter the novel, and the author paints a vivid picture of a tightly knit farming community with its feast days and famine, its gossip and dark secrets.

The First World War heralds the end of their way of life. The old songs are replaced by American blues and even the landscape itself seems to undergo a profound change. Gibbon traces these changes without sentimentality in this frank account of the harshness of people's lives at a time of great social change. Based on his home town of Arbuthnott, and informed by his own experiences, the story is a celebration of the beauty of Scotland and a paean to the natural world.

In 2005, *Sunset Song* was voted Scotland's favourite book. The trilogy, entitled *A Scots Quair* (*A Scots Book*), is completed by *Cloud Howe* (1933) and *Grey Granite* (1934).

# THE CROW ROAD (1992)

Iain Banks

Prentice McHoan returns to his home town of Gallanach, in Argyll, for his grandmother's funeral. He has the opportunity to examine his family's baneful history, as well as his own turbid present. His troubled relationships with his immediate family members are brought into sharp focus, particularly the relationship he has with the atheist and communist father who disowned Prentice after his son admitted a nagging agnosticism. He stays with his uncle Hamish, a rather vengeful Christian, and hears of the odd disappearance of his Uncle Rory and the suspicious death of his Aunt Fiona. Amid this emotional disorder, he takes comfort in lusting after his lovely cousin, Verity, until his older brother also turns his attentions on her.

Banks weaves the threads of his story with skill and the themes of God, death and the search for meaning in life are handled without artifice. Prentice's descent into penury and isolation is described in an amusing and touching way, while his subsequent recovery and redemption handled judiciously. This is a mature and thoughtful book that has the west Highland landscape at its heart.

*It was adapted into a highly successful TV Series by the BBC in 1996. Other Iain Banks novels with a Scottish flavour are* Espedair Street *(1987), about a has-been rock star living in Glasgow, and* Complicity *(1993), a coruscating diatribe against all things Tory, and* The Steep Approach to Garbadale *(2007).*

## 📖 Read ons

*Like*, Ali Smith
This intriguing novel, set in Scotland and Cambridge, recounts the childhood friendship between two women. The obsessive behaviour of one of them has serious repercussions for the other.

*The Sopranos*, Alan Warner
A day in the lives of five vivacious, alcohol-fuelled schoolgirls who travel from their dead-end coastal town to the big city for the inter-school choir finals. A witty, astute and poignant depiction of adolescence.

*The Lymond Chronicles*, Dorothy Dunnett
A sweeping six-book saga that follows the life of charismatic Francis Crawford of Lymond in sixteenth-century Scotland and Europe. The series begins with *The Game of Kings.*

*The Bruce Trilogy*, Nigel Tranter
Tranter takes the reader deep into Scotland's fourteenth-century past with this gripping and well-researched trilogy of novels, bringing to life the struggles and triumphs of the great Scottish king, Robert the Bruce.

*Consider the Lilies*, Iain Crichton-Smith
A beautiful novel about the dark period of the Higland Clearances, told through the memories of old Mrs Scott, who finds comfort not in religion, as she expects, but in her atheist neighbour.

*Young Adam*, Alexander Trocchi
Heroin addict and Beat writer Trocchi focuses this existential and erotic masterpiece on a hired hand working on a barge on the River Clyde. He expertly seduces the skipper's wife and also finds a floating corpse.

*Electric Brae*, Andrew Greig
A spare and evocative page-turner, set in various locations around Scotland, that revolves around mountain climbing, the political landscape of the 1980s and the complex relationships between four friends.

*The Cone-Gatherers*, Robin Jenkins
This modern Scottish classic is set on a Highland estate during the Second World War. When two brothers collect cones for their seeds, their activities inspire hatred and loathing in the estate's gamekeeper.

*Greenvoe*, George Mackay Brown
An ominous military project planned for the small Orcadian isle of Hellya looks set to change forever the ancient way of life of a tightly knit community.

*The Silver Darlings*, Neil M Gunn
Uprooted after the Clearances, Finn, the mythical main character, is one of many Highland crofters who re-establish themselves on the coast and learns to fish in order to survive.

*The House with the Green Shutters*, George Douglas Brown
In nineteenth-century Ayrshire, a powerful and unlikeable merchant, John Gourlay, is outmanoeuvred in business and violently confronted by his own downtrodden son.

*Docherty*, William McIlvanney
A moving novel set in Kilmarnock (labelled Graithnock in the book), about a miner, Tam Docherty, and his son during the depression in the 1930s. *The Kiln* details the life of Tam's grandson, Tom.

# EDINBURGH

*The Prime of Miss Jean Brodie*, Muriel Spark

## THE PRIME OF MISS JEAN BRODIE (1961)
Muriel Spark

Edinburgh is an elegant backdrop to this deservedly famous novel set in a girls' school in the thirties, and Miss Jean Brodie herself is one of the most famous characters in modern British literature. She is indeed a woman in her prime, with her wisdom and insight at their peak. She considers that her role in life is to mould young girls into her version of cultured ladies. Her favourites become known as the Brodie Set and it is they who tell the story of her singular tutelage and rather sad downfall.

Miss Brodie is a bully and a pedant whose fascination with fascism and penchant for romantic love set her at odds with the headmistress, Miss McKay. During the course of the novel, Miss Brodie encourages one of her girls, Rose, to become the lover of the one-armed art teacher, Mr Lloyd. Another charge, Joyce, is encouraged to join her brother in fighting in the Spanish Civil War: she is promptly killed.

The demise of the Brodie Set is an unavoidable climax, hastened when Miss McKay enlists one of the girls, the wonderfully named Sandy Stranger, to betray their mistress.

This sparkling story is told in original and witty prose rich with acute observation. It was adapted for the stage, and notably filmed in 1969, with the excellent Maggie Smith in the lead role. A less successful TV series was made in 1978.

## 🌊Read ons

*Trainspotting*, Irvine Welsh
An era-defining novel that reveals the sleazy side of the genteel city of Edinburgh. Mark Renton and his friends indulge in liberal amounts of hard drugs. *Porno* follows the same characters in later life.

*Born Free*, Laura Hird
A feisty, witty story of a dysfunctional tenement family looking to escape their dreary lives. Petulant teenager Jake, boy-hungry sister Joni, alcoholic mum Angie, and impotent dad Vic, all tell their sides of the story.

*The Lamplighter*, Anthony O'Neill
Savage murders are being committed all over Edinburgh in the late nineteenth century. Evidence points to Evelyn Todd, who knows about the killings intimately but denies any involvement.

*44 Scotland Street*, Alexander McCall Smith
Originally published in serial format in *The Scotsman* newspaper, this light-hearted and extremely popular novel follows the exploits of various well-to-do residents of an upmarket area of Edinburgh. Three sequels are also available.

*Knots and Crosses*, Ian Rankin
Edinburgh is richly described in this first instalment in the John Rebus series, which delves deep into the detective's past, offering explanations for his gruff and gloomy disposition.

# GLASGOW

*Lanark: A Life in Four Books*, Alasdair Gray

## LANARK (1981)
### Alasdair Gray

A devilishly quirky and fantastical novel written by an author regarded as being at the vanguard of a new Scottish renaissance. The stories of the two main protagonists, Lanark and Duncan Thaw, are compelling but seemingly unrelated individual tales.

In the first part of the novel, a fantasy alternative Glasgow, labelled Unthank, is a world in which people disappear and/or develop the skin disease Dragonhide which eventually turns them into dragons. Lanark arrives, with no memory of his past life. He has great difficulty understanding the world around him and finds himself working to save the city from the creeping menace of capitalism.

An unrelated Part Two presents a realistic portrayal of the life of young Duncan Thaw, growing up in 1950s Glasgow and failing to become an artist. He ends up mentally unstable and incapable of love.

Over twenty-five years in the writing, *Lanark* is a book of grand scope that is endlessly inventive and genuinely funny, a manifesto that places the need for love – for others and for ourselves – at the heart of the community. It is illustrated with the author's own drawings (as are all his books). Other works include the award-winning gothic Frankenstein pastiche, *Poor Things* (1992), set in Victorian Glasgow.

GLASGOW

## 📖Read ons

*The Cutting Room*, Louise Welsh
A captivating novel about a Glasgow auctioneer who comes across a collection of violent pornographic images and feels compelled to find out more about their deceased owner.

*How Late it Was, How Late*, James Kelman
A powerful stream-of-consciousness novel, told in working-class Glaswegian vernacular, about a con who goes blind after a drunken binge and a police beating and his stumbling attempts to understand his life and the welfare system. 1994 Booker Prize winner.

*Hen's Teeth*, Manda Scott
A Glasgow therapist tries to solve the mystery of her ex-lover's suspicious death and finds herself grappling with genetic engineering, veterinary science and missing chickens. The first novel in a series.

*So I Am Glad*, A L Kennedy
Magic realism, sadomasochistic sex, quirky humour and emotional complexity all feature in this remarkable story of a woman who meets the ghost of Cyrano de Bergerac and falls in love.

*Laidlaw*, William McIlvanney
Inspector Jack Laidlaw, a disgruntled philosophy buff, pursues a murderer through a gloomy, Chandleresque Glasgow. Two sequels are also available.

*Swing Hammer Swing*, Jeff Torrington
The novel follows a week in the life of father-to-be, Tam Clay in the late 1960s, as he meanders around the Gorbals slums, a place soon to be demolished.

*A Glasgow Trilogy*, George Friel
An omnibus of Friel novels that are convincing and humanistic portrayals of raw emotions and Glasgow working-class life in the 1950s and 60s.

# WALES

KEYTITLES

*How Green Was My Valley*, Richard Llewellyn
*On the Black Hill*, Bruce Chatwin

## HOW GREEN WAS MY VALLEY (1939)

Richard Llewellyn

A poetic and political story about the Morgan family in rural South Wales, beautifully told through the eyes of the youngest boy, Huw, in vibrant and powerful prose.

As he is preparing to leave the family home, Huw tells the story of this mining family, a story that begins around the turn of the twentieth century as the coal industry becomes unionised. Huw's academic abilities once offered him an escape, but he chooses to join his father and five brothers in the pit.

A eulogy for the Welsh countryside and community life mixes with a vivid portrayal of the harsh conditions of the mineworkers. The influence of the church on everyday lives is juxtaposed with the realities of dealing with the bosses at the pit, and schisms occur within the family when the workers strike in response to cutbacks and closures. There are poignant tales of love, unrequited or misdirected. National pride and hostility towards the English are sympathetically portrayed sentiments that always fall short of fanaticism, and the whole is unashamedly nostalgic in tone.

This is the first novel of a quartet. It is followed by *Up, Into The Singing Mountain* (1960); *Down Where The Moon is Small and Green* (1966), in which Huw Morgan lives among Welsh settlers in Patagonia; and *Green, Green My Valley Now* (1975), in which Huw returns to South Wales.

In 1941, John Ford made a powerful film that was nominated for five Oscars. An impressive BBC serial aired in 1978.

# ON THE BLACK HILL (1982)

Bruce Chatwin

This is a pastoral novel that tells the story of two eighty-year-old twins who spend their whole life in the immediate vicinity of their Welsh border farm. The story begins in 1899, with the courting and marriage of their ill-suited parents, Amos and Mary, he an irascible peasant farmer with conventional ideas, she the educated and cultured daughter of an English clergyman, with spiritual needs her husband is incapable of fulfilling.

The lives and personalities of the identical twins mirror those of their parents, with Benjamin content to stay at home while Lewis is restless and frustrated. Despite the murderous love they feel for each other, the twins are interdependent, feeling each other's pain, remaining in voluntary isolation from the outside world, and sleeping together in their parents' bed for forty-two years. When anything threatens to separate them, their reactions are visceral: Lewis suffers his younger brother's distress when Benjamin is called up to fight; later, when Lewis talks of marriage, Benjamin's grief brings him close to death.

The book has a tremendous sense of place and the minutiae of country life is lovingly displayed, often through other well-drawn eccentric characters: local beauty, Rosie Fifield, who catches Lewis's eye but cannot capture his heart, and 'Theo the Tent', a red-bearded giant who preaches Buddhism and eventually leaves to live in Thailand.

*The author, who is perhaps better known for his travel books, provides a rich and vivid portrait of Welsh country life.* On The Black Hill *was successful as both a stage play and in a 1987 film.*

## 📖 Read ons

*One Moonlit Night*, Caradog Prichard
A dark and sad story, poetically told, about a man who returns to the Welsh slate-quarrying village of his youth during the First World War and reminisces about his deprived childhood and his troubled fellow villagers.

*Collected Stories*, Dylan Thomas
This edition gathers together all of Thomas's masterful and humorous short stories, including the semi-autobiographical tales from *Portrait of the Artist as a Young Dog* and *Adventures in the Skin Trade*.

*Eve Green*, Susan Fletcher
A moving and atmospheric novel about a pregnant woman looking back on her difficult youth spent with her grandparents in a remote Welsh valley, after the suicide of her mother.

*The Hiding Place*, Trezza Azzopardi
Family secrets resurface when Dolores Gauci meets her sisters for the first time in thirty years at their mother's funeral. A fascinating look at Maltese immigrant life in 1960s' Cardiff.

*Sheepshagger*, Niall Griffiths
A bleak and compelling tale about a group of disenchanted and drug-fuelled youths in Aberystwyth, and their hatred for the English infiltrators.

*Aberystwyth Mon Amour*, Malcolm Pryce
The first in a series of Chandleresque comic thrillers starring Private Investigator Louie Knight solving crimes on the mean streets of Aberystwyth. Followed by *Last Tango in Aberystwyth*.

*The Cardiff Trilogy*, John Williams
An omnibus edition of Williams's pacy crime novels and stories set in the seedier districts of the author's hometown. It includes *Five Pubs, Two Bars and a Nightclub*, *Cardiff Dead*, and *The Prince of Wales*.

*Fairy Tale*, Alice Thomas Ellis
Mystical and magical things happen to seventeen-year-old Eloise and her boyfriend, Simon, after they move to a rural idyll in remote Wales, in this quirky and comic modern fairy tale.

*Border Country*, Raymond Williams
One of a series of Welsh classics recently republished by the Library of Wales, which tells the moving semi-autobiographical story of a father-son relationship in rural South Wales.

*The Old Devils*, Kingsley Amis
A booze-soaked novel that is both humorous and poignant. Alun Weaver, a semi-successful poet, and his beautiful wife, Rhiannon, return to their Welsh homeland and stir up the lives of their old friends.

*The Fall*, Simon Mawer
A climber falls to his death during a solo ascent of Snowdonia. His estranged friend drives to Wales to comfort the grieving widow, his former lover, and journeys into his own past.

*Rape of the Fair Country*, Alexander Cordell
A nineteenth-century family struggles to survive whilst working for the brutal English owners of the local iron works. The saga continues in *The Hosts of Rebecca* and *Song of the Earth*.

# ENGLAND

## GENERAL ENGLAND

---

**KEY**TITLES

*A Dance to the Music of Time*, Anthony Powell
*Room at the Top*, John Braine

---

## A DANCE TO THE MUSIC OF TIME (1951–1975)
Anthony Powell

A twelve-novel cycle that chronicles the lives of a group of Eton schoolfriends from 1914 to 1971, as observed by the permanently perplexed Nick Jenkins. The friends and lovers continually come together, drift apart, and meet up again as the effects of time, nature and society take their toll. The story follows four upper-class characters from adolescence to senescence through the eyes of Jenkins, a cipher who recalls and assesses his life through his relationships with the others as he follows them in their initiations into sex and love, through their first marriages and jobs and the Second World War, and into the exigencies of old age.

Historical events are not dwelt upon. Rather it is personal relationships that provide the material for this ironic, sophisticated social comedy about the changing British establishment and the effects such change has on individuals.

The novels can be read independently, but the joy of the series, named after a painting by Nicolas Poussin, is the development and fate of the characters at its centre. The cycle is now also published in four volumes of three novels apiece, each one bearing the title of a season of the year, beginning with *Spring*. The whole series was dramatised to good effect by Channel 4 in 1997.

# ROOM AT THE TOP (1957)

## John Braine

Joe Lampton is looking back, ten years later, on his road to the top, which began just after he was demobbed from the army at the end of the Second World War. Both his parents were killed in a bombing raid and he has come down from Dufton to the fictitious town of Warley to work in the Municipal Treasury. Lampton joins an amateur theatrical society where he meets, and immediately sets out to pursue, Susan Brown, the only daughter of a successful local businessman. Lampton also begins a casual affair with an older woman, Alice Aisgill, which develops into an authentic love that contrasts sharply with the sterility of his relationship with the boss's daughter.

As he climbs the social ladder, Lampton changes his language and his dress. He becomes increasingly isolated from the outside world and insulated from his true self, a realisation that he does come to in time. It is a brilliantly scathing and psychologically astute novel that perfectly illustrates the aspirations of the postwar working class.

*John Braine was one of the original Angry Young Men, along with playwright, John Osbourne, writer Colin Wilson and fellow Yorkshire novelist, Stan Barstow, whose novel* A Kind of Loving *(1960) is another excellent barometer of the times.*

An award-winning film was made in 1959, with Laurence Harvey giving the performance of a lifetime and Simone Signoret winning an Oscar. A worthy sequel, *Life at the Top* (1962), was also made into a successful film.

**Read ons**

*England, England*, Julian Barnes
In this witty satire on English culture and nationality, the Isle of Wight has been turned into an 'England' theme park as an antidote to the real thing, whose glory days have faded into the past.

*Cold Comfort Farm*, Stella Gibbons
This gloriously comic novel is a clever parody of Hardy and Lawrence. An orphaned townie tries to bring order to the chaotic lives of her hapless country relatives in rural Sussex.

*The Remains of the Day*, Kazuo Ishiguro
A staid and ageing butler reminisces about his life of personal disappointments and self-deceptions in his dedication to duty, as he journeys around southwest England on holiday. Poignant and beautifully crafted.

*Brideshead Revisited*, Evelyn Waugh
A nostalgic novel that paints a portrait of England between the wars. Charles Ryder looks back at his life and his fixation with a doomed aristocratic family.

*The Pursuit of Love*, Nancy Mitford
A hugely enjoyable comic novel about the romantic pursuits of Linda Radlett and her eccentric, aristocratic family, narrated by cousin Fanny. *See also* **Love in a Cold Climate** and *The Blessing*.

*Lady Chatterley's Lover*, D H Lawrence
Famously banned in Britain for many years, Lawrence's frank and controversial tale of passion between people from different social classes is a fascinating study of English social mores in the early twentieth century.

*What a Carve Up!*, Jonathan Coe
A brilliant satire on Britain in the 1980s. Funny, clever and political, it is destined to be a classic of the future.

*If Nobody Speaks of Remarkable Things*, Jon McGregor
On an unremarkable day in an ordinary, unnamed northern town, a disaster occurs that changes the lives of everyone who witnesses it. An award-winning debut novel.

*The Enigma of Arrival*, V S Naipaul
Exile, belonging and change are the main themes in this melancholy autobiographical tale of a young Trinidadian Indian who settles into life in rural Wiltshire. The countryside and its characters are beautifully described.

*Mrs Dalloway*, Virginia Woolf
Set in London in the 1920s, and told in Woolf's stream-of-consciousness style, this novel charts the inner thoughts, feelings and impressions of Clarissa Dalloway during one day, as she prepares to host a dinner party.

*The Ragged-Trousered Philanthropists*, Robert Tressell
A passionate Socialist novel, set in the second decade of the twentieth century, about a group of painters and decorators in southeast England made aware of their subjugation and the evils of capitalism by the prophet-like Frank Owen.

*Small Island*, Andrea Levy
This excellent, moving story of Jamaicans in Britain in the 1940s is told by four very different narrators – two white, two West Indian – whose lives collide and interweave. Winner of the Orange Prize and the Whitbread Novel Award.

*The Radiant Way*, Margaret Drabble
Book One of a trilogy, this is the story of three middle-aged women, friends from university, and their changing lives in Thatcher's Britain in the early 1980s. The companion volumes are *A Natural Curiosity* and *The Gates of Ivory*.

# NORTHERN ENGLAND

---

**KEY**TITLE

*This Sporting Life*, David Storey (Yorkshire)

---

## THIS SPORTING LIFE (1960)
David Storey

David Storey's first published novel concerns Arthur Machin as he makes his way into the moneyed world of rugby football in Yorkshire. A true existential hero, he despises the games played by local worthies to win influence and wealth, yet he adores the prestige he receives as a result of his success on the field.

However, his relationship with his recently widowed landlady, Mrs Hammond, is problematic. The object of much local gossip, it is founded on genuine love but frustrated by the cards that life has dealt them. Arthur is unsure how to behave, torn between the urge to imitate the macho heroes of the cheap novels he reads and the need to explore his true feelings. Constantly betrayed by his own inarticulacy, he resorts to the brutishness he has relied on all his life.

Storey's novel is a powerful portrait of a man attempting to resolve the conflict between his inner needs and the pressures and desires of the outside world. Although its treatment of the working class seems a little dated now, it continues to have a strong psychological impact on the reader.

*David Storey also wrote the screenplay for the film of the novel, made by Lindsay Anderson in 1963, with a young, brooding Richard Harris in the lead role. Storey's Booker-Prize-winning novel* Saville *(1976) is set in a Yorkshire mining village in the 1930s and moves into the postwar period and beyond.*

## ✒Read ons

*A Month in the Country*, J L Carr **(Yorkshire)**
A short, tender novel about a man, damaged by his war experiences, who finds peace and renewal in a small village while helping to restore a church mural.

*My Summer of Love*, Helen Cross **(Yorkshire)**
Two troubled teenage girls spend a sultry summer together in the 1980s, lost in their own world of drink and debauchery and forming a dangerous love-hate relationship. A shocking yet humorous coming-of-age story.

*Behind the Scenes at the Museum*, Kate Atkinson **(Yorkshire)**
A sparkling debut novel that is gripping from its first quirky paragraph. It tells the story of Ruby, brought up above a pet shop in York, and of four generations of her family.

*A Kind of Loving*, Stan Barstow **(Yorkshire)**
A bittersweet and compelling portrait of working-class life in the late 1950s, which spawned two sequels.

*The Taxi Driver's Daughter*, Julia Darling **(Newcastle)**
Cracks in the family façade cause problems for fifteen-year-old Caris. Her mother is sent to prison for shoplifting and she becomes involved with a dangerous boy called George.

*Union Street*, Pat Barker **(Teesside)**
An unnamed industrial city in the northeast in the 1970s is the setting for this hard-hitting novel about the difficult lives of seven women.

*The Maid of Buttermere*, Melvyn Bragg **(Cumbria)**
John Hatfield, scoundrel and con man, marries local beauty, Mary, but has to flee when he is exposed as an impostor. A historical novel, set in the nineteenth century, that expertly combines fact and fiction.

*Cold Water*, Gwendoline Riley **(Manchester)**
Carmel McKisco works in a bar and dreams of an exciting and glamorous life. A gritty and assured novella set in an atmospherically wet and wintry Manchester.

*The Wrong Boy*, Willy Russell **(Manchester)**
Raymond is a misunderstood lad who believes his only ally is the musician, Morrissey. He writes letters to his idol, describing his lonely plight. A comic tour de force from the acclaimed playwright.

*The Craze*, Paul Southern **(Manchester)**
Revolving around three main characters, this is a gripping and violent story of drugs, murder and the Asian underworld in Manchester's sleazy underbelly.

*Outlaws*, Kevin Sampson **(Liverpool)**
Scousers meet Scorcese in this graphic and witty tale of Liverpool's underworld. Three ageing old-school gangsters plan to do one last job before entering the world of retirement and respectability.

*Love On the Dole*, Walter Greenwood **(Lancashire)**
The struggles of love and survival during the depression are the subject of this classic novel. It is a gritty depiction of mass unemployment and poverty in a northern town in the 1930s.

*Thursbitch*, Alan Garner **(Cheshire)**
Two intersecting narratives, set in a Pennine valley, span three centuries, with dialogue in the local vernacular helping to create an acute sense of place.

*Oranges Are Not the Only Fruit*, Jeanette Winterson
An excellent semi-autobiographical tale of a girl growing up in a northern town in a strict religious family. Her nascent preference for other girls outrages her domineering mother.

# THE MIDLANDS

KEYTITLE

*Precious Bane*, Mary Webb **(Shropshire)**

## PRECIOUS BANE (1924)
### Mary Webb

Set in rural southwest Shropshire in the first half of the nineteenth century, this novel tells of Prue Sarn's life on her family's country farm. Her brother, Gideon, has lightning in his blood and a greed for gold. He dreams of the family living in finery, with himself as 'chief among ten thousand'. When their father dies, Gideon becomes a Sin Eater in order to obtain ownership of the family farm. Prue is cursed with a harelip, which prompts locals to suspect that she turns into a hare at midnight or into a witch when the moon is full.

The humble Prue finds peace in every situation, her spiritual core strengthened by her disfigurement and the community's hostility. She agrees to work hard for her brother on the understanding that, when they have enough money, they will find a cure for her harelip. When she falls in love with a local weaver, Kester Woodseaves, she feels constrained to keep herself hidden away. The story of their burgeoning love sees Kester learning that real beauty is on the inside.

Mary Webb's imaginative mixture of folklore, bible story and romance novel make this a timeless book that remains a much-loved classic. The sense of place is enhanced by the use of local dialect, which also adds to the rhythmic and sensual feel of the book.

*All of Mary Webb's novels are set in Shropshire.* Gone to Earth *(1917) is recommended.*

## 📖Read ons

*Sons and Lovers*, D H Lawrence **(Nottinghamshire)**
A classic autobiographical novel, set in the author's native county, about the difficult marriage of Gertrude and Walter Morel and Gertrude's suffocating plans for their children.

*Saturday Night, Sunday Morning*, Alan Sillitoe **(Nottingham)**
An excellent story of working-class life in the 1950s. Arthur Seaton is a hard-drinking, womanising, 'angry young man' who works at the local factory but wants something more out of life.

*Living*, Henry Green **(Birmingham)**
Written in a distinctive and deliberately sparse style designed to emulate working-class speech, this vivid novel examines the class distinctions of the 1930s through the lives of a group of workers in an iron foundry.

*The Rotters' Club*, Jonathon Coe **(Birmingham)**
Adolescence in Birmingham in the 1970s is superbly captured in this eloquent and entertaining comic novel of young Benjamin Trotter and his schoolfriends trying to find their place in the world.

*Anna of the Five Towns*, Arnold Bennett **(Staffordshire)**
Set in the Potteries in the 1890s, this is a story of the moral and romantic dilemmas faced by a young woman who inherits her miserly father's fortune and his business interests.

*Anita and Me*, Meera Syal **(Midlands)**
In this entertaining novel, nine-year-old Meena, growing up in a Midlands mining village in the 1960s, is caught between the expectations of her traditional Punjabi family and modern English culture, personified by the tearaway Anita.

*Hurry On Down*, John Wain
A landmark novel from 1953 which was a precursor to the Angry Young Men novels. Charles Lumley rejects his university education to do various menial jobs, hoping to find his true path in life.

# EASTERN ENGLAND

**KEY** TITLE

*Waterland*, Graham Swift **(The Fens)**

## WATERLAND (1983)

### Graham Swift

History teacher, Tom Crick is about to be forced into early retirement when his wife, Mary kidnaps a baby from a local supermarket. The ensuing publicity and her subsequent breakdown make him examine his life in detail, an examination paralleled by the soul-searching prompted by an inquisitive pupil who makes him question the value of history and the need to reclaim the past. Tom abandons the curriculum and tells his class stories about the Norfolk Fens where he grew up forty years ago, during the Second World War.

Various episodes from his past are recalled, in particular those from 1943, a year in which the intense rivalry between his mentally subnormal brother, Dick, and local boy Freddie Parr resulted in the latter's death. He tells of Mary, the wife who was his childhood sweetheart, and how her pregnancy, and subsequent abortion at the hands of a neighbourhood 'witch', rendered her infertile. He also reflects mournfully on his widowed father's valiant attempt to bring up his two sons properly, and the profound guilt he felt at failing.

Tom Crick retreats further in time, giving his students an account of his forebears that goes back to the eighteenth century. Tales of the reclaiming of waterlogged land are brought alive magnificently: the cyclical battle with nature to keep the land dry and the fields productive in this bleak landscape is integral to the novel and its effect on the various characters is profound.

Through a web of madness, incest, murder and romance, this complex book moves back and forth in time, linking the past to the present and describing each scenario with vigour and elan. Included in the narrative are numerous philosophical meditations on various subjects, from empire building to the breeding habits of eels, and all are expertly handled.

Swift's writing is impressively assured. A brooding menace slowly builds around the flat lands of East Anglia and the development of the narrative adds layers of chilling apprehension.

## 📖 Read ons

*Watch Me Disappear*, Jill Dawson **(The Fens)**
Tina Humber returns to the village where, thirty years earlier, her childhood friend disappeared. Old memories and emotions rise to the surface in this spine-tingling novel that skilfully evokes the atmosphere of the 1970s.

*The Rector's Daughter*, F M Mayor **(East Anglia)**
Set in the 1930s in a bleak East Anglian landscape, adroitly described, this is the tale of spinster Mary Jocelyn, and the dull and selfless life she leads. When she meets curate Robert Herbert, her suppressed passions are ignited, though not fulfilled.

*The Rings of Saturn*, W G Sebald **(Norfolk)**
Part fiction, part memoir, part travel journal, this is a fascinating book following the author's journey around Norfolk. Each place visited triggers off digressions, memories, historical happenings, and imaginings. A wonderful book.

*The Go-Between*, L P Hartley **(Norfolk)**
An old man looks back to a summer holiday he spent as a child at a friend's house, a holiday that ended tragically. It is beautifully evocative of the Edwardian era.

*The Chymical Wedding*, Lindsay Clarke **(Norfolk)**
Two narratives, a hundred years apart, are woven together in this atmospheric and intriguing novel of alchemy, obsession, love and poetry, set in a small East Anglian village.

*The Bookshop*, Penelope Fitzgerald **(Suffolk)**
Despite the opposition of various ruthless locals, widow Florence Green is determined to open a bookshop in the insular East Anglian seaside town of Hardborough. A slim novel that deftly depicts small-town life.

*Something Might Happen*, Julie Myerson **(Suffolk)**
A novel that explores the effects of the murder of a mother of two on the victim's family and friends in a small Suffolk town.

*The Sea House*, Esther Freud **(Suffolk)**
A young woman rents a quiet cottage by the sea and reads an architect's love letters to his wife, written a generation ago, as part of her thesis research. They force her to confront her own life and her aspirations for the future.

# SOUTHERN ENGLAND

*Brighton Rock*, Graham Greene

## BRIGHTON ROCK (1938)
### Graham Greene

Teenage sociopath, Pinkie Brown, is one of literature's great anti-heroes. When Fred Hale comes to Brighton to distribute cards for a newspaper competition, Pinkie murders him in retaliation for Hale's betrayal of Kite, the former leader of the gang that Pinkie now controls. Sure of the justice of his actions, Pinkie reckons without Hale's fiery guardian angel, Ida Arnold, a pub landlady who is suspicious of Hale's demise and who pursues Pinkie with relentless determination.

In order to secure an alibi for Hale's murder, Pinkie takes up with Rose, a timid and innocent waitress who believes Pinkie loves her. The struggle between good and evil played out in the minds of Pinkie and Rose, both Roman Catholics, is contrasted with Ida's atheistic moral certainty.

Pinkie's background is unknown to the reader and his motivations are unclear. Uninterested in drink and women, he seems to be motivated purely by hatred. Rose regards her love for Pinkie as paramount in her life, outweighing her religion and her regard for the law. Ida is disturbed by Rose's involvement with Pinkie and tries to save her, while Pinkie's criminality intensifies and his downfall approaches.

Greene, a film critic as well as a novelist, frames his scenes with a cineaste's eye and the story as a whole is wonderfully evocative of the seedy side of life in a seaside town in a drab England of the 1930s. Both the atmospheric menace of gangland warfare and the intimate existential struggle are portrayed with chilling immediacy.

The earlier *A Gun For Sale* (1936) describes the rift between the rival gangs and Fred Hale's role as an informer.

An excellent film, starring a young Richard Attenborough, was made in 1947, for which Greene wrote the screenplay, along with Terence Rattigan.

## 📖 Read ons

*All Souls*, Javier Marías **(Oxford)**
A witty and perceptive tale of academic life in Oxford, in which a visiting Spanish lecturer divulges his thoughts on the foibles of the community around him, while indulging in an affair with a married woman.

*Last Bus to Woodstock*, Colin Dexter **(Oxford/Oxfordshire)**
Inspector Morse, Oxford's erudite, Jaguar-driving, crossword-solving detective, searches for the key to a murder with help from sidekick Lewis, in this first novel in the long-running series.

*Last Orders*, Graham Swift **(Kent)**
Four friends of recently deceased Jack Dodds drive from London to Margate to scatter his ashes out at sea. On the way, the friends reassess their lives, their friendships, and the opportunities they missed, as old age encroaches.

*The Darling Buds of May*, H E Bates **(Kent)**
The first in Bates' series of adventures featuring Pop and Ma Larkin and their brood of children living in rustic charm in the Kent countryside in the 1950s.

*Wide Open*, Nicola Barker **(Kent)**
Set on the flat and bleak Isle of Sheppey, this comic and poignant tale is the first of a 'Thames Gateway' series of novels.

*The Country Life*, Rachel Cusk **(Sussex)**
Stella Benson leaves London to become an au pair in a small Sussex village. Disaster and humiliation befall her as she tries to adapt to her new rural life, in this funny and astute novel.

*In the Springtime of the Year*, Susan Hill **(Buckinghamshire)**
An inspiring novel about a young woman trying to come to terms with the sudden death of her husband. The grieving process and the rural setting are described in detail.

# LONDON

KEYTITLES

*Capital*, Maureen Duffy
*London Fields*, Martin Amis

## CAPITAL (1975)
Maureen Duffy

A curious novel about the history of London, seen not through the eyes of the important and feted but through those of the underdogs, the unknowns, those who lived anonymous lives.

Meepers, an amateur archaeologist, walks the streets of London hearing voices from the past beneath his feet, becoming convinced that they are attempting to communicate a warning about the future. He is a singular and obsessive character who lives in a friend's shed and works at a London college as a porter.

Emery is a university historian whose story is told through the letters he sends to his absent wife. He once rejected a 'crackpot' article submitted by Meepers for his historical journal. When he sees Meepers at a lecture he is giving, he begins to wonder if he is being stalked.

Meepers' thesis is that London came through the Dark Ages intact, and he believes that this fact will somehow guarantee the city's survival from nuclear annihilation or ecological damnation. The tales of these two characters are interspersed with the history of London itself, beginning with its prehistoric past as a virgin forest.

When Meepers finds his shed padlocked one day, he is forced to move from abode to abode, like a ghostly figure from his own past, mirroring the displaced and the forgotten to the point of invisibility. Through a chain of coincidences, he and Emery become involved in each other's lives and form an unlikely friendship that leads to an unexpected, yet satisfactory resolution of both their futures.

This is grim history revisited, written with a poets' eye and a sly humour. *Capital* is the second volume of Duffy's loose trilogy of London novels. The companion volumes, *Wounds* (1969) and *Londoners* (1983), are sadly both out of print.

# LONDON FIELDS (1989)

Martin Amis

A young woman is planning a murder – her own. The action opens in the year preceding the Millennium and the end of the world is nigh, but Nicola Six would rather die now than drift into a loveless old age. Her psychic abilities give her the clear knowledge that her killing is going to happen (she even knows the date of her murder – her thirty-fifth birthday) but she does not know which of two men – Keith Talent or Guy Clinch – will be her murderer. Talent is a working class-yob with a penchant for pornography and darts, while Clinch is an upper-class milksop bored with life. She spends the novel trying to work these two men into a frenzy of lust, jealousy or pique that may motivate them to kill her when the day comes.

However, this situation appears to be the plot of a novel being finished by Samson Young, a New York writer in London (having swapped apartments with a more successful British writer, Mark Asprey) to complete the work before he dies of the wasting disease that has rendered him almost impotent. Sam engages directly with the lives of the three protagonists of his novel and interrupts the narrative to check details, give bad advice and generally get in the way. When it transpires that Mark Asprey (Martin Amis?) is Nicola's former lover, the reader is left wondering who is controlling the action.

Written in Amis's cartwheeling, crackerjack prose, this is a cynical and amusing novel designed to highlight the foulness lurking behind London's grand facades. The book's original title was *The Death of Love*.

## 📖 Read ons

*Mother London*, Michael Moorcock
A captivating and humane history of the capital, from the Blitz to the 1980s, told through the eyes of three characters who wander the city hearing in their heads the voices of ordinary Londoners from the past.

*The Lonely Londoners*, Samuel Selvon
This was one of the first novels to chronicle the lives of black people in 1950s' Britain. Written in Creole it recounts the disillusionment of a Trinidadian, whose real-life experiences confound his cherished image of London.

*The Heat of the Day*, Elizabeth Bowen
Bowen captures the angst and confusion of London's inhabitants in a city under siege during the Blitz, in this complex story of espionage, sacrifice and doomed love.

*Hawksmoor*, Peter Ackroyd
A modern-day Nicholas Hawksmoor investigates murders in churches designed by the eighteenth-century Nicholas Dyer and uncovers occult foundations. A clever mix of mystery and history.

*Twenty Thousand Streets Under the Sky*, Patrick Hamilton
A trilogy that captures the bleakness of London life in the 1930s: a world of pubs, prostitution, cheap lodgings and desperate love. Also recommended is the sleazy *Hangover Square*.

*Brixton Rock*, Alex Wheatle
Teenager Brenton's troubled life in Brixton around the time of the 1980 riots is relayed with excellent period detail in Jamaican patois, in this updated version of Graham Greene's *Brighton Rock*.

*The London Novels*, Colin MacInnes
Set around Notting Hill and Soho, these books reveal a rapidly changing 1950s' Britain with the blossoming of a multiracial culture. A trilogy, which begins with *Absolute Beginners* and continues with *City of Spades*, *Mr Love and Justice*.

*Jack Maggs*, Peter Carey
In this re-imagining of *Great Expectations*, an escaped convict returns from Australia to track down the young man whose fortune he has helped to secure. He meets a would-be writer who uses the convict's story for his own purposes.

*Up the Junction*, Nell Dunn
Set in Battersea in the 1960s, this is a collection of vignettes of working-class women's lives in a bleak and battered landscape. *See also **Poor Cow***.

*Downriver*, Iain Sinclair
Twelve interconnected, multi-layered tales centred on the Thames. The reader journeys to the heart of the city and glimpses its rich and varied history.

*253*, Geoff Ryman
An innovative collection of stories in which the reader is given the outward appearance and inner thoughts and feelings of each of the 253 passengers on a packed London underground train (all seats full, no-one standing). Each vignette is 253 words long.

*Bleeding London*, Geoff Nicholson
Three people traverse the highways of London, each armed with a London A-Z and each on their own obsessive mission. Eventually their paths cross in this thoughtful homage to London and its history.

*Skin-Lane*, Neil Bartlett
An excellent evocation of 1960s' London from an outstanding writer. A man is troubled by dreams and strange longings. He begins to wander the streets in search of answers.

# SOUTH-WEST ENGLAND

*Jamaica Inn*, Daphne du Maurier

## JAMAICA INN (1936)
Daphne du Maurier

A pastiche of gothic horror, set in 1815. An innocent farmer's daughter, Mary Yellen, fulfils her mother's dying wish and leaves her home in Helford to live with her aunt and uncle in the inn they run near Bodmin Moor. Mary is unnerved by a coach driver's assertion that respectable people avoid Jamaica Inn. Her aunt, the aptly named Patience, is a sallow and docile individual, while she finds her Uncle Joss to be a drunken bully.

It emerges that Joss Merlyn is a smuggler who uses his inn as a base from which to peddle smuggled goods around the area. Futhermore, he confesses to luring people to their death and, one stormy night, forces Mary down to the beach to recover loot from a ship dashed against the rocks.

Du Maurier has a great deal of fun with shadows and light and the windswept bleakness of the Cornish moors, and she produces an appealingly feisty main character in Mary, supported by a host of suitably villainous and colourful characters, including an albino vicar, Francis Davey, and Joss Merlyn's enigmatic brother, Jem. The denouement is fabulously unlikely but entirely in keeping with the romantic spirit of the book.

*It was made into a popular film by Alfred Hitchcock in 1939. Daphne du Maurier's other Cornish novels include* Frenchman's Creek *(1941), set during the Restoration.*

## 📖 Read ons

*Ulverton*, Adam Thorpe **(Wessex Downs)**
The story of a fictional village on the Wessex Downs is told by twelve different narrators throughout the past five centuries, in this fascinating and imaginative novel of history and place.

*The Harvest*, Christopher Hart **(Dorset/Wiltshire)**
An elegy to the English countryside and the death of rural life. Young Lewis Pike, living on the Dorset/Wiltshire border, struggles to adapt to a rapidly changing world.

*The Children of Dynmouth*, William Trevor **(Dorset)**
A bizarre and darkly humorous novel about a troubled boy growing up in a run-down seaside town in the 1970s, daydreaming about finding fame and embarking on a trail of destruction and despair.

*Wolf Solent*, John Cowper Powys **(Dorset)**
The story of a man in his mid-thirties who returns to his small hometown after a prolonged period in London. He enjoys a spiritual rejuvenation in the idyllic countryside of his native Dorset. *See also* ***A Glastonbury Romance***.

*The French Lieutenant's Woman*, John Fowles **(Lyme Regis)**
A classic novel that interweaves postmodern techniques with the traditions of nineteenth-century storytelling. An amateur palaeontologist becomes obsessively enamoured of a 'fallen' woman.

*In The Place of Fallen Leaves*, Tim Pears **(Devon)**
A thirteen-year-old girl slowly awakens to the ways of the world around her and her life is changed forever. A beautiful tale of the history of a family and a rural community.

*Borrowed Light*, Joolz Denby **(Cornwall)**
Like an updated Du Maurier with surfboards, Astra has to cope with having to care for her ill mother and her family. When her best friend's beautiful and mesmerising sister arrives, her life starts to unravel.

*Zennor in Darkness*, Helen Dunmore **(Cornwall)**
Mixing fact and fiction, this is the story of three girls growing up in Cornwall during the First World War. D H Lawrence and his German wife are accused by the locals of being spies.

## READ**ON**A**THEME**

### LIFE IN THE UK – BLACK/ASIAN/MUSLIM IN BRITAIN

*26a*, Diane Evans
A moving and perceptive coming-of-age novel about twins born to a Nigerian mother and an English father. They grow up in Neasden and dream of other worlds and 'flapjack empires'. One day, their idyll is shattered.

*A Distant Shore*, Caryl Phillips
An African ex-soldier and a lonely divorcee become neighbours in an English village. Gradually, in spite of their different characters and backgrounds, they seek solace from each other.

*Second-Class Citizen*, Buchi Emecheta
A semi-autobiographical story of a woman who leaves Nigeria for London. She encounters racism and sexism as she struggles to make a living and bring up her children. *See also* Emecheta's previous novel, *In the Ditch*.

*Some Kind of Black*, Diran Adebayo
An award-winning and stylish story of a young black student at Oxford who frequently visits London and indulges in all the pleasures the city has to offer, eventually becoming involved in black activist politics.

*Disappearance*, David Dabydeen
A powerful novel that explores themes of memory, history and change through the story of a Guyanese engineer in south-east England, working on sea defences to protect an endangered village, and his relationship with the lady with whom he boards.

*White Teeth*, Zadie Smith
This is Smith's impressive debut novel about family relations and multiculturalism in the UK, spanning three generations.

*Brick Lane*, Monica Ali
This novel chronicles the life of a Bangladeshi girl uprooted from her home country by an arranged marriage. She tries to make sense of her new surroundings in London's East End.

*The Buddha of Suburbia*, Hanif Kureishi
An energetic story of racial conflict and youth culture in an ethnically diversifying Britain in the 1970s. The reader follows the escapades of Anglo-Indian Karim in the suburbs of London.

*Maps for Lost Lovers*, Nadeem Aslam
A fascinating and brutal novel that recounts a year in the life of a Pakistani community in a northern English town. Two lovers disappear, presumed murdered.

*Londonstani*, Gautam Malkani
A vibrant and linguistically clever novel about a gang of young Asians on the streets of Hounslow in west London, struggling to assert an identity that straddles two different cultures.

*Minaret*, Leila Aboulela
Najwa, a Sudanese Muslim, leads an anonymous life in London, cleaning houses for a living: it is a far cry from her once-privileged life in Sudan. She seeks solace in her religion, but the possibility of love brings renewed hope.

*Only in London*, Hanan Al-Shaykh
The lives of three Arabs and one Islamic scholar all become intricately connected after arriving in London on the same flight. A tender tale of love, life and estrangement.

*A Concise Chinese-English Dictionary For Lovers*, Xiaolu
A delightful book about a Chinese girl coming to London for the first time and systematically learning about language and love.

*Sour Sweet*, Timothy Mo
Mo assuredly weaves themes of cultural identity and tradition into this saga of the Chen family, Chinese immigrants in London's triad-controlled Chinatown in the 1960s.

*Small Island,* Andrea Levy, *see* **England: General England.**
*The Lonely Londoners*, Samuel Selvon, *see* **England: London.**
*Brixton Rock*, Alex Wheatle, *see* **England: London.**
*The Enigma of Arrival*, V S Naipaul, *see* **England: General England.**
*Anita and Me*, Meera Syal, *see* **England: Midlands.**

# READONATHEME

## ANGLO-SAXON ATTITUDES – ENGLISH HISTORY

*Credo*, Melvyn Bragg
A story of the battle between Christian and Pagan ideologies in the north of England in the Dark Ages. A well-researched and thought-provoking adventure.

*The Last English King*, Julian Rathbone
Walt, the only surviving bodyguard to Harold, the last Anglo-Saxon King of England, recounts the events leading up to the battle with William the Conqueror, at Hastings in 1066. A familiar tale, impressively retold.

*The Seventh Son*, Reay Tannahill
An immensely readable and even-handed account of the life of the infamous Richard III.

*The Autobiography of Henry VIII*, Margaret George
In the words of the king himself, with occasional insights from his court jester, Henry's life is recounted, from young prince to bloated monarch.

*Virgin*, Robin Maxwell
The third in Maxwell's trilogy of Tudor novels tells the story of the young Elizabeth I and the difficult and unstable years of the English monarchy following her father's death.

*Nothing Like the Sun*, Anthony Burgess
One of the English heavyweights of the twentieth century takes on the life of William Shakespeare. The Bard's relationships are laid bare in this thrilling romp.

*Year of Wonders*, Geraldine Brooks
The year is 1666 and the Great Plague is ravaging England. A village in Derbyshire decides to isolate itself from the outside world and a year of hardship and constraint begins.

*As Meat Loves Salt*, Maria McCann
This richly detailed, compelling story, set during the English Civil War, describes the dark, passionate and manipulative relationship between two men, from battlefield to communal settlement.

*Restoration*, Rose Tremain
Robert Merivel joins the court of Charles II but is cast aside when he falls in love with the king's mistress. He falls further from grace thereafter, before eventually finding redemption and personal salvation.

*Slammerkin*, Emma Donoghue
Set in the eighteenth century and inspired by a true story, this is the memorable tale of ambitious Mary Saunders, whose life takes her from a London whorehouse to a country town, and eventually to disaster.

*The Crimson Petal and the White*, Michel Faber
A widely acclaimed and weighty tome on the life of Sugar, a prostitute in Victorian London. The city and its colourful characters are consummately described in this masterful evocation of the period.

# INDEX

26a 342
42nd Parallel, The 39
44 Scotland Street 315
101 Reykjavik 236
253 339
1876 41
1919 39

Abdolah, Kader 152
Abductor 191
Abe, Kobo 120
Abella, Alex 77
Aberystwyth Mon Amour
  320
Abish, Walter 246
Abodehman, Ahmed 156
Aboulela, Leila 343
Absalom, Absalom! 53
Absolute Beginners 338
Abyssinian Chronicles 167
Accidental Tourist, The 42
Accordion Crimes 40
Achebe, Chinua 164 (Ed.),
  186
Ackroyd, Peter 338
Across the River and Into
  the Trees 270
Adair, Gilbert 283
Adam Runaway 293
Adama 156
Adebayo, Diran 342
Adichie, Chimamanda Ngozi
  187
Africa Bar, The 167
African Short Stories 164
After a Funeral 196
Afterlands 240
Age of Innocence, The 47
Age of Iron 176

Age of Reason, The 281
Ageyev, M 210
Agony and the Ecstasy, The
  285
Agualusa, José Eduardo 293
Ahmad, Aisha 151
Aidoo, Ama Ata 185
Aira, Cesar 9
Aïtmatov, Chinghiz 153
Akasaka, Mari 63
Akunin, Boris 210
Akutagawa, Ryunosuke 120
Al Aswany, Alaa 195
Al-Hamad, Turki 156
Al-Khatib, Muhammad Kamil
  157
Al-Shaykh, Hanan 156, 343
Alai 133
Alain-Fournier 278
Alarcon, Daniel 15
Alchemist, The 146
Alchemy of Desire,
  The 140
Alexander, Caroline 240
Alexander: Child of a
  Dream 200
Alexandria Quartet, The 195
Alexandria Semaphore, The
  195
Alexie, Sherman 82
Algren, Nelson 55
Ali and Nino 153
Ali, Monica 343
Ali, Tariq 148, 288
Alias Grace 91
All Quiet on the Western
  Front 245
All Souls 335
All Souls' Day 250

All-True Travels and
  Adventures of Lidie
  Newton, The 57
Allende, Isabel 3, 5
Almond, The 191
Alvtegen, Karin 231
Ambjornsen, Ingvar 233
Amercian Pastoral 41
Amis, Kingsley 321
Amis, Martin 227, 337
Ammaniti, Niccolò 265
Among Women Only 262
Amongst Women 296
An Olympic Death 291
Anam, Tahmima 145
Anand, Mulk Raj 139
Anatomy School, The 308
Anchee Min 126
Ancient Evenings 196
And Quiet Flows the Don
  206
And We Sold The Rain –
  Contemporary Fiction of
  Central America 31
Anderson, Barbara 105
Anderson Dargatz, Gail 93
Anderson, Sherwood
  60
Andreas, Neshani 173
Andric, Ivo 220
Anecdotes of Destiny 238
Angela Carter's Book of
  Fairy Tales 180
Angels on the Head of a Pin
  210
Angle of Repose 67
Anita and Me 330
Anna of the Five Towns 330
Annie John 22

*Another Country* 50
*Antarctic Navigation* 240
*Anthills of the Savannah* 186
Antoni, Robert 26
*Antwerp* 254
*Apothecary's House, The* 252
Appelfeld, Aron 257
*Apprenticeship of Duddy Kravitz, The* 94
Aquin, Hubert 94
*Arabian Nights and Days* 179
*Aristotle Detective* 201
Arlt, Roberto 9
Armah, Ayi Kwei 184
Arnim, Elizabeth von 246, 294
Arthur, Elizabeth 240
*As I Lay Dying* 53
*As Meat Love Salt* 345
*Ask the Dust* 77
Aslam, Nadeem 145, 343
*Assault, The* 251
*Astonishing the Gods* 147
Asturias, Angel 31
*At Swim-Two Birds* 305
*At Swim, Two Boys* 304
*Athenian Murders, The* 200
Athill, Diana 196
Atkinson, Kate 327
*Atomised* 279
Atwood, Margaret 90-91, 180
Atxaga, Bernardo 291
*Audrey Hepburn's Neck* 124
*August* 294
*Augustus* 272
*Aunt Julia and the Scriptwriter* 15
*Aurelio Zen series* 266
Auster, Paul 51, 79, 134

*Autobiography of an Ex-Coloured Man, The* 84
*Autobiography of Henry VIII, The* 344
Aw, Tash 108
*Awakening, The* 55
*Away From You* 170
Azim, Firdous (Ed.) 145
Azzopardi, Trezza 320

Bâ, Mariama 183
Babel, Isaac 207
*Baby No Eyes* 105
Bach, Richard 146
Bach-Wiig, Harald (Ed.) 233
*Back When We Were Grownups* 42
*Badenheim 1939* 257
Bail, Murray 98
Bainbridge, Beryl 95, 240
Baldwin, James 50, 84, 283
*Balkan Trilogy, The* 225
*Ballad of the Sad Café, The* 55
Ballard, J G 107, 130
*Balthasar's Odyssey* 259
*Balzac and the Little Chinese Seamstress* 130
Bánffy, Miklós 225
*Bangkok 8* 112
Banks, Iain 311
Banville, John 301
Baricco, Alessandro 121
Barker, Nicola 335
Barker, Pat 327
Barnes, Julian 324
Barrett, Andrea 212
Barry, Sebastian 300
Barstow, Stan 327
Bartlett, Neil 339
*Bastard Boy, The* 259
Bateman, Colin 309

Bates, H E 335
*Baumgartner's Bombay* 142
Bawden, Nina 125
*Beach Boy* 142
*Beach, The* 112
*Bean Trees, The* 61
*Beasts of No Nation* 184
*Beatles* 232
Beauvoir, Simone de 280
Beckett, Samuel 304
Bedford, Sybille 245
*Beer in the Snooker Club* 196
*Beginning of Spring, The* 210
*Behind the Scenes at the Museum* 327
*Beirut Blues* 156
*Beka Lamb* 32
Bellow, Saul 59
*Beloved* 40
*Belshazzar's Daughter* 203
*Belt, The* 156
Bely, Andrei 211
Ben Jellon, Tahar 189
*Bend in the River, A* 182
*Benjamin* 13
Bennett, Arnold 330
Bennett, Ronan 182
Berger, John 260
Berger, Thomas 68
*Bering* 212
*Berlin Alexanderplatz* 249
*Berlin Noir Trilogy, The* 249
Bernièrs, Louis de 4, 199, 203
*Bethany Bettany* 17
Beti, Mongo 182
*Beware of Pity* 257
*Beyond Illusions* 115

Beyond Sleep 233
Beyond the Great Indoors 233
Big Money, The 39
Big Sleep, The 76
Big Sur 73
Bird Artist, The 93
Birds of America 41
Birds of Passage 195
Birds Without Wings 203
Birthday Boys, The 240
Bitter Fruit 177
Bjerck, Birgit (Ed.) 233
Black Narcissus 140
Black Robe 93
Blackbird House 45
Blackwater 231
Blackwater Lightship, The 300
Bleeding London 339
Blind Assassin 90
Blind Owl, The 152
Blindfold, The 48
Blonde 41
Blood in the Sun 166
Blood Meridian 65
Blood Sisters 170
Blue Afternoon, The 110
Blue Bedspread, The 140
Blue Flower, The 245
Blue Movie 78
Bly 232
Boase, Roger 151
Body Snatcher 6
Bolano, Roberto 5
Bolger, Dermot 125, 304
Bombay Ice 142
Bone People, The 103
Bonesetter's Daughter, The 131
Bonfire of the Vanities, The 51

Bonjour Tristesse 275
Boogaloo on 2nd Avenue 37
Book of Fathers, The 224
Book of Illusions, The 79
Book of Imaginary Beings, The 180
Book of Laughter and Forgetting, The 217
Book of Not, The 171
Book of Saladin: A Novel 148
Book of the Heathen, The 182
Books of Disquiet, The 293
Bookshop, The 332
Border Country 321
Borges, Jorge Luis 7, 180
Born Free 315
Borrowed Light 341
Bowen, Elizabeth 125, 299, 338
Bowles, Jane 31
Bowles, Paul 190
Boy 167
Boy's Own Story, A 61
Boyd, William 110, 167, 184
Boyle, T C 213
Böll, Heinrich 245
Bradbury, Malcolm 211
Bragg, Melvyn 327, 344
Braine, John 323
Brautigan, Richard 73
Brazzaville Beach 184
Breadwinner, The 151
Breaking Ice: An Anthology of Contemporary African-American Fiction 84
Brennan, Maeve 304
Brick Lane 343
Brideshead Revisited 324

Bridge of San Luis Rey, The 15
Bridge on the Drina, The 220
Brief Stay with the Living, A 278
Bright Lights, Big City 50
Brighter Sun, A 26
Brighton Rock 334
Brink, Andre 177
Brink, H M van den 252
Brixton Rock 338
Brookner, Anita 258
Brooks, Geraldine 345
Brothers, The 13
Brown, Alan 124
Brown, George Douglas 313
Brown, Stewart (Ed.) 23
Bruce Trilogy, The 312
Bruges-la-Morte 254
Buarque, Chico 13
Buchan, James 246
Büchler, Alexandre (Ed.) 216
Buddenbrooks 245
Buddha of Suburbia, The 343
Buenos Aires Quintet, The 9
Bukowski, Charles 77, 78
Bulgakov, Mikhail 209
Bull From the Sea, The 179
Burdett, John 112
Burgess, Anthony 109, 345
Burmese Days 113
Burns, Anna 306
Burnt-Out Case, A 182
Burr 41
Buru Quartet 111
Bus Driver Who Wanted to be God and Other Stories 161
Butcher Boy, The 300

*Butcher's Wife, The* 133
*Butterfly Effect, The* 234
*Butterfly's Tongue* 287
*Buxton Spice* 17
*By the Grand Canal* 270
*By Night in Chile* 5
Byers, Michael 82

Cabrera Infante, Guillermo 28
Cade Bambara, Toni 84
Cain, James M 73
*Cairo Trilogy, The* 194
Calasso, Roberto 179
*Call of the Wild, The* 82
Calvino, Italo 179, 268
Cameron, Peter 6
Camilleri, Andrea 266
Camus, Albert 191
*Cannery Row* 71
*Capital* 336
*Captain Corelli's Mandolin* 199
*Cara Massimina* 267
*Caramelo* 35
*Caravaggio: A Novel* 284
*Cardiff Trilogy, The* 320
Carey, Peter 97, 135, 339
*Carnival* 26
*Carpenter's Pencil* 287
Carpentier, Alejo 29
Carr, J L 327
*Carter Beats the Devil* 73
Carter, Angela 180
Cartwright, Justin 169, 177
Carver, Raymond 40
Cary, Joyce 186
*Casa Rossa* 265
Casares, Adolfo Bioy 10
*Case of Comrade Tulayev, The* 208
*Cassada* 18

*Castle, The* 219
*Catastrophist, The* 182
*Catcher in the Rye, The* 50
Cather, Willa 61, 66
Cela, Camilo Jose 288
*Celestial Harmonies* 224
*Century in Scarlet* 226
Cercas, Javier 288
Chabon, Michael 45
Chamoiseau, Patrick 23
Chandler, Raymond 76
Chandler, Robert (Ed.) 207
Chandra, Vikram 142
Chandrartna, Bandula 148
*Changes* 185
Chang-Rae Lee 88
Chatwin, Bruce 185, 219, 319
Chaudhuri, Amit 139
Chavarría, Daniel 29, 201
*Cheese* 254
Cheever, John 44
Chevalier, Tracy 284
*Children of Dynmouth, The* 341
Chinodya, Shimmer 173
*Chirundu* 175
Chopin, Kate 55
*Chosen, The* 41
Christensen, Lars Saabye 232
Christie, Agatha 18
Chwin, Stefan 223
*Chymical Wedding, The* 332
*Cider House Rules, The* 46
Cisneros, Sandra 35, 86
*City of God* 11–12
*City of Spades* 338
*City of Your Final Destination, The* 6
Clarke, Austin 23
Clarke, Lindsay 180, 332

*Claudine in Paris* 282
Claus, Hugo 254
Clavell, James 121
*Clear Light of Day* 139
Clement, Catherine 147
*Close Quarters* 96
*Close Range – Brokeback Mountain and Other Stories* 82
*Closely Observed Trains* 19
*Cloud Howe* 310
*Cloudstreet* 101
*Club of Angels, The* 13
*Coast of Good Intentions, The* 82
Cobbold, Marika 231
Coe, Jonathan 324, 330
Coelho, Paul 146
Coetzee, J M 107, 176, 211
*Coffee Trader, The* 36
Cohen, Albert 258
*Cold Comfort Farm* 324
*Cold Skin* 241
*Cold Water* 327
Colette 282
*Collected Fictions* (Jorge Luis Borges) 7
*Collected Short Stories* (Michael McLaverty) 308
*Collected Stories* (William Trevor) 301
*Collected Stories* (Dylan Thomas) 320
*Collected Stories, The* (Grace Paley) 51
Collen, Lindsey 167
*Color Purple, The* 55
*Colour, The* 105
*Colour of a Dog Running Away, The* 291
*Comedians, The* 25
*Comedy Writer, The* 78

*Comfort of Strangers, The* 270

*Comfort Woman* 87

*Coming To Birth* 170

*Commitments, The* 303

*Complicity* 311

Condé, Maryse 23

*Cone-Gatherers, The* 313

*Confederacy of Dunces, A* 54

*Confederate General from Big Sur, A* 73

Connolly, Joseph 294

Conrad, Joseph 5, 95, 182

*Conservationist, The* 174

*Consider the Lilies* 312

*Constant Gardner, The* 170

*Contempt* 265

*Conversations in Sicily* 265

*Cooking with Fernet Branca* 36

Coraghessan Boyle, T 71

Cordell, Alexander 321

Cornwell, Bernard 239

*Coroner's Lunch, The* 110

Cortazar, Julio 9

Cotterill, Colin 110

*Counting House, The* 17

*Country Girls, The* 297

*Country Girls Trilogy, The* 297

*Country Life, The* 335

Coupland, Douglas 94

Courtmanche, Gil 167

Couto, Mia 173

*Cow, The* 258

Cowper Powys, John 341

*Cowrie of Hope* 173

Cozarinsky, Edgardo 10

Crace, Jim 36, 135, 162

Craig, Christine 27

*Craze, The* 328

*Credo* 344

*Creole* 293

Crichton, Michael 107, 226

Crichton-Smith, Iain 312

*Crimson Petal and the White, The* 345

*Croatian Nights* 220

Crockett, Edward John 212

Cross, Helen 327

*Cross Stitch* 227

*Crow Road* 311

Crummey, Michael 94

Cruz, Angie 86

*Cry, the Beloved Country* 177

*Crying of Lot 49, The* 73

*Cuba and the Night* 29

*Cure for Death by Lightning, The* 93

*Curious Earth, A* 294

*Curriculum Vitae of Aurora Ortiz, The* 288

Curtis Ford, Michael 200

Cusk, Rachel 335

*Cutting Room, The* 317

*Cyclone, The* 31

D'Aguiar, Fred 17

Dabydeen, David 17, 342

Dai Sijie 130

Dalby, Liza 121

*Dalva* 61

*Dance to the Music of Time, A* 322

*Dancer Upstairs, The* 15

Daneshvar, Simin 152

Dangarembga, Tsitsi 171

*Dangling Man, The* 59

Dangor, Achmat 177

Daniel, A B 15

Danticat, Edwidge 25

*Dark Bride, The* 5

*Dark Clue, The* 285

*Dark, The* 296

*Dark Labyrinth, The* 199

*Dark Room, The* 243

*Darkroom of Damocles, The* 252

*Darkness at Noon* 210

*Darling Buds of May, The* 335

*Darling, Julia* 327

Darrieussecq, Marie 240, 278

*Daughters of the House* 279

Davenport, Will 284

Davey, Maggie (Ed.) 177

Davies, Robertson 93

Dawson, Jill 332

*Day of the Locust, The* 78

Deane, Seamus 308

*Death in the Andes* 14-15

*Death of Artemio Cruz* 34

*Death Comes for the Archbishop* 66

*Death in Danzig* 222

*Death at La Fenice* 270

*Death and Nightingales* 309

*Death and the Penguin* 225

*Death in Venice* 269

*Death of Vishnu, The* 142

*Debatable Land* 96

*Debt to Pleasure, The* 36

Deighton, Len 249

Delaney, Frank 301

Deledda, Grazia 266

DeLillo, Don 40

*Delta Wedding* 55

Denby, Joolz 341

Desai, Anita 139, 142, 146

*Desperadoes* 31

Desqueyroux, Thérèse 278

*Devil in the Blue Dress* 77

*Devil in the Flesh, The* 282
*Devil in the Hills, The* 262
*Devil's Larder, The* 36
Dexter, Colin 335
*Dharma Bum, The* 147
Diamant, Anita 162
Diaz, Junot 25, 86
Dibdin, Michael 266
Dickey, Eric Jerome 85
Didion, Joan 73
*Difficult Daughters* 140
Diliberto, Gioia 285
*Dinaane: Short Stories of South African Women* 177
Dinesen, Isak 238
*Dinner at the Homesick Restaurant* 42–43
*Dirty Havana Trilogy* 28
*Disappearance* 342
*Discovery of Chocolate, The* 227
*Discovery of Slowness, The* 212
*Disgrace* 176
Diski, Jenny 162
*Distant View of a Minaret and Other Stories* 195
*Distant Shore, A* 342
Divakaruni, Chitra Banerjee 36
*Divine Husband, The* 31
*Divorcing Jack* 309
Docherty 313
*Doctor Glas* 230
*Doctor Zhivago* 204
Doctorow, E L 50
Dodge, Jim 63, 73
Doherty, Paul 196
*Don Flows Home to the Sea, The* 206
*Don't Look Back* 234

Donleavy, J P 304
Donoghue, Emma 345
Doody, Margaret 201
*Door, The* 224
Dorrestein, Renate 252
Dos Passos, John 38
*Double Tongue, The* 200
*Down Where the Moon is Small and Green* 318
*Downriver* 339
Doyle, Roddy 303
Döblin, Alfred 249
Drabble, Margaret 325
*Dream of Sukhanov, The* 210
*Dream Story* 257
*Dreamers* 233
Dreiser, Theodore 61
*Drown* 25, 86
Druzhnikov, Yuri 210
*Dry White Season, A* 177
Du Maurier, Daphne 226, 340
*Dublin: Foundation* 305
*Dubliners* 302
Dubus III, Andre 73
Dudman, Clare 212
Duff, Alan 105
Duffy, Maureen 336
Duncker, Patricia 260
Dunmore, Helen 211, 229, 342
Dunn, Nell 339
Dunnett, Dorothy 312
Duong Thu Huong 115
Duras, Marguerite 115
Durrell, Lawrence 195, 199

*Eagle and the Crow, The* 222
Earth and Ashes 151
*Earthquake Bird, The* 124

*East of Eden* 71
*Easter Island* 106
Easton Ellis, Bret 75
*Eating Chinese Food Naked* 87
Eco, Umberto 265
*Edge of the Alphabet, The* 104
Edgell, Zee 32
Edric, Robert 182
*Efuru* 188
Eggers, Dave 259
Eidson, Thomas 68
*Eight Months on Ghazzah Street* 155
Ekman, Kerstin 231
El Saadawi, Nawal 193
*Electric Brae* 312
*Elizabeth and Her German Garden* 246
Ellis, Deborah 151
Ellison, Ralph 40
Ellroy, James 77
Elphinstone, Margaret 239
Elsschot, Willem 254
*Embers* 223
Emecheta, Buchi 187, 342
*Emigrants, The* 246
*Emperor's Tomb* 256
*Emperor: The Gates of Rome* 272
*Empire* 41
*Empire Falls* 45
*Empire of the Sun* 130
*Empress Orchid* 126-127
*Enchanted April, The* 294
*Enchantment of Lily Dahl, The* 48
*End of a Family Story, The* 224
*Engineer of Human Souls, The* 216

*England, This England* 324
*English Passengers* 102
*English Patient, The* 191
*Enigma of Arrival* 325
*Enormous Radio, The* 44
Enquist, Per Olov 238
Enright, Anne 5, 304
Erdich, Louise 41, 61
Erofeyev, Victor 207
Espedair Street 311
Esquivel, Laura 36
*Essential Jennifer Johnston, The* 300
Esterhazy, Peter 225
*Eucalyptus* 98-99
Eugenides, Jeffrey 62
*Eureka Street* 307
*Europa* 63
*Eva Luna* 5
Evans, Diane 342
Evans, Nicholas 82
*Eve Green* 320
*Even Cowgirls Get the Blues* 64
Everett, Peter 285
*Every Man for Himself* 95
*Everyman's Rules for Scientific Living* 101
*Everything is Illuminated* 225
*Explorers of the New Century* 213
*Explosion in a Cathedral* 29
*Extremely Loud and Incredibly Close* 51
*Eye of Cybele, The* 201
*Eyes of the Interred* 31

Faber, Michel 64, 345
*Faceless Killers* 231
*Faces in the Water* 104
Fagerholm, Monika 229

*Fairy Grandmother, The* 282
*Fairy Tale* 321
*Fall, The* 321
*Family Matters* 141
*Famished Road, The* 187
Fante, John 77
Faqir, Fadia 157
*Far Journey of Oudin, The* 17
*Far Tortuga* 23
Farah, Nuruddin 166
*Farewell My Concubine* 130
Farhi, Moris 5, 203
*Farming of Bones, The* 25
Farrell, J G 109
Farrelly, Peter 78
*Fascination of Evil, The* 196
*Fatelessness* 224
Faulkner, Willliam 53
Faulks, Sebastian 279
*Fear and Loathing in Las Vegas* 74
*Fear and Trembling* 121
*Feast of the Goat, The* 25
Ferrante, Elena 266
Fesperman, Dan 220
*Few Things I Know About Glafkos Thrassakis, The* 199
*Fictions of Bruno Schulz, The* 222
*Fifth Business* 93
*Fig Eater, The* 257
Figiel, Sía 106
*Finbar's Hotel* 125
*Fine Balance, A* 141
Finn, Melanie 170
*Fire Down Below* 96
*Fire from Heaven* 200
*First Man in Rome, The* 272
Fischer, Tibor 225
Fisher, Carrie 78

Fitch, Janet 77
Fitzgerald, F Scott 46, 78, 279
Fitzgerald, Penelope 210, 245, 332
*Five Forty-Eight, The* 44
*Flag for Sunrise, A* 31
*Flamethrowers, The* 9
Flanagan, Richard 102
*Flea Palace, The* 203
Fletcher, Susan 320
*Floating Book, The* 271
Foden, Giles 167
*Foe* 107
*Folding Star, The* 254
*Following Story, The* 252
Fonseca, Rubem 13
*For Whom the Bell Tolls* 289
Forbes, Leslie 142
Ford, Richard 35, 40, 45, 82
*Foreign Bodies* 109
*Foreign Parts* 63
Forster, E M 140, 266
Forster, Margaret 285
*Fortress Besieged* 131
*Fortress of Solitude, The* 50
Fossum, Karin 234
*Foundation Pit, The* 205
*Four Meals: A Novel* 160
*Four Walls* 199
Fowles, John 198, 341
*Fox Girl* 133
*Fragrant Harbour* 133
Frame, Janet 104
Franco, Jorge 5
*Frangipani* 106
Franklin, Miles 101
Frayn, Michael 135, 210
Fredriksson, Marianne 231
*Freedom Song* 139
*French Lieutenant's Woman, The* 341

*Frenchman's Creek* 340
Freud, Esther 191, 333
*Frieda and Min* 177
Friel, George 317
*Friends and Lovers* 85
*Fringe of Leaves* 101
*From a Crooked Rib* 166
*Frozen Music* 231
*Fruit of the Lemon* 27
Fuentes, Carlos 34
Fugard, Athol 178
*Fugitive Pieces* 94
*Funeral in Berlin* 249
*Fup* 73

Gabaldon, Diana 227
*Gabriel, Clove and
 Cinnamon* 12
Gaines, Ernest J 56, 84
Galgut, Damon 177
Gallant, Mavis 282
Galloway, Janice 63
*Galpa: Short Stories by
 Bangladesh Women* 145
Gao Xingjian 129
Garcia-Roza, Luiz Alfredo 13
*Garden of the Finzi-
 Continis, The* 263
*Garden Part and Other
 Stories*, The 104
Garland, Alex 112
*Garlic Ballads* 130
Garner, Alan 328
Garros-Evdokimov 221
*Gate of the Sun* 156
*Gates of Fire* 200
*Gates of Ivory, The* 325
*Gathering of Old Men, A* 56
Gee, Maurice 105
*Geisha of Gion* 119
*General in His Labyrinth,
 The* 2

Genet, Jean 278
George, Margaret 162, 196,
 344
Germain, Sylvie 219
*Gesture Life, A* 88
*Get Shorty* 79
Ghali, Waguih 196
Ghosh, Amitav 113, 139
Gibbons, Stella 324
Gide, André 278
*Gift, The* 208
*Ginger Man, The* 304
*Giovanni's Room* 283
*Girl at the Lion D'Or, The*
 279
*Girl Who Married a Lion,
 The* 179
*Girl Who Played Go, The* 131
*Girl With the Green Eyes,
 The* 297
*Girl With the Pearl Earring*
 284
*Girlfriend in a Coma* 94
*Girls in Their Married Bliss*
 297
Glanville, Jo (Ed.) 157
*Glasgow Trilogy, A* 317
*Glass Palace, The* 113
Glauser, Friedrich 258
*Go-Between, The* 332
*Go Tell It on the Mountain*
 84
*Goat's Song, The* 300
*God of Small Things, The*
 136–137
*God Who Begot a Jackal,
 The* 191
*God's Bits of Wood* 185
*Gods, Demons and Others*
 179
*God's Medicine Men and
 Other Stories* 188

Gold, Glen David 73
*Golden Age, A* 145
*Golden Age, The* 41
Golden, Arthur 119
Golding, William 96, 107, 200
Goldman, Francisco 31
*Golem, The* 219
Golshiri, Hushang 149
Gombrowicz, Witold 223
*Gone to Earth* 329
*Good Behaviour* 301
*Good Doctor, The* 177
*Good Man in Africa, A* 184
*Good Man is Hard to Find,
 A* 52
*Good Morning, Midnight*
 283
*Good Soldier Svejk,
 The* 215
*Goodbye My Brother* 44
*Goodbye to Berlin* 248
Goodwin, Jason 203
Goosen, Theodore W (Ed.)
 120
Gordimer, Nadine 174
Gorky, Maxim 207
*Gospel According to Jesus
 Christ, The* 162
*Gould's Book of Fish* 102
Gowdy, Barbara 94
Goytisolo, Juan 291
Grace Metalious 45
Grace, Patricia 105
*Grain of Wheat, A* 168-169
*Grandfather's Tale* 157
Grant, Linda 160
*Granta Book of the
 American Short Story,
 The* 40
*Grapes of Wrath, The* 70
*Grass Is Singing, The* 172
Grass, Günter 244

Grassic Gibbon, Lewis 273, 310
Graves, Robert 272
Gray, Alasdair 316
Gray, Stephen (Ed.) 164
*Great Gatsby, The* 46
*Green Pope, The* 31
*Green, Green My Valley Now* 318
Green, Henry 330
Greene, Graham 10, 19, 25, 29, 35, 115, 182, 185, 257, 259, 334
*Greenlanders, The* 239
*Greenvoe* 313
Greenway, Alice 133
Greenwood, Walter 328
Greig, Andrew 312
Grenville, Kate 99
Grey Granite 310
Grey, Zane 68
Griffiths, Niall 320
Grondahl, Jens Christian 238
Grossman, David 159
Grossman, Vassily 207
Grushin, Olga 210
Guene, Faïa 283
Gun For Sale, A 334
Gunesekera, Romesh 144
Gunn, Kirsty 105
Gunn, Neil M 313
Gurnah, Abdulrazak 167
Guterson, David 81
Gutierrez, Pedro Juan 29
Guyana Quartet, The 17
Gwyn, Richard 291

Habiby, Emile 161
Habila, Helon 188
Half Brothers, The 232
Halikowska, Teresa (Ed.) 223
Hallucinating Foucault 260

Ham on Rye 77
Hamid, Mohsin 145
Hamilton Case, The 145
Hamilton, Patrick 338
Hamilton-Paterson, James 36
Hamsun, Karl 233
Hanania, Tony 156
*Hangover Square* 338
*Hanna's Daughters* 231
*Hare, The* 9
*Harland's Half Acre* 100
*Harmony Silk Factory, The* 108–109
Harris, Robert 273
Harris, Wilson 16
Harrison, Jim 61
Harrison, Kathryn 82, 289
Hart, Christopher 341
Hartley, L P 332
Haruf, Kent 68
*Harvest, The* 341
*Harvest of Thorns* 173
Hašek, Jaroslav 215
Hatoum, Milton 13
Hatziyannidis, Vangelis 199
*Haunting of L, The* 93
*Hav* 135
*Havana Red* 29
*Havana World Series* 29
Hawes, James 134
*Hawksmoor* 338
Head, Bessie 173
*Headcrusher* 225
*Healers, The* 184
Healy, Dermot 300
*Heart of Darkness* 182
*Heart of the Matter, The* 185
*Heart of Stone, A* 252
*Heart's Journey in Winter* 246
*Heat and Dust* 140
*Heat of the Day, The* 338

Heath, Roy 17
Hedayat, Sadegh 152
Heerden, Etienne van 177
Heighton, Steven 240
Helgason, Hallgrimur 236
Hemingway, Ernest 270, 289
Hemon, Aleksandar 220
*Hen's Teeth* 317
*Henderson's Spear* 106
Hensher, Philip 151, 249
*Her Lover (Belle de Seigneur)* 258
Hermans, W F 233, 252
*Herzog* 59
Hesse, Herman 146, 245
Hiaasen, Carl 56
Hickey, Elizabeth 284
*Hideous Kinky* 191
*Hiding Place, The* 320
*High Wind in Jamaica, A* 27
Highsmith, Patricia 192, 266
*Highways to a War* 109
Hijuelos, Oscar 86
*Hikayat: Short Stories by Lebanese Women* 156
Hill, Susan 335
Hilton, James 134
Himes, Chester 51
Hird, Laura 315
Hislop, Victoria 199
*History's Fiction* 133
*History: A Novel* 265
Hitiura, Célestine 106
*Hive, The* 288
Høeg, Peter 237
Hoffman, Alice 45
Hollinghurst, Alan 254
*Hollywood* 78
*Hollywood: a Novel of the Twenties* 41
Holt, Thomas 239, 273
Holt, Tom 200

*Holy Innocents, The* 283
*Home and the World, The* 137
*Homestead* 257
*Honorary Consul, The* 10
*Hopscotch* 9
*Horse Whisperer, The* 82
Hosseini, Khaled 150
*Hosts of Rebecca, The* 321
*Hot Water Man* 145
*Hotel, The* 125
*Hotel Honolulu* 83
*Hotel du Lac* 258
*Hotel New Hampshire, The* 126
*Hotel Savoy* 125
*Hotel World* 125
*Hothouse, The* 245
Houellebecq, Michel 279, 294
*House of Day, House of Night* 222
*House Guest, The* 105
*House on Mango Street, The* 86
*House of Mirth, The* 47
*House for Mr Biswas, A* 20–21
*House of Orphans* 229
*House of Sand and Fog* 73
*House of the Spirits, The* 3
*House on the Strand, The* 226
*House With the Green Shutters, The* 313
*Housekeeping* 80-81
*How German Is It?* 246
*How Green Was My Valley* 318
*How Late It Was, How Late* 317

Hradal, Bohumil 19, 216
Hubank, Roger 240
Huelle, Pawel 223
Hughes, Richard 27
Hulme, Keri 103
*Humboldt's Gift* 59
Humphreys, Helen 18
*Hungry Tide, The* 139
*Hunter, The* 102
*Hurry on Down* 330
Husain, Shakrukh 180
Hustvedt, Siri 48
Huxley, Aldous 107
Huxley, Elspeth 170
Hwee Hwee Tan 109
Hyde, George (Ed.) 223

*I Am a Cat* 121
*I Am Madame X* 285
*I, Claudius* 272
*I Could Read the Sky* 301
*I, Fatty* 78
*I'll Go To Bed At Noon* 294
*I'm Not Scared* 265
*I Served the Kong of England* 216
*Icarus Girl, The* 188
*Ice Cream War, An* 167
*Ice Palace, The* 233
*Ice Road, The* 208
*Idea of Perfection* 99
Idilbi, Ulfat 157
*If Nobody Speaks of Remarkable Things* 324
Iggulden, Conn 272
Ihimaera, Witi 104
*Imago* 238
*In Babylon* 253
*In-Between World of Vikram Lall, The* 170
*In the Castle of My Skin* 23
*In Corner B* 175

*In the Country of Last Things* 134
*In the Country of Men* 192
*In a German Pension* 246
*In the Miso Soup* 124
*In the Place of Fallen Leaves* 341
*In Search of Lost Time* 274–275
*In the Skin of a Lion* 93
*In the Springtime of the Year* 335
*Indecision* 6
*Independence Day* 45
*Independent People* 235
*Indigo* 23
Indridason, Arnaldur 236
*Infante's Inferno* 28
*Inferno* 13
*Infinite Possibilities* 219
*Infinite Riches* 187
*Ingenious Pain* 259
*Inishowen* 300
Innes, C L (Ed.) 164
*Innocent, The* 249
*Inside Daisy Clover* 79
*Interior* 169
*Interpreters, The* 188
*Interruption of Everything, The* 85
*Invention of Morel, The* 10
*Invisible Cities* 268
*Invisible Man* 40
*Invitation to a Journey* 219
*Ireland: A Novel* 301
Irving, John 46, 126
Isegawa, Moses 167
Isherwood, Christopher 248
Ishiguro, Kazuo 324
*Island* 107
*Island, The* 199
*Islands* 178

Ismailov, Hamid 153
*Italian Folktales* 179
Iwasaki, Mineko 119
Iweala, Uzodinma 184
Iyer, Pico 29
Ja Jin 130
Jack Maggs 339
Jacq, Christian 196
*Jamaica Inn* 340
*Jamilia* 153
James, Henry 270
*Janissary Tree, The* 203
Janoda, Jeff 239
Jansson, Tove 228
Japin, Arthur 253
Japrisot, Sebastien 278
Jarrar, Nada Awar 157
Jarrett-Macauley, Delia 185
*Jasmine* 87
*Jasmine Isle, The* 199
*Jazz* 50
Jelinek, Elfriede 257
*Jen Gish* 88
Jenkins, Robin 313
Jensen, Liz 135, 226
Jha, Raj Kamal 140
Johnson, James Weldon 84
Johnson-Davies, Denys (Ed.)
    148
Johnston, Jennifer 300, 308
Jokanovic, Vladimir 220
*Joke, The* 217
Jones, Susanna 124
Jooste, Pamela 177
*Journey Home, The* (Olaf
    Olaffson) 236
*Journey Home, The* (Dermot
    Bolger) 304
*Journey to Ithaca* 146
*Journey by Moonlight* 264
*Journey Through the
    Wilderness* 5

*Joy Luck Club, The* 87
Joyce, James 302
*Joys of Motherhood,
    The* 187
*Julian* 272
*Jurassic Park* 107
*Just Like a River* 157
*Just Like Tomorrow* 283

*Ka: Stories of the Mind and
    Gods of India* 179
Kadare, Ismail 195, 214
Kafka, Franz 219
Kanehara, Hitomi 124
Kapur, Manju 140
Karnezis, Panos 199, 203
*Kartography* 143
Karystiani, Ioanna 199
Kaufman, Alan 160
Kavanagh, Patrick 301
Kawabata, Yasunari 120
Kazantzakis, Nikos 162, 197
Kazuo Ishiguro 130
Keane, Molly 301
Keating, Barbara and
    Stephanie 170
*Keepers of the House* 6
*Keeping the World Away*
    285
Keillor, Garrison 62
Keller, Okja 133
Kelman, James 317
Kemal, Yashar 203
Kempadoo, Oonya 17
Keneally, Thomas 101, 241
Kennedy Toole, John 54
Kennedy, A L 317
Kenzaburo Oe 118
Keret, Etgar 161
Kerouac, Jack 63, 73, 147
Kerr, Philip 249
Kertesz, Imre 255

Khadra, Yasmina 151
Khalaf, Roseanne Saad (Ed.)
    156
Khalifeh, Sahar 157
Khoury, Elias 156
Kiely, Benedict 309
*Killing of the Saints,
    The* 77
Kincaid, Jamaica 22
*Kind of Loving, A* 327
*Kindness to the Children,
    A* 27
*King Must Die, The* 179
*King, Queen, Knave* 250
*King's Last Song, The* 109
Kingsolver, Barbara 56, 61,
    181
*Kiss of the Spider
    Woman* 9
*Kitchen* 122
*Kite Runner, The* 150
Kjærstad, Jan 233, 234
Klíma, Ivan 218
Kneale, Matthew 102, 124
*Knots and Crosses* 315
Knox, Elizabeth 37
Koch, Christopher 109, 111
Koeppen, Walter 245
Koestler, Arthur 210
Kohn, Rebecca 163
Koji Suzuki 120
Kollontai, Alexandra 208
Kourouma, Ahmadou 185
Krabbé, Tim 18, 252
Kretser, Michelle de 145
*Kristin Lavransdatter* 233
Kross, Jaan 221
Kundera, Milton 217
Kunkel, Benjamin 6
Kureishi, Hanif 343
Kurkov, Andrey 221
Kurlansky, Mark 37

*LA Confidential* 77
*Labyrinth of Solitude, The* 35
*Labyrinths* 7-8
*Ladies' Man* 50
*Lady Chatterley's Lover* 324
Lahiri, Jhumpa 86
*Laidlaw* 317
*Lake Beyond the Wind, A* 157
*Lake Woebegon Days* 62
Lambert, Gavin 79
Lamming, George 23
Lampedusa, Giuseppe 261
*Lamplighter, The* 315
*Lanark* 316
Lanchester, John 36, 133
*Land of the Green Plums, The* 225
*Lang* 229
*Lanzarote* 294
Lapcharoensap 112
Larson, Charles, R (Ed.) 164
Larsson, Bjorn 95
*Last Bus to Woodstock* 335
*Last English King, The* 344
*Last Exit to Brooklyn* 49
*Last Flight of the Flamingo* 173
*Last Kabbalist of Lisbon, The* 293
*Last King of Scotland, The* 167
*Last Kingdom, The* 239
*Last Orders* 335
*Last September, The* 299
*Last Song of Dusk, The* 142
*Last Tango in Aberystwyth* 320
*Last Temptation of Christ* 162
*Last Tycoon, The* 78

*Last of the Wine, The* 201
*Late-Night New, The* 199
Latour, José 29
Laurence, Margaret 94
Lawrence, D H 324, 330
Laxness, Halldór 235
*Lay of the Land, The* 45
Laye, Camara 185
Le Carré, John 31, 161, 170, 249
*Le Grand Meaulnes* 278
*Leaving Earth* 18
Lee, Harper 55
Lee, Lilian 130
*Legacy, A* 245
Leigh, Julia 102
*Leisure* 294
Lennon, J Robert 68
*Leo the African* 191
Leon, Donna 270
Leonard, Elmore 79
*Leopard V – An Island of Sound* 224
*Leopard VI – The Norwegian Feeling for Real* 233
*Leopard, The* 261
*Les Liaisons Culinaires* 36
*Less Than Zero* 75
Lessing, Doris 172
*Lesson Before Dying, A* 84
Lethem, Jonathan 50
*Levant Trilogy, The* 195
Levy, Andrea 27, 325, 344
Lewis, Sinclair 61
Li Ang 133
*Lichen* 89
*Licks of Love* 40
*Lie in the Dark* 220
*Life is Elsewhere* 217
*Life and Fate* 207
*Life of Insects, The* 207

*Life and Times of Michael K* 176
*Life With an Idiot* 207
*Life With a Star* 219
*Life's Music, A* 207
Liffner, Eva-Marie 238
*Light in August* 53
*Light Comedy, A* 291
*Light Years* 46
*Like* 312
*Like Nowhere Else* 157
*Like Water for Chocolate* 36
*Lila: An Inquiry Into Morals* 146
*Lincoln* 41
Lindsay, Joan 101
Lins, Paulo 11
Lippi, Rosina 257
Liss, David 36
*Little Big Man* 68
*Little Drummer Girl, The* 161
*Little Infamies* 199
*Live from Golgotha* 227
Lively, Penelope 195
*Living* 330
*Lizard Tails* 291
Llamazares, Julio 288
Llewellyn, Richard 318
Llosa, Mario Vargas 13, 14, 25, 284
Lodge, David 83
*London Fields* 337
London, Jack 82, 95
*London Novels, The* 338
*Londonstani* 343
*Lone Man, The* 291
*Lonely Girl, The* 297
*Lonely Hearts Club, The* 291
*Lonely Londoners, The* 338
*Lonely Passion of Judith Hearne* 308
*Lonesome Dove* 68

*Long Day Wanes, The* 109
*Long John Silver* 95
*Long Silence of Mario Salviati, The* 177
Loo, Tessa de 252
*Look Homeward, Angel* 56
*Lord Jim* 95
*Lord of the Flies* 107
*Lost Honour of Katharina Blum* 245
*Lost Horizon* 134
*Lost Manuscript, The* 13
*Love on the Dole* 328
*Love and Garbage* 218
*Love and Longing in Bombay* 142
*Love Medicine* 61
*Love in the Time of Cholera* 2
*Love of Worker Bees* 208
Lovelace, Earl 26
*Lovely Green Eyes* 216
*Lover, The* (Marguerite Duras) 115
*Lover, The* (A B Yehoshua) 158
*Loving Che* 86
Lovric, Michelle 271
Lowry, Malcolm 35
*Lucca* 238
Lustig, Arnost 216
*Lymond Chronicles, The* 312

*M'hashish* 191
Ma Jian 130, 134
Maalouf, Amin 154, 191, 259
Macauley, Rose 203
Macgoye, Marjorie Oludhe 170
MacInnes, Colin 338
MacKay Brown, George 313

MacLaverty, Bernard 308
MacLaverty, Michael 308
MacLeod, Alistair 94
Madden, Deirdre 309
*Made in Yugoslavia* 220
Maes, Nick 167
Magnan, Pierre 278
*Magus, The* 198
Mahfouz, Naguib 179, 194
Mahjoub, Jamal 63
*Maid of Buttermere, The* 327
Mailer, Norman 196
*Main Street* 61
Makine, Andreï 207
*Makioka Sisters, The* 117
Makiya, Kana 160
*Malayan Trilogy, The* 109
*Malgudi Omnibus, A* 139
Malkani, Gautam 343
Malouf, David 100
*Mambo Kings Play Songs of Love, The* 86
*Man of Feeling, A* 288
*Man Without Qualities, The* 255
*Man's Head, A* 283
*Mandarins, The* 280
Manfredi, Valerio Massimo 200
Manguel, Alberto 106
Manicka, Rani 109
Mankel, Henning 231
Mann, Thomas 245, 269
Manning, Olivia 195, 221
*Manon des Sources* 277
Mansfield, Katherine 104, 246
Mantel, Hilary 155, 279
*Map of Glass, A* 93
*Maps for Lost Lovers* 343
*Map of Love, The* 195

Márai, Sándor 224
Marciano, Francesca 170, 265
Marias, Javier 288, 335
Markaris, Petroas 199
Markovits, Benjamin 212
*Marks of Identity* 291
Marouane, Leila 191
Márquez, Gabriel García 1
*Marriage of Cadmus and Harmony, The* 179
*Marrying Buddha* 127
Marsé, Juan 291
Martin, Andrew 19
Martin, Valerie 55
Martínez, Tomás Eloy 8
*Mary, Called Magdalene* 162
*Masai Dreaming* 169
*Mask of Ra, The* 196
*Mason and Dixon* 41
Mason, Daniel 113
Massie, Allan 272
*Master of Go, The* 120
*Master and Margarita, The* 209–210
*Master of St Petersburg, The* 211
*Masters of the Dew* 25
Matar, Hisham 192
*Matches* 160
Mathews, Adrian 252
Matthiessen, Peter 23
Maupin, Armistead 72
Mauriac, Françoise 278
Mawer, Simon 321
Maxwell, Robin 345
Maxwell, William 58
Mayor, F M 332
*Maze, The* 203
McCabe, Eugene 309
McCabe, Patrick 300

IcCall Smith, Alexander 179, 315

McCann, Maria 345

McCarthy, Cormac 65

McCullers, Carson 55

McCullough, Colleen 272

McEwan, Ian 249, 270

McGahern, John 296

McGrath, Patrick 32

McGregor, Jon 324

McIlvanney, William 313, 317

McInerney, Jay 50

McLarty, Ron 18

McLiam Wilson, Robert 307

McMillan, Terry 84, 85

McMurtry, Larry 68

McNamee, Eoin 308

McWilliam, Candia 96

Mda, Zakes 178

*Meadowland* 239

Meek, James 208

Mei Ng 87

Melo, Patricia 13

Melville, Pauline 17

*Mema* 182

*Memed, My Hawk* 203

*Memoirs of Cleopatra, The* 196

*Memoirs of a Geisha* 119

*Memoirs of Hadrian* 272

*Memory of Running, The* 18

Mendoza, Eduardo 291

Menendez, Ana 86

Mengara, Daniel M 182

*Mercedes-Benz* 222

*Mermaid and the Drunks, The* 5

Metha, Gita 139

Mexica 35

Meyrink, Gustav 219

Meziekia, Nega 191

Michael, Ib 238

Michaels, Ann 94

Michèle, Roberts 162, 279

*Midnight's Children* 138–139

Miller, Andrew 259

Miller, Henry 282

Mills, Magnus 134, 213

*Minaret* 343

*Ministry of Pain, The* 220

*Mint Tea and Other Stories* 27

*Miracle of Life of Edgar Mint, The* 68

*Mirage* 148

*Misericordia* 288

Mishra, Pankaj 140

*Miss Garnet's Angel* 270

*Miss Smilla's Feeling for Snow* 237

*Missing* 231

*Mister Johnson* 186

*Mistress of Spices, The* 36

Mistry, Rohinton 141

Mitchell, David 123

Mo Yan 130

Mo, Timothy 111, 132, 344

*Modern Baptists* 56

*Modern Utopia, A* 134

Moggach, Deborah 145

*Moldavian Pimp, The* 10

*Monkey King, The* 132

*Monkfish Moon* 144

Montalbán, Manuel Vázquez 9

Montero, Mayra 25

*Month in the Country, A* 327

*Moon and the Bonfires, The* 262

*Moon and Sixpence, The* 106

*Moon Tiger* 195

*Moonlight Shadow* 122

Moorcock, Michael 338

Moore, Brian 93, 308

Moore, Lorrie 41

Morante, Elsa 265

Moravia, Alberto 265

*More Pricks Than Kicks* 304

Morgan, Marlo 146

Morris, Jan 135

Morrison, Toni 23, 40, 50, 61

*Moscow Stations* 19

*Moses, Citizen and Me* 185

Mosley, Walter 77

*Mosquito Coast, The* 30

*Moth Smoke* 145

*Mother* 207

*Mother, The* 266

*Mother London* 338

*Moviegoer, The* 55

Mphahlele, Es'kia 175

Möring, Marcel 253

*Mr Norris Changes Trains* 248

*Mr Foreigner* 124

*Mr Fortune's Maggot* 106

*Mr Golightly's Holiday* 295

*Mr Love and Justice* 338

Mrabet, Mohammed 191

*Mrs Chippy's Last Expedition: The Remarkable Journal of Shackleton's Polar-Bound Cat* 240

*Mrs Dalloway* 325

*Mrs Palfrey at the Claremont* 125

Mukherjee, Bharati 87

*Mulberry Empire, The* 151

Mulisch, Harry 251

Muller, Herta 220

Munro, Alice 89

Murakami, Haruki 117, 123

Murakami, Ryu 124

*Murder on the Orient Express* 18
*Murdered House, The* 278
*Murderer, The* 17
Murdoch, Iris 304
Murr, Naeem 87
*Musashi* 120
*Museum Guard, The* 93
Music and Silence 238
Musil, Robert 255
*Mutant Message Down Under* 146
*My Antonia* 61
*My Brilliant Career* 101
*My Dirty Little Book of Stolen Time* 226
*My Father's Notebook* 152
*My Michael* 160
*My Name is Red* 202
*My Name Was Judas* 163
*My Oedipus Complex and Other Stories* 298
*My Summer of Love* 327
*My Uncle Napoleon* 152
Myerson, Julie 333
*Mystic Masseur, The* 21

Nabokov, Vladimir 208, 250
Nadas, Peter 225
Nadel, Barbara 203
Nadolny, Sten 212
Naipaul, V S 20, 182, 325
*Naked Pueblo* 68
Nakhjavani, Bahiyyih 156
*Name of the Rose, The* 265
*Namesake, The* 86
Narayan, R K 139, 179
*Narratives of Empire series* 41
*Narziss and Goldmund* 245
*Native Son* 84
Natsuo Kirino 123

*Natural Curiosity, A* 325
*Nautical Chart, The* 95
Neale Hurston, Zora 84
*Necropolis Railway, The* 19
Nedjdma 191
Némirovsky, Irène 278
*Neon Bible, The* 54
*Nervous Conditions* 171
*New Life, The* 202
*New Life, The* 64
*New York Trilogy* 51
*Next Episode* 94
Nguyen, Kien 115
Nice Change, A 125
Nicholson, Geoff 294, 339
Niekerk, Marlene van 178
Niemi, Mikael 231
Niffenegger, Audrey 227
*Night Flight* 18
Ninh, Bao 114
*No Bones* 306
*No Great Mischief* 94
*No Highway* 18
*No Signposts in the Sea* 96
*Noodle Maker, The* 130
Nooteboom, Cees 250, 252
Norman, Howard 93
*North* 240
*Norwegian Wood* 124
*Nostromo* 5
*Not Before Sundown* 229
*Not Fade Away* 63
*Notebooks of Don Rigoberto* 15
*Nothing Happens in Carmincross* 309
*Nothing Like the Sun* 345
Nothomb, Amélie 121
*Novel With Cocaine* 210
*Number 5* 308
*Number9dream* 123
Nunez, Raul 291

Nwapa, Flora 188

O'Brien, Edna 297
O'Brien, Flann 300, 305
O'Brien, Tim 115
O'Connor, Flannery 52
O'Connor, Frank 298
O'Connor, Joseph 31, 95, 300
O'Grady, Timothy 301
O'Neill, Anthony 152, 315
O'Neill, Jamie 304
*O, Pioneers* 61
Oates, Joyce Carol 41
*Of Mice and Men* 70
Ojaide, Tanure 188
Okja Keller, Nora 87
Okri, Ben 147, 187
Olafsson, Olaf 236
*Old Devils, The* 312
*Old Man Who Read Love Stories, The* 6
*Old New York* 47
*Olympiad* 200
*On the Black Hill* 319
*On the Night Plain* 68
*On The Road* 63
*On the Water* 252
*Once and Future King, The* 180
*Once Were Warriors* 105
Ondaatje, Michael 93, 145, 191
*One: A Novel* 146
*One Day in the Short Life of Ivan Denisovich* 207
*One Hundred Years of Solitude* 1-2
*One Moonlit Night* 320
*One by One in the Darkness* 309
Onetti, Juan Carlos 6
*Only Human* 162

*Only in London* 343
*Open Door and Other Stories* 9
*Operation Shylock* 160
*Oranges Are Not the Only Fruit* 328
*Orlando* 226
Orwell, George 113
Otsuka, Julie 87
*Our Man in Havana* 29
*Our Weddings* 160
Ousmane, Sembene 185
*Out* 124
*Out Stealing Horses* 233
*Outerbridge Reach* 96
*Outlaws* 328
*Outsider, The* 191
*Owls Do Cry* 104
*Oxford Book of Caribbean Short Stories, The* 23
*Oxford Book of Japanese Short Stories, The* 120
*Oxford Book of Sea Stories, The* 95
Oyeyemi, Helen 188
*Oyster* 101
Oz, Amos 160

Paasilinna, Arto 229
*Paddy Clarke Ha Ha Ha* 303
Padura, Leonardo 29
Pagnol, Marcel 277
*Painted Kiss, The* 284
*Painter, The* 284
*Palace of the Peacock* 16–17
*Palace, The* 271
Paley, Grace 51
*Palm-Wine Drinkard, The* 188
Pamuk, Orhan 64, 202
*Paper Eater, The* 135

*Paradise* (Abdulrazak Gurnah)167
*Paradise* (Toni Morrison) 61
*Paradise News* 83
*Paris Stories* 282
Parks, Tim 63, 267, 294
Parsipur, Shahrnush 152
*Pashtun Tales: From the Pakistan-Afgan Frontier* 151
*Passage to India, A* 140
*Passion of Artemesia, The* 284
*Past Continuous* 160
Pasternak, Boris 204
Paton, Alan 177
Patterson, Glenn 308
Pavese, Cesare 262
Paz, Octavio 35
Peachment, Christopher 284
Pears, Tim 341
Pedro Páramo 33–34
Pelevin, Victor 207
*Penelopiad, The* 180
Pennac, Daniel 282
Penney, Stef 93
*People's Act of Love, The* 208
Pepetela, Mayombe 173
Percy, Walker 55
Pérez Galdós, Benito 288
Perez-Reverte, Arturo 95, 287
*Perfect Man, The* 87
*Perfume* 276
Perlman, Elliot 102
*Persian Brides* 152
*Persian Requiem, A* 152
Pessoa, Fernando 293
*Petersburg* 211
Petterson, Per 233
*Peyton Place* 45
Pezeshkzad, Iraj 152

Phillips, Caryl 24, 342
*Photographer's Wife, The* 195
*Piano Teacher, The* 257
*Piano Tuner, The* 113
*Picador Book of African Stories* 164
Pickett, Rex 37
*Picnic at Hanging Rock* 101
Pierre, D B C 69
*Pigs in Heaven* 61
*Pillars of Salt* 157
Pirsig, Robert M 64, 146
*Place of Greater Safety, A* 279
*Plainsong* 68
Platonov, Andrey 205
*Play It As It Lays* 73
*Playmaker, The* 101
*Pleasure of Eliza Lynch, The* 5
*Pleasured* 249
*Plumb* 105
*Poet, The* 133
Poirier, Mark 68
*Poisonwood Bible, The* 181
*Polished Hoe, The* 23
*Pompeii* 273
*Poor Things* 316
*Pop. 1280* 69
*Popular Music* 231
*Pornografia: A Novel* 222
*Port Mungo* 32
*Portable Virgin, The* 304
*Postcards from the Edge* 78
Poster, Jem 213
*Postman Always Rings Twice, The* 73
Potok, Chaim 41
Powell, Anthony 322
*Power and the Glory, The* 35

*Prague Orgy, The* 219
*Prague Trilogy, The* 219
Prawer Jhabvala, Ruth 140
*Precious Bane* 329
Pressfield, Steven 200
Price, Richard 50
Prichard, Caradog 320
*Prime of Miss Jean Brodie, The* 314
*Prince* 238
Prince, Peter 293
*Prince, The* 149-150
*Prodigal Summer* 56
*Property* 55
Proulx, E Annie 40, 82, 92
Proust, Marcel 274
Pryce, Malcolm 320
*Ptolemies, The, Book 1: The House of the Eagle* 196
Puig, Manuel 9
*Puma's Shadow, The* 15
*Purple Hibiscus* 187
*Purple Violet of Oshaantu, The* 173
*Pursuit of Love, The* 324
Pyke, Steve 301
Pynchon, Thomas 41, 73
Pyramid, The 195

Qian Zhongshu 131
*Qissat: Short Stories by Palestinian Women* 157
*Quarantine* 162
Queneau, Raymond 282
*Querelle of Brest, The* 278
*Quest for Christa T, The* 246
*Question of Bruno, The* 220
*Question of Power, A* 173
Quieroz, Eça de 293
*Quiet American, The* 115

Raban, Jonathan 82

*Rabbit series* 39
Rabinyan, Dorit 152, 160
*Radetsky March, The* 256
*Radiant Way, The* 325
*Radience of the King, The* 185
Radiguiet, Raymond 282
*Rage in Harlem, A* 51
*Ragged-Trousered Philanthropists, The* 325
*Ragtime* 50
Rahimi, Atiq 151
*Railway, The* 153
*Rain* 105
*Raise the Red Lantern* 131
*Ramses series, The* 196
Rankin, Ian 315
*Rape of the Fair Country* 312
*Rapids* 294
*Rashomon* 120
Rathbone, Julian 344
*Razor's Edge, The* 146
*Reader, The* 242
*Reading in the Dark* 308
*Rector's Daughter, The* 332
*Red Cavalry and Other Stories* 207
*Red Dust* 178
*Red and the Green, The* 304
*Red Poppies: A Novel of Tibet* 133
*Red Strangers* 170
*Red Tent, The* 162
*Redundancy of Courage, The* 111
*Reef* 144
*Remains of the Day, The* 324
Remarque, Erich Maria 245
*Remembering Babylon* 100
Renault, Mary 179, 200, 201
*Republic of Love, The* 91

*Restoration* 345
Restrepo, Laura 5
*Return from Troy, The* 180
*Return of the Water Spirit, The* 173
*Reunion* 246
*Revolutionary Road* 43
Rhys, Jean 21, 283
*Rice Mother, The* 109
Richards, Ben 5
Richler, Mordecai 94
*Rider, The* 18
*Riders of the Purple Sage* 68
*Riders, The* 260
Rifaat, Alifa 195
*Rifling Paradise* 213
*Right and Left* 249
Riley, Gwendoline 327
Riley, Jane 27
*Ring* 120
*Rings of Saturn, The* 332
*Rites of Passage* 96
Rivas, Manuel 286
*River Sutra, A* 139
*River Thieves* 94
Rivière, William 270
*Road Home, The* 61
Robbins, Tom 64
Roberts, Gregory David 142
Robinson, Marilynne 80
*Rock of Tanois, The* 154–155
Rodenbach, Georges 254
Rogers, Jane 96
*Romantic, The* 94
*Romantics, The* 140
*Room at the Top, A* 323
*Room With A View, A* 266
*Rosario Tijeras* 5
*Roseanna* 231
Roth, Joseph 125, 249, 256
Roth, Philip 41, 160, 219

*Rotters' Club, The* 330
Roumain, Jacques 25
Roy, Arundhati 136
Royle, Nichols 254
Ruiz Zafón, Carlos 290
*Rules of the Wild* 170
Rulfo, Juan 33
*Rum Diary, The* 24
Runice, James 227
*Running in the Family* 145
Rushdie, Salman 138, 145
*Rushing to Paradise* 107
Russell, Willy 328
*Russian Interpreter, The* 210
*Russian Short Stories from Pushkin to Buida* 207
Russo, Richard 45
Rutherford, Edward 305
Rygg, Pernille 234
Ryman, Geoff 109
Ryman, Geoff 339

Sackville-West, Vita 96
*Saddam City* 151
*Saddlebag, The* 156
Saeed, Mahmoud 151
Safran Foer, Jonathan 51, 221
*Saga – A Novel of Medieval Iceland* 239
Sagan, Françoise 275
Said, Kurban 153
*Sailor Who Fell From Grace With The Sea* 120
Saint Exupery, Antoine de 18
Salih, Tayeb 165
Salinger, J D 50
*Salt* 26
*Salt Eaters, The* 84
Salter, James 18, 46, 279
Sampson, Kevin 294, 328

Sánchez Piñol, Albert 241
Sansom, C J 288
Santos, Rosario (Ed.) 31
Saramago, José 162, 292
Saro-Wiwa, Ken 188
Sartre, Jean-Paul 281
*Satan in Goray* 221
*Saturday Night, Sunday Morning* 330
*Saville* 326
*Saving Fish from Drowning* 113
*Scarlet Moving Van, The* 44
*Scarlet Song* 183
*Scheherazade* 152
Schlink, Bernhard 242
Schneider, Peter 247
Schnitzler, Arthur 257
Schulz, Bruno 223
Sciascia, Leonardo 265
*Scientific Romance, A* 227
*Scots Quair, A* 310
Scott, Lawrence 26
Scott, Manda 317
*Sea Glass* 45
*Sea House, The* 239, 333
*Sea, The* 301
*Sea-Wolf, The* 95
*Seal Wife, The* 82
*Season of Migration to the North* 165–166
*Season of the Rainbirds* 145
Sebald, W G 246, 332
*Second-Class Citizen* 342
*Secret History, The* 45
*Secret Ladder, The* 17
*Secret Life of Saeed: The Pessoptimist, The* 161
*Secret River* 99
*Seducer, The* 234
See, Lisa 131
Seiffert, Rachel 243

Selby Jr, Hubert 49
*Selected Stories* (Alice Munro) 89–90
Selvon, Samuel 26, 338
Senior, Oliver 27
*Señor Vivo and the Coca Lord* 4
Sepulveda, Luis 6
Serge, Victor 208
Seth, Vikram 138
*Seven Days to the Sea* 163
*Seven Madmen, The* 9
*Seventh Son, The* 344
Severin, Tim 239
*Seville Reunion, The* 287
Shabtai, Yaakov 160
*Shadow Walker, The* 133
*Shadow of the Wind* 290
*Shadows of the Pomegranate Tree* 288
*Shadows on Our Skin* 308
Shafak, Elif 203
Shakespeare, Nicholas 15
Shalev, Meir 160
*Shame* 145
Shamsie, Kamila 143
*Shanghai Baby* 127
Shanghvi, Siddharth Dhanvant 142
Shan So 131
*Shantaram* 142
*Shape of Water, The* 266
*Sheepsagger* 320
*Sheltering Sky, The* 190
Shields, Carol 91
Shields, Jody 257
*Shipping News, The* 92
*Shipyard, The* 6
*Shogun* 121
Sholokhov, Mikhail 206
Shreve, Anita 45
Shusaku Endo 120

Shute, Nevile 18, 101
*Shyness and Dignity* 234
*Siddartha* 146
*Sideways* 37
*Siege, The* 211
*Siege of Krishnapur* 109
*Sightseeing* 112
*Silence* 120
*Silence of the Rain, The* 13
*Silent Cry, The* 118
*Silk* 121
Sillitoe, Alan 330
*Silver Darlings, The* 313
Simenon, Georges 283
Sinclair, Iain 339
*Singapore Grip, The* 109
Singer, Isaac Bashevis 222
*Singing Whakapapa, The* 105
Sinisalo, Johanna 229
Sinyangwe, Binwell 173
*Sister Carrie* 61
*Six* 135
Sjowall, Maj 231
*Skin-Line* 339
Skvorecky, Josef 216
*Slammerkin* 345
Slaughterhouse 5 226
Sleigh, Dan 178
Slovo, Gillian 178, 208
*Small Island* 325, 344
Smiley, Jane 57, 239
Smith, Ali 125, 312
Smith, Betty 50
Smith, Wilbur 196
Smith, Zadie 343
*Smouldering Charcoal* 173
*Snakes and Earrings* 124
*Snapper, The* 303
*Snow Falling on Cedars* 81
*Snow Flower and the Secret Fan* 131

*So I Am Glad* 317
*So Long a Letter* 183
*So Long, See You Tomorrow* 58
Solana, Almudena 288
*Soldiers of Salamis, The* 288
Sole, Robert 195
*Soledad* 86
Solstad, Dag 234
Solzhenitsyn, Aleksandr 207
*Some Kind of Black* 342
Somerset Maugham, W 106, 146
*Something I've Been Meaning to Tell You* 89
*Something Might Happen* 333
*Somewhere, Home* 157
*Song for Nero, A* 273
*Song of the Earth* 312
*Songs of Enchantment* 187
*Sons and Lovers* 330
*Sopranos, The* 312
*Sorrow of Belgium, The* 254
*Sorrow of War, The* 114
*Sort of the Madman, The* 182
Soseki, Natsume 121
Soueif, Ahdaf 195
*Soul* 205
*Soul Mountain* 128
*South, The* 289
*Southern Mail* 18
Southern, Paul 328
Southern, Terry 78
Soyinka, Wole 188
*Sozaboy* 188
*Space Between Us, The* 142
Spark, Muriel 314
*Spartacus* 273
Söderberg, Hjalmar 230

*Speak for England* 134
Spinoza, José Carlos 200
Spinrad, Norman 35
*Sport and a Pastime, A* 279
*Sportswriter, The* 45
*Spring Flowers, Spring Frost* 214–215
Sprott, Duncan 196
*Spy Who Came in From the Cold, The* 249
St Aubin de Terán, Lisa 6, 271
*St. Agnes' Stand* 68
Stahl, Jerry 78
Staïkos, Andreas 36
*Stamboul Train* 19
*Star of the Sea* 95
*State of Independence, A* 24
Stead, C K 105, 163
*Steep Approach to Garbadale, The* 311
Steinbeck, John 70
Sterchi, Beat 258
*Stevenson Under the Palm Trees* 106
*Stick Your Tongue Out* 134
*Stone Angel, The* 94
*Stone Virgin, The* 270
Stone, Irving 285
Stone, Robert 30, 96
Storey, David 326
*Stories of Eva Luna* 5
*Stories of John Cheever, The* 44
*Story of the Night, The* 9
*Strait is the Gate* 278
*Strangers* 123
*String of Pearls, The* 256
Su Tong 131
*Such a Long Journey* 141
*Suitable Boy, A* 138

*Suite Française* 278
*Summer Affair, A* 218
*Summer in Baden-Baden* 259
*Summer Book, The* 228
*Summer Lightning and Other Stories* 27
*Summer Things* 294
*Sunday at the Pool in Kigali, A* 167
*Sunset Song* 310
*Surfacing* 91
Suri, Manil 142
*Surveillance* 82
Süskind, Patrick 276
*Sutton Place Story, The* 44
Svevo, Italo 266
*Swallows of Kabul* 151
*Sweet Dreams* 135
*Sweet Sour* 344
*Sweet Thursday* 71
Swift, Graham 331–332, 335
*Swimmer, The* 44
*Swing Hammer Swing* 317
*Sword in the Stone, The* 180
Syal, Meera 330
*Syme Paper, The* 212
Szabó, Magda 225
Szerb, Antal 264
Szirtes, George 225

Tagore, Rabindranath 137
*Tailor of Panama, The* 31
*Tainted Blood* 236
*Tale of Murasaki, The* 121
*Talented Mr Ripley, The* 266
*Tales and New Tales from the Mountain* 293
*Tales from Firozsha Baag* 141
*Tales of the City* 72

Tan, Amy 87, 113, 131
*Tango Singer, The* 8
*Tango for a Torturer* 29
Tannahill, Reay 344
Tanner, Tony (Ed.) 95
Tanzaki, Junichiro 117
*Tapestries, The* 115
*Tar Baby* 23
*Tarry Flynn* 301
Tartt, Donna 45
*Taxi Driver's Daughter, The* 327
Taylor, Elizabeth 125
*Ten Little Indians* 82
*Ten Thousand, The* 200
*Tender is the Night* 279
*Tenderness of Wolves, The* 93
*Tent of the Miracles* 12
Tepal, Tarun J 140
*Texaco* 23
*That They May Face the Rising Sun* 296
*The Rock: A Tale of Seventh-Century Jerusalem* 160
*Their Eyes Were Watching God* 84
*Theo's Odyssey* 147
Theroux, Paul 30, 83
*They Came Like Swallows* 58
*They Were Counted* 225
*They Were Divided* 225
*They Were Found Wanting* 225
*They Who Do Not Grieve* 106
*Things Fall Apart* 186
*Things They Carried, The* 115
Thiong'o, Ngugi Wa 168

*Third Man, The* 257
*Third Policeman, The* 300
*This Blinding Absence of Light* 189–190
*This Side of Reality: Modern Czech Writing* 216
*This Sporting Life* 326
*This Thing of Darkness* 212
*This Was Old Chief's Country* 172
Thomas Ellis, Alice 321
Thomas, Dylan 320
Thompson, Harry 212
Thompson, Hunter S 24, 74
Thompson, Jim 69
Thorpe, Adam 341
*Thousand Acres, A* 57
*Thousand Orange Trees, A* 289
*Thousand Splendid Suns, A* 150
*Thousand Years of Good Prayers* 131
*Three Dollars* 102
*Three to See the King* 134
*Three Trapped Tigers* 28
Thubron, Colin 260
*Thumbprint* 258
*Thunder God* 239
*Thursbitch* 328
Tiffany, Carrie 101
*Time Traveller's Wife, The* 226
*Time Will Darken It* 58
*Time's Arrow* 227
*Timeline* 226
*Tin Drum, The* 244
*To a God Unknown* 70
*To Kill a Mockingbird* 55
*To the Ends of the Sea: A Sea Trilogy* 96

*To The Hermitage* 211
*To the Last City* 260
*To the Wedding* 260
Toer, Pramoedya Ananta 111
Tóibín, Colm 9, 289, 300
Tokarczuk, Olga 223
*Torch Song* 44
Torga, Miguel 293
Torrington, Jeff 317
*Tortilla Curtain, The* 71–72
*Tortilla Flat* 70
*Tourist Season* 56
*Towers of Tredizond, The* 203
*Town Called Alice, A* 101
Townsend Warner, Sylvia 106
*Tracks* 41
*Tragedy of the Street of Flowers, The* 293
*Trainspotting* 315
*Transylvania Trilogy* 224
Tranter, Nigel 312
*Travelling with Djinns* 63
*Travels with My Aunt* 259
*Treading Air* 225
*Tree Grows in Brooklyn, A* 50
Tremain, Rose 105, 238, 282, 345
*Tremor of Forgery, The* 192
Tressell, Robert 325
Trevor, William 301, 341
*Triomf* 178
Trocchi, Alexander 312
*Tropic of Cancer* 282
*Troubles* 109
*Troublesome Offspring of Cardinal Guzman* 4
*Troubling Love* 266
*True History of the Kelly Gang, The* 97–98

*Tsotsi* 178
Tsypkin, Leonid 259
Turner Hospital, Janette 101
Tutuola, Amos 188
*Twenty Thousand Street Under the Sky* 338
*Twins, The* 252
*Two Hearts of Kwasi Boachi, The* 253
*Two Serious Ladies* 31
Tyler, Anne 42
*Typical American* 88

Udall, Brady 68
Ugresic, Dubravka 220
Uhlman, Fred 246
*Ultimate Good Luck, The* 35
*Ultras, The* 308
*Ulverton* 341
*Ulysses* 302
Umrigar, Thrity 142
*Unbearable Lightness of Being, The* 217
*Under African Skies: Modern African Stories* 164
*Under the Frog* 224
*Under the Naked Sky: Short Stories from the Arab World* 148
*Under the Skin* 64
*Under the Tongue* 173
*Under the Volcano* 35
*Underworld* 40
Undset, Sigrid 233
*Union Street* 327
*Unreal Towns* 156
Unsworth, Barry 270
*Untouchable* 139
*Unusual Life of Tristram Smith, The* 135
*Up the Junction* 339

*Up, Into the Singing Mountain* 318
Updike, John 39
Urquhart, Jane 93
*USA* 38–39
*Utz* 219

Vakil, Ardashir 142
Valenzuela, Luisa 9
Vámos, Miklós 225
*Van, The* 303
Vanderbes, Jennifer 106
*Vanishing, The* 252
Vassanji, M G 170
Vassilikos, Vassilis 199
Vázquez Montalbán, Manuel 291
*Ventriloquist's Tale, The* 17
Vera, Yvonne 173
Verissimo, Luis Fernando 13
*Vernon Little God* 69
*Very Long Engagement, A* 278
Vesaas, Tarjei 233
*Vibrator* 63
*Viceroy of Ouidah, The* 185
Vickers, Salley 270, 295
*Victim of the Aurora* 241
Vidal, Gore 41, 227, 272
*Viking: Odinn's Child* 239
*Vintner's Luck, The* 37
*Violent Bear it Away, The* 52
*Virago Book of Erotic Myths and Legends* 180
*Virgin* 345
*Virgin Suicides, The* 62
*Visit of the Royal Physician, The* 238
*Visitor, The* 304
Vittorini, Elio 265
Vonnegut, Kurt 226
*Voss* 212

*Voyage Home, The* 96
*Voyage of the Narwhal, The* 212
*Voyages of Alfred Wallis, The* 285
Vreeland, Susan 284

Wahloo, Per 231
Wain, John 330
*Waiting* 130
*Waiting for an Angel* 188
*Waiting for Leah* 216
*Waiting for the Wild Beasts to Vote* 185
*Walk on the Wild Side, A* 55
*Walker Brothers Cowboy* 89
Walker, Alice 55
Walters, Michael 134
*Wall Jumper, The* 247
*War at the End of the World, The* 13
*War at Troy, The* 180
*War by Candlelight* 15
War of Don Emmanuel's Nether Parts, The 4
*Warlock* 196
Warner, Alan 312
Warner, Marina 23
*Washington DC* 41
*Watch Me Disappear* 332
*Water Music* 213
*Water of the Hills, The* 277
*Waterland* 331
Watkins, Paul 239
Waugh, Evelyn 324
*Way I Found Her, The* 282
*Way to Paradise, The* 284
Webb, Mary 329
*Wedding, The* 45
*Weeping Woman on the Streets of Prague, The* 219

*Wegener's Jigsaw* 212
Wei Hui 127
Weil, Jiri 219
Wells, H G 134
Welsh, Irving 315
Welsh, Louise 317
Welty, Eudora 55
West, Dorothy 45
West, Nathanael 78
Westo, Kjell 229
*Whale Caller, The* 178
*Whale Rider, The* 104
Wharton, Edith 47
*What A Carve Up!* 324
*What I Loved* 48
*What We Did on Our Holidays* 294
*What We Talk About When We Talk About Love* 40
Wheatle, Alex 338
*When I Lived in Modern Times* 160
*When the Emperor Was Divine* 87
*When the Grey Beetles Took Over Baghdad* 151
*When We Were Orphans* 130
*Whereabouts of Eneas McNulty, The* 300
*White* 240
*White Ghost Girls* 133
*White Lightning* 169, 177
*White Oleander* 77
*White Teeth* 343
White, Edmund 61
White, Patrick 101, 212
White, T H 180
*Whole Armour, The* 17
Wickham, John (Ed.) 23
*Wide Open* 335
*Wide Sargasso Sea* 21

Wilcox, James 56
*Wild Girl, The* 162
*Wild Thorns* 157
Wilder, Thornton 15
*Wildlife* 82
Williams, John 320
Williams, Raymond 321
Wilson, James 259, 285
*Wind-up Bird Chronicle, The* 116
*Windward Heights* 23
*Wine-Dark Sea, The* 265
Winesburg, Ohio 60
*Wings of the Dove, The* 270
*Winter Book, The* 228
*Winter Breaks* 294
*Winter in Madrid* 288
*Winter Queen, The* 210
*Winter's Bone* 62
Winterson, Jeanette 328
Winton, Tim 101, 260
*Wise Blood* 52
*Witchbroom* 26
*Without a Name* 173
Wolf, Christa 246
*Wolf Solent* 341
Wolfe, Thomas 56
Wolfe, Tom 51
*Woman in the Dunes* 120
*Woman and the Priest, The* 266
*Woman at Point Zero* 193
*Woman in White, The* 285
*Women Without Men* 152
*Wonder Boys* 45
*Wonderful Women by the Water* 229
Woodrell, Daniel 62
Woods, Denyse 157
Woodward, Gerard 294
Woolf, Virginia 226, 325
Wright, Richard 84

Wright, Ronald 106, 227
Wrong Boy, The 328

Xu Xi 133

Yacoubian Building, The
   195
Yahia, Mona 151
Yakhlif, Yahya 157
Yamada, Taichi 123
Yates, Richard 43
Year of Living Dangerously,
   The 111
Year of the Death of
   Ricardo Reis 292
Year of the Hare,
   The 229

Years of Wonders 345
Years With Laura Díaz,
   The 34
Yehoshua, A B 158-159
Yellow Ruin, The 288
Yerofeev, Venedikt 19
Yi Mun-yol 133
Yiyun Li 131
Yoshikawa, Elji 120
Yoshimoto, Banana 122
You Shall Know Our
   Velocity 259
You, Darkness 25
Young Adam 312
Young Turk 203
Yourcenar, Marguerite 272
Yukio Mishima 120

Zaman, Niaz (Ed.) 145
Zazie in the Metro 282
Zeleza, Tiyambe 173
Zeller, Florian 196
Zen and the Art of
   Motorcycle Maintenance
   64
Zennor in Darkness 342
Zeno's Confidence 266
Zilahy, Lajos 226
Zimler, Richard 293
Zorba the Greek 197-198
Zweig, Stefan 257